HV 1626 B37 1992

1993 2010
994

VISUAL HANDICAPS & LEARNING

THIRD EDITION

NATALIE C. BARRAGA

JANE N. ERIN

pro·ed

8700 Shoal Creek Boulevard
Austin, Texas 78758

Printed in the United States of America

Library of Congress Cataloging-in-Publication Data

Barraga, Natalie.
   Visual handicaps and learning / Natalie C. Barraga, Jane N. Erin.
— 3rd ed.
     p. cm.
   Includes bibliographical references and index.
   ISBN 0-89079-515-0
   1. Visually handicapped children—Education. I. Erin, Jane N.
II. Title.
   HV1626.B37 1992
   362.4′1—dc20   91-27820
                                             CIP

pro·ed

8700 Shoal Creek Boulevard
Austin, Texas 78758

1 2 3 4 5 6 7 8 9 10   95 94 93 92 91

Contents

Foreword

One often asks how different a revision of a book is from its predecessor. This text, the second revision since the original *Visual Handicaps and Learning* (1976, 1983), retains a blend of research, philosophy, professional trends, and concepts about blindness and visual impairments with the lives of children. The children Carlos, Lucy, Ching Lan, and Michael (of earlier editions) are joined in this book by Sharon, who brings to the reader an understanding of living, developing, and learning with severe multiple handicaps in addition to blindness.

Since 1983, numerous legal and pedagogical changes have occurred in the field of special education in general, and in educational services to children who are blind and visually disabled in particular. In this text, these changes have been included, discussed, and sometimes challenged. New teaching materials and approaches are included. Research findings have been updated. We are touched by the increasing possibilities and opportunities for learning that special education can offer to children who are visually disabled. We also are deeply concerned for those children who may not have the early experiences that are being provided for Carlos or the visual stimulation program that is helping Lucy to utilize her functional low vision. We worry about youngsters who may not have the inner strength and insights of Ching Lan or the alternative learning approaches sought for Michael. Through these children, we also come to know their parents and to discover the many ways in which parents of children with visual handicaps become the most important teachers of all for their children.

Early development is emphasized throughout the text, to stress the importance of early foundations on later learning. Ching Lan is able to retain visual imagery to help her learn new ways of traveling, although we know she will lose her vision. Carlos moves freely about as a 3-year-old who is blind as he is "piecing together" an understanding of the world through which he is moving. Sharon presents a different set of sensory perceptions due to her multiple impairments, and we try to understand how her experiences differ from those of the other children and from our own memories of childhood.

This edition also has the insight of a second author. Jane Erin joins Natalie Barraga in helping the reader become not only involved in the lives of the children, but also in the issues that perplex educators faced with the challenges and the delights of teaching children with visual disabilities. Dr. Erin adds her expertise as a teacher and an administrator of programs serving multiply handicapped and deaf–blind youngsters. Her many years of preparing future teachers of children with visual handicaps and multiple handicaps complement Dr. Barraga's knowledge and easy style for imparting information and concern for parents and children with visual impairments.

Even the reader who has studied earlier editions of *Visual Handicaps and Learning* will surely want to reread this text cover to cover. Only then will the reader be stimulated to have new ideas about the potential for a quality education for children with visual handicaps . After all, these children will live most of their lives in the 1990s and beyond. As teachers, as parents, and as concerned individuals, we need to be ready.

Anne L. Corn
The University of Texas at Austin

Preface

Historical documents and literature throughout the ages have expressed a concern about impairments in sensory organs, especially the eyes. Some philosophers have theorized that the eyes are mystical organs related to the soul; some have supported legal sanctions for destruction of those without sight; others have advocated veneration and worship of blind persons; and a few have actually suggested isolated care as a benevolent societal attitude. Not until the 17th century was consideration given to the idea of educating persons with severe visual impairments. Even then, the major concern for hundreds of years was to train these people for service to society in asylums, residential schools, or workshops. Concentration on public education during the 20th century has helped to change some of the societal attitudes around the world. However, superstitions and emotionally laden attitudes regarding visual impairment or blindness can be found in many parts of the world, even in the more advanced countries.

The passage of Public Law 94-142, The Education of All Handicapped Children Act in the United States (retitled in 1990 as IDEA, Individuals with Disabilities Education Act), has facilitated progress in public attitudes throughout the world beyond expectations. Similar legislation has been passed in several other countries. The passage in 1986 of PL 99-457, Disabled Infants and Toddlers Act, extended services down to birth. Today, many preschool children and their parents have the opportunity to know personally and interact with a child with a visual impairment. However, the causes of visual impairment frequently present damage in other parts of the body as well, sometimes resulting in severely multihandicapped children with visual impairments whose futures may not be optimistic. The advent of infant and early childhood programs makes possible intervention at a much earlier age; thus, children and parents have received very positive assistance, which has eliminated many of the lags encountered previously.

To understand the areas of development most vulnerable to visual impairment, we must think objectively about the role of vision in incidental learning and plan interventions appropriate to the nature and degree of limitations. Preventing lags in any area of development is possible when substitutions and adaptations are made to foster learning and development to the child's maximum capacity. What the child has is far more important than the impairment or the condition of the eyes. To redirect thinking toward this goal, attention should be shifted from the causes or medical diagnoses of eye conditions, which stress visual damage and incapacity, and toward healthy organs and the potential for development and learning through alternative senses and processes.

The discussions in this text are addressed to education students and teachers, generic special education teachers, clinical and educational vision specialists, parents, and support personnel, such as psychologists, occupational and physical therapists, and social workers. One major objective of this book is to present a new way of thinking about individuals with visual impairment so that they are viewed as participating members of a "seeing world" despite their reduction in visual functioning.

Developmental and learning processes are presented from a descriptive and functional frame of reference rather than as generalized characteristics, factual data, or statistical information relying heavily on measurement criteria. Some ideas discussed in the text are based on the personal experiences of the authors; others have emerged through study, observation, and research. As teacher educators (the first author is also the mother of a person with a visual handicap), we have tried to translate theory into practice. Our philosophy includes a firm belief that measurements, labels, materials, equipment, and legislation are less important than the personal factors in human beings—both teachers and students—as they relate to or influence development and learning. Regardless of impairments or labels, educators' major concern must be to develop to the fullest each student's potential for learning.

The vignettes presented in Chapter 1 are purely fictional and do not describe any real persons known to us through personal experience or from reading actual case histories. The children depicted represent the variability in severity of visual impairments and the range and diversity of the influence that these conditions have on development and learning. Children similar to those portrayed are likely to be found in almost any community or school setting in any part of the world. Frequent reference to the children described in the vignettes is for the sole purpose of illustrating ideas and should not be associated with any real person.

Chapter 2 examines the problem of the multiplicity of descriptive terms still in use, making an appeal for the adoption of consistent terminology in an attempt to substitute stability of thought for stereotypic notions.

Because environmentally influenced development and learning in all children begin immediately at birth, Chapters 3 and 4 identify the concerns of the earliest years of life and present both a theoretical basis and empirical evidence for evaluating developmental patterns reflected in learning behavior. Chapter 5 addresses an ever increasing percentage of the population of visually handicapped children—those with multiple disabilities. The interaction of a visual impairment with other medical and developmental problems is sometimes greater than the sum of the discrete conditions; there are likely to be interruptions in emotional and physical development, as well as a marked limitation in the potential for mental development.

Chapter 6 focuses on the sensory aspects of learning and the sequences and processes through which children develop the highest level of efficiency possible. Chapter 7 examines the range of present educational settings and the variety of services provided in each. The issue of assessment and other evaluative approaches to intellectual and personal functioning is explored in Chapter 8.

Chapter 9 provides a comprehensive discussion of the necessary curriculum adaptations and the specialized materials appropriate for students with visual handicaps. The culmination of school learning is applied to achieving the goals of independent living and vocational success in Chapter 10, prior to offering a look to the future in Chapter 11. Some of the major issues, facilitating and restraining forces affecting their resolution, dreams, and challenges conclude the discussion.

Because these ideas have been fostered by many persons and evolved out of a wide variety of literary sources, documentation of references is more often general than specific. When appropriate, the reader is directed to specific literature for in-depth study. The authors assume full responsibility for inaccuracies, provocative controversy, and limitations in discussions. Grateful appreciation is expressed to all the children, teachers, students, and colleagues who have had a part in generating and shaping these thoughts through the years. We are deeply indebted to Anne Corn, Coordinator of the Program to Prepare Teachers of the Visually Handicapped at The University of Texas at Austin. She has taken time to read the entire manuscript and offer suggestions as well as to write the foreword.

Natalie C. Barraga
Jane N. Erin
The University of Texas at Austin
January 1991

1

To See or Not To See

Most of the things we learned as children came to us through vision. Life was full of incidental learning experiences. Billboards and street signs, adults working or going to work, photographs, paintings, television shows, and the faces of friends were so common that we learned to take them for granted by the time we were aware of the world around us.

The idea that a child may not have access to all this visual information may seem unjust or tragic. Those people who have never met a child with a visual disability may imagine the child in one dimension, as a person who is responding only to a loss and not as someone who is learning about a world full of sounds, tastes, textures, or visual forms that are perceived in different ways. In reading this book, you will learn about a world you may not have experienced, but one that can excite the curiosity of a child with visual handicaps just as keenly as a world full of visual detail can excite children with sight. As you read this book, keep in mind that children with visual impairments have only their visual handicaps in common. They have individual interests, motivations, and experiences. They are more like their brothers and sisters and as much like their playmates next door as they are like any other child who has a visual impairment.

The similarities among children with visual impairments are few, and the differences are many. Some are totally blind from birth or become blind shortly thereafter. Many have serious structural or pathological conditions of the eye or visual system at birth, but are still able to learn to function visually throughout their lives. A few have medical conditions that become progressively serious until total blindness occurs at some time during their school years. In other cases, accidents may be responsible for sudden blindness. Still other children have serious visual impairments at birth because of unknown factors, such as possible intrauterine viruses, interruptions in embryonic development, underdevelopment of visual and related systems because of premature birth, and/or drugs taken by the mother during pregnancy. To emphasize the differences among children identified as visually handicapped, the following vignettes depict several typical children who have visual impairments.

CARLOS

As the counselor for children with visual handicaps and the young college student who was accompanying him approached the door, they could hear a little boy say, "Car stop—somebody come," and his mother responded with, "Thank you, I'll be there." The student looked at the counselor with a puzzled expression since she had understood that they were going to see a totally blind child soon to have his third birthday. She wondered how he knew they were coming to his house.

They rang the doorbell, and when the mother opened the door, the counselor spoke. Immediately, Carlos squealed the counselor's name and rushed to grab him in a big hug before the mother could invite the visitors to enter. The student was introduced as the counselor's friend, and by the time they sat down, Carlos was asking the young girl one question after another, as if she were already his friend too.

Events of the past few moments had shattered the student's preconceived notions of blindness. She became so enchanted with Carlos that all anxieties seemed to flow away as she sat quietly, watching and listening. She began to realize how much there was to learn by observing Carlos as he moved about, played with his toys, and interacted with the adults. He was totally blind, but this fact was forgotten as soon as the mother and the counselor began a conversation. They responded to Carlos's questions or addressed him occasionally, when he was not completely absorbed in his own play. At times, he would seek contact by approaching one of them or calling their names to determine whether they were still nearby.

In many ways, Carlos seemed much like any other child of almost 3, as he talked to himself, then to his toys, and at times to one of the adults. Other children might look for a smile or a wave of the hand for assurance or to maintain contact, but Carlos frequently asked a question or made a comment to reassure himself that an adult was present.

Although the student had not expected to see a child who would be moving from place to place so freely, she noted that when Carlos moved, he often seemed to move to a voice. Also, as he moved away from the voice, he was able to avoid chairs and other objects in the room just as if he could see them. When he was near another person, Carlos would usually touch the person or the person's chair to maintain close contact as he talked or questioned. He sometimes asked for help in playing or for assistance in finding a particular toy. Frequently, Carlos's mother described verbally where he would find the toy or instructed him that he could look in a particular place in his room for what he wanted. Encouraged and reassured by his mother, Carlos searched with his hands until he found things and continued with his play or went to another room and came back with the object he wanted. If he left the room, he put out his hands to verify the location of doorways. He used his feet to find toys that he thought were located in his general vicinity.

The student was somewhat surprised to hear the mother ask Carlos to bring things to her, to take objects to the counselor, or to tell the visitors something about what he was doing. She even let him go outside by himself to ride his tricycle, after reminding him to ride only to the end of the sidewalk and then back to the front steps.

By the time she found herself outside with the counselor after cheerful goodbyes, the student's thoughts were going in all directions. She had so many questions: Are all 3-year-old children who are totally blind like Carlos? Do all parents relate to their blind children as Carlos's mother did? How did he know to avoid a chair or to stop before he bumped into the door? Did he listen for cues as to his location?

Continuing to reflect on the visit, she began to recall ways in which Carlos differed from sighted 3-year-old children whom she had known. As he played or moved around, he seemed to hold his head down rather than up, unless reminded, and he made more than the usual amount of noise as he handled his toys and played with them, sometimes using them simply for the purpose of making a sound. Were all blind children so noisy in their play? She recalled also that if the conversation stopped and the room was very quiet, Carlos would usually be the first one to say something, to ask a question, or to find some way to interact with an adult. Did she imagine this, or was it really so? Other things appeared to be unusual—Carlos frequently used his toys differently from most children and not always for the purposes they were intended, and he seemed to change often from one toy to another and to misplace them, at which time he would return to the adults to be a part of the group. What were the reasons for these seemingly discrepant behaviors?

Looking back over the total experience, the student had a good feeling, although she still felt confused and was unable to resolve all her questions. Nevertheless, she recognized some of her misconceptions and expected she would be quite comfortable with other blind children she might encounter.

Not all young children who are blind are like Carlos, nor are all parents like his mother in attitude and interactions with their children. She had the benefit of continuous support and assistance from specially trained educational personnel shortly after Carlos's birth. This was possible because shortly before Carlos was born, services to children with visual impairment were extended to infants and young children and their parents through legislation in the state where they lived. Now, legislation in the United States, through the Handicapped Infants and Toddlers Act of 1986 (retitled in 1990 as Disabled Infants and Toddlers Act), Public Law (PL) 99-457, makes it possible for services to be provided to infants and young children in all states with assistance from grants provided by the federal government.

By the time Carlos and his mother arrived home from the hospital after his birth, a counselor and a specially trained teacher of children with visual handicaps contacted them. Despite this support, both of Carlos's parents experienced mixed feelings of sorrow, insecurity, guilt, and even resentment that their baby was blind. The counselor tried to discuss with them that shock, denial, and resentment could be therapeutic and that they should not resist these feelings (Gardner, 1982). Dealing with and acknowledging these feelings could lead to a rapid, stable adjustment. Even then, Carlos's mother sometimes doubted her own ability to do all that was expected of her. As she began working with Carlos and trying to look carefully for his responses, she felt more comfortable and gradually gained confidence in her ability to interpret his movements and other behaviors. A child without vision, she realized, had more subtle and quite different communicative responses than those of a child with vision. She learned how to help Carlos use his other senses and began to think of him as a baby who was cuddly and interesting to play with. She spent a lot of time teaching him to use his hands and his ears, but she noticed very early how quickly he learned to discriminate sounds. Every time she had a question, teachers helped her find an answer, and she enjoyed the relationships with other parents of children who had visual impairments. All these resources may have made a real difference in Carlos's behavior at 3 years of age, as well as his mother's attitude. She also learned that not all children with visual impairments are totally blind, as can be seen from the following description of Lucy, who was born with a severe visual impairment but showed evidence of developing some usable vision.

LUCY

At the age of 2, Lucy was still a puzzle to her parents; they had many conflicting thoughts about her development and behavior. At the most unexpected moments she appeared to reach out toward things as if she could see them, and at other times she seemed unable to see at all. Because of her prematurity and the many medical procedures necessary, she seemed to exhibit little visual behavior in the early weeks. The doctor had told the parents to observe her visual development carefully because some damage to the eyes might have occurred. The doctor also had said, "There is nothing medically that we can do now, and I don't know anything to tell you to do." Fortunately for Lucy, her parents wanted a baby very much, and although they were confused and upset, she was so lovable and responsive that they found it possible much of the time to think of her as they would have thought of any other baby.

Much to their surprise, a few weeks after they took her home from the hospital, they received a call from a teacher of children with visual handicaps who offered to help them learn how to observe and work with Lucy. During the teacher's first visit, she told them to give Lucy lots of love and attention and to keep a record of anything she did that suggested she might be responding visually. When Lucy was a few weeks old, they noticed that she turned her head repeatedly to the light in the room or toward the window when near it. Was it possible that she could see the light? When the teacher returned, she told them to dim the light in a room, and hold a penlight at different distances and angles from her face to get Lucy to try to look for the light. As soon as she was attending to the light each time, they used mobiles and small multicolored objects with a light shining on them to which she also began to respond. Several months later, when Lucy was playing with her mother, she tried to reach out toward her mother's face. But she never followed her mother around the room with her eyes, and often her eyes seemed to move as if she had little control of them. At 6 months, when Lucy could sit up alone, she would often reach toward the soap in the bath water or extend an arm in the direction of her feet when being dressed. Surely these actions were indications that she was visually aware of certain objects. At the age of 1 year,

Lucy picked up objects or toys and moved them back and forth in front of her eyes, holding them very close to her face. However, if she dropped or lost something with which she was playing, she never seemed to be able to find it easily, and would either cry or "feel around" as if she could not see at all. Crawling, standing, and walking posed no unusual problems, although she was a bit hesitant to move very far and seldom directed her body purposefully, except within a very limited area.

Despite a few lingering doubts and many questions, Lucy's parents knew that she was beginning to learn to see quite a few things, but just how much was still not clear. They played games with her, trying to get her to focus on objects, to encourage her to find things. They showed her every possible object in the house and outside. Soon they developed the habit of calling her attention to interesting things by saying, "Look Lucy "and helping her direct her gaze toward the object. When she was only about 18 months old, Lucy looked up at the moon one night and said, "Light." This was remarkable behavior for a child who could hardly see the food on her plate and who seemed always to be reaching for things by grasping too far to the right or left or not far enough, frequently knocking the object to the floor in her efforts.

When Lucy was 2 years old she was able to attend a morning class with other children 2 days a week. The teachers could evaluate the developmental progress of the children, as well as their visual and orientation behaviors. During this time, the parents could observe through a two-way mirror and listen to the interaction. Some mornings there were discussion groups, and other times there were speakers or consultants with whom the parents could discuss problems or ask questions. At first, the school team planned the activities, but soon parents were taking the leadership in deciding what they needed and wanted during the 3-hour period, which became a real learning experience for them. As mentioned previously, such educational services had been available in their state for several years, but with the passage of federal legislation, children with impairments in all states in the United States can now receive educational services from birth.

At the age of 3, Lucy began to look voluntarily through magazines she found in the house, and she also showed much more interest in exploring. She began to attend a daily morning class for preschoolers with visual impairments. In a few months, she was so active and independent in her movements and exploration abilities that she was invited to spend a small part of each morning in the regular early childhood preschool class with children who did not have visual impairments. It was quite a challenge for her to keep up with children who could see much better and at greater distances. Lucy learned to listen to them and move to the sound of their voices. In classroom activities, she asked many questions, and the other children were eager to "help" her and to respond to her need to move closer to the teacher or to find toys on the shelves. She learned to make marks with crayons, although she used them a bit differently than the other children. Her pictures were not so much imitations of people or things as they were marks with many colors. She seemed to enjoy the experience of drawing and painting, just as the other children did.

On the playground, where all the preschool classes were together, Lucy could move from one piece of equipment to another and take turns with other children, who were eager to give her assistance even when she did not really need it. The teachers encouraged them to let Lucy find her own way and to get in line by herself. There were some things she could not do as readily as the children who could see. For example, she was inclined to approach the swing without listening or looking carefully to see if someone was swinging toward her, and she often tripped over things directly in front of her in her eagerness to "keep up" with the others. However, she could move several feet directly ahead to an object that was dominantly visible. She made great progress in the early childhood programs, and she became a curious, busy little girl who wanted to be a part of every activity at home and to help her mother and father with whatever they were doing. Their joy increased daily when they saw her doing so many things and gaining self-confidence. She even began to play outside with other children in the neighborhood and to move around the block with caution.

The teachers gradually increased her time in the preschool class with normally seeing children until she spent 2 hours each day with them. Her time in the special class was spent in developing greater visual efficiency and in refining orientation and movement skills, as well as in making discriminations at greater and greater distances.

When it was time to visit the eye specialist, the parents were apprehensive, but quite relieved when the doctor showed great delight with Lucy's evident "looking and seeing" behavior. She told them Lucy could see at about 10 inches what a child with normal vision could see at 20 feet. That meant that she could function visually quite well at a very close range, but would continue to have difficulty seeing at greater distances, especially in large spatial areas such as the playground. Even that news was very encouraging. The doctor told them to continue what they were doing with her, always encouraging her to "look" closely and carefully. They could help her by moving her closer to objects or people or bringing them closer to her when possible. She also suggested that Lucy have a stand magnifier at home, such as the one they had in the classroom at school, so that she could examine details of household objects and designs on her clothing, and/or she could begin to make pictures of things she had seen.

As the time for kindergarten approached, the teacher recommended that Lucy be enrolled in the class with normally seeing children. With only minor attention from the teacher, and occasional assistance in learning new skills from her vision-specialist teacher, she was soon participating in most activities. While the other children were working with letters and flash cards, Lucy's special teacher sat with her and helped her to hold them close enough to see easily. It took her longer to do things that required vision, but she was persistent and her teachers were patient.

Lucy usually used the regular materials, and if she had difficulty seeing them, she would take them to the stand magnifier to verify the details. She also learned to make her letters by placing her paper under the magnifier and copying those her special teacher provided as a model. She could match pictures and letters and numbers with little difficulty when she could bring them as close to her eyes as needed. Her progress was rapid, and she was able to keep pace with the other children with a minimum of special help.

As the time neared for Lucy to begin first grade, her parents still had many questions about how well she was able to see. They wondered whether she would be able to see all her schoolwork and to learn to read visually. Would she learn to use braille? These were questions that could not be answered now—only time would tell. With Lucy's love of learning, her vibrancy with other children, and her winning ways with the teachers, whatever was best for her school progress would be fine with the parents. She might even read some things in print, but learn to read braille also, enabling her to use all her senses and have more materials available to her. By learning braille, she could rest her eyes if they became tired or use braille if the light was insufficient for her to see the print easily.

Many children with severe visual handicaps are similar to Lucy. The prospects for such a child's future remain somewhat unclear; the child may behave sometimes as a seeing child and at other times as a child who cannot see at all. Parents, educators, and vision specialists can make few conclusive statements or predictions. Nevertheless, one possibility is evident—a child who demonstrates an ability to see may be able to learn to function more efficiently visually. Certainly, no child who can see to do the things that Lucy has been described as doing could be considered a "blind" child, even though this term was once used to describe her.

As Lucy develops, there will continue to be many unanswered questions. For the moment, Lucy is a child who sees and is learning to explore her world visually and to find her place among her friends who have much better vision. With continued improvement and her evident speed in learning, Lucy may complete high school and go on to college. This is in contrast to another child in Lucy's neighborhood, Sharon, who will always need a specialized program to enhance her learning.

SHARON

When Sharon's mother entered her daughter's room to get her up each morning, she always went to the window and opened the curtains before going to Sharon's bedside. A few months ago, Sharon had begun to notice the patch of light that widened when the curtains opened. Now, each morning, she turned her head toward the window, waved her arms with their tiny fisted hands, and called out in loud, excitable sounds. To her mother, those sounds meant, "Good morning, mother, I love you! I can't wait to get up!"

At 4 years old, Sharon was beginning to do many new things. There was a time when Sharon's mother had not believed that the child could learn at all. Soon after Sharon's birth, when one doctor said, "Put her in a home for handicapped children," Sharon's parents had wondered whether that might not be best for both Sharon and her family. She would require a great deal of special care, the doctor said, and she might never even recognize her family. During Sharon's delivery, her brain was deprived of oxygen for several minutes; this resulted in severe cerebral palsy, profound mental retardation, and a loss of vision which the ophthalmologist called "cortical visual impairment." Sharon had remained in the hospital for several months. When she did come home, she required almost constant care. She was often ill, and for the first 18 months, all her nutrition was provided through a tube placed into an opening in her stomach. Sharon's parents often wondered whether they had done the right thing by bringing her home to live, with two active older brothers who also needed their parents' attention.

But now, at 4 years of age, Sharon was an important member of the family; her mother could not imagine life without her. Almost weekly, Sharon learned or tried something new: She smiled when her brothers or parents spoke to her; she reached with her right hand for brightly colored toys like her clown doll; and she eagerly ate soft or chopped foods that were fed to her, often what the rest of the family was eating. She was usually a healthy little girl, although her mother was careful not to expose her to others with colds or flu because Sharon's lack of muscle control made it difficult for her to cough or reposition herself for sinus drainage.

Perhaps the most exciting change over the last year had been the development of Sharon's vision. Sharon's doctor had said she had no vision as an infant, so her family had tried to communicate with her through sound and touch. However, when a teacher for infants with special needs began coming to the house when Sharon was less than 1 year old, the teacher pointed out that Sharon sometimes seemed to look at bright lights and shiny toys; although Sharon's mother had noticed this before, it was so slight that she thought that it might be her imagination. A teacher of children with visual handicaps had come to the house with the infant teacher on several occasions, and he showed Sharon's mother ways to help Sharon understand that she could reach out for the forms and colors that she perceived. The family began to collect objects that Sharon might be able to see, and they placed them above and beside her bed.

By Sharon's second year, when she began to attend a day program several mornings a week, her parents were sure that she could see much more than light and forms. She sometimes smiled when one of her brothers silently tiptoed toward her from the side, and she bounced and waved her arms when her mother removed her yellow bath wedge from the closet a few feet from Sharon's bed. Along with Sharon's teacher, her parents developed a list of daily routines in which they could include familiar, visible objects to help Sharon connect visual images to real events and people. Although the ophthalmologist could not be very clear about exactly how much Sharon was seeing, her family now felt sure that vision would be an important way for Sharon to learn and communicate.

As Sharon's mother turned her daughter on her side and prepared to change and dress her, she thought of how far Sharon had come over the last 4 years. Although her mother would never have wished to have a child with severe disabilities, Sharon had opened new worlds for her family. Her mother had formed important friendships with other parents of children with disabilities, and she had learned that her two older sons could capably take some responsibilities in helping to care for Sharon. Perhaps most important, raising Sharon had strengthened her parents' marriage as both parents learned that they could cope with the special challenges of parenting Sharon. There was no doubt that Sharon had enriched all their lives.

Sharon babbled loudly as her mother sat her up against her own stomach and began to unfasten her daughter's pajama top. Her mother asked, "Hey, what's new, little girl? Going out to conquer the world today?" Sharon answered with a smile and a squeal of delight. To her mother, that was enough. In the story that follows, however, Michael's mother would expect more of her son, a boy with seemingly minor problems.

MICHAEL

Sitting at the kitchen table, Michael's mother was reading his report card. She was relieved to note that, for the first time, he had no failing grades. He had received a C in reading, and she hoped that this was a sign that Michael was finally beginning to comprehend the puzzle of the printed word. Perhaps this term she would not have to leave work as often for school conferences. Her boss was becoming concerned about the work she had missed for meetings with Michael's teachers, but as a single mother, she believed that she played an important role in her child's education.

Thinking back, she could remember what an energetic, active boy Michael had been before he entered kindergarten. At that time, the parents thought the only difficulty that might affect his learning was his visual impairment. She and Michael's father had known that their son's vision was poor before he was 3 years old; the doctor had told them that the condition was called "progressive myopia" and that Michael might need to hold things closer to his eyes and might have problems in spotting the ball in playground games or in seeing detail when watching movies. Following the diagnosis, Michael had been given glasses to be worn all day; although he was a rough-and-tumble child, he never broke or lost his glasses and always remembered to put them on first thing in the morning. As a preschooler, Michael played actively with other children and never seemed to miss much of what was going on in his neighborhood. Although he got into more than his share of fights with other children, his father dismissed it, saying that his son was just "all boy" and that Michael knew how to "stick up for himself."

Two years ago, when Michael entered kindergarten, everything seemed to happen at once. Shortly after Michael's baby sister was born, his parents divorced and his mother went to work for an insurance firm. So much had to be done that at first Michael's mother did not pay much attention to the notes from his teacher. Her son was unable to listen and follow directions; his handwriting was slow, and he made many letters backward or upside down; he could not pay attention in class; he could not tell his name from the names of other children whose first initial was M. The teacher had talked about keeping him in kindergarten for another year, but Michael's mother did not want to see her son left behind his classmates. She remembered how uncomfortable she was at having to meet with the teacher and the principal, but she did go to talk with them. When the mother explained that things were very difficult at home and that Michael's vision might be making his work more difficult, the school agreed to pass him along to first grade and to try to get him some help from a special teacher for children with visual handicaps.

First grade began with similar difficulties: Michael was in the slow reading group, although he loved number problems and would often choose games and books with mostly numbers to work in after school. The picture brightened a little when Ms. Jackson began to visit Michael each week. As an itinerant teacher of children with visual handicaps, she worked with him to encourage him to use his vision efficiently. She taught him a special way of printing and helped him use a little telescope called a monocular, which allowed him to copy from the chalkboard without leaving his seat. However, even Ms. Jackson said that Michael's school problems did not seem to be caused by his visual condition, and she suggested that Michael have a more thorough assessment to determine whether he might also have a learning disability.

Michael's mother remembered how difficult it had been for her to agree to have the school psychologist evaluate Michael. She knew that Michael's vision was poor, and she expected schoolwork to take him a little longer. But what if there was another reason, something wrong with Michael's thinking or learning abilities? What if he was retarded? The idea was very frightening to her, and when Michael was evaluated as having a learning disability, she at first felt angry and annoyed. Her child was not slow; perhaps the diagnostician had not taken the time to make Michael comfortable enough to show the things he could do.

She even felt a little angry when she went to another conference, this one to help arrange special education services for Michael. But she also was desperate; her active, playful child felt like a failure in school, and many mornings he would complain of a stomachache when it was time to leave for school. At the meeting, Michael's first-grade teacher suggested that he spend 2 hours in a resource room each day to work on language arts and that Ms. Jackson continue to work with him in using his vision effectively. Michael's mother had agreed with some hesitation. In only a few months, however, Michael had begun to regain some of his interest in learning and the stomachaches had disappeared completely.

As she glanced at her son playing in the living room with a set of racing cars, she laughed a little at her own apprehensions. Michael was beginning to enjoy figuring out new words now. He was hunched over the racetrack, printing a sign that said, "Races today!" He had to lean forward so his eyes were a few inches from his own printing, and he had an extra "o" in the word "today," but he had printed the sign on his own initiative. Six months ago, he tried to avoid reading and writing even when he was playing. Now he recognized the importance of printed words in daily activities; this morning he had even read the name of the prize robot contained in the cereal box. As she got up to watch the beginning of the races, she was grateful that there were ways to adapt learning for children like Michael who might take a different route to success in learning. His problems seemed much less serious, however, than those of a young girl down the street who might be blind in a short time.

CHING LAN

Although Ching Lan had been wearing glasses since she was 4, and had received the services of a special teacher for children with visual handicaps since second grade, her parents were not prepared when the doctor told them that Ching Lan, now 11, was losing her vision rapidly. He said that Ching Lan could be totally blind in as short a time as a few months and certainly in a few years. As they sat stunned by the news, they suddenly remembered what another doctor had told them when Ching Lan was a baby: "I'm not sure how much she sees and how long she will retain her sight. She will be fine for several years, but the time will come when she will start to lose her vision." That time had come!

They had hoped their doctor was wrong. After all, he was only human—there might be some kind of mistake. Ching Lan seemed to get along fine in school, and she seemed to enjoy playing outdoors with her friends just as much as she always had. They made an appointment with another doctor, who had been recommended by a mother they met at a recent meeting of the National Association for Parents of the Visually Impaired (NAPVI). Perhaps a different doctor could give them better news. But after the new doctor examined Ching Lan, his prognosis was the same: "I'm sorry, but her condition is degenerative, and we can't be sure how rapidly the loss of vision will progress." He offered to explain the condition to Ching Lan, but her parents said they would do it themselves.

As the days passed, however, they found themselves putting off talking with their daughter. What would it do to her if she knew? Would she become depressed and unable to function in school? Would her friends still play with her? Would she lose the ability to do things for herself, such as dressing or making her own sandwich for lunch? New worries came to them each day, but they were reluctant to share them with Ching Lan; she seemed so young to have to deal with such a problem.

Several weeks later, Ching Lan came home from school one day with less enthusiasm than usual and acted a bit strange. She went to her room, saying she was tired and would rest before dinner. At dinner, her parents were surprised when she said, "Did those doctors say anything about me losing my vision? I know I must be, because everything gets harder to see each day, and I can hardly do my schoolwork." Finally her father said falteringly, "The doctor did say that your eyes were not doing as well as they have been." Ching Lan sat for a moment and said, "I knew it, but you didn't tell me because you didn't want to talk about it. Well, I've known it for a long time, and my teacher and I talked about it. He showed me a big television that I can use later that will make the printing in my books look very large. It even makes my fingernails look big!

"The kids all help me, too, and when I drop something that I can't find, they tell me where it is until I get close enough to see it. That doesn't bother me since I never could see some things if the sun was shining or the light was too bright or they were far away. Last week, John Martin hid my pencil, but I heard right where he put it and I found it right away!"

Ching Lan's mother wanted to take her daughter in her arms and tell her how sorry she was that Ching Lan would not be able to see for much longer, but she could not bring herself to do it because she knew that Ching Lan would realize how sad she felt. She remembered when Ching Lan was very young, soon after the doctor told them of the vision problem, how much she had worried about what might have caused the problem; she tried to think about whether she had taken any medicine when she was pregnant, and she even asked her husband's sister if she knew of anyone in her family who had a problem with their eyes. But after a while, she began to see how much Ching Lan could do, and she thought less often about why her daughter's vision was different. Maybe they would come to accept this change in the same way.

As Ching Lan continued to talk, her mother noticed how much wiser than her years she sounded: "Ever since I noticed that I couldn't see as well, I've been practicing. Sometimes I close my eyes and try walking around by myself, and you know what? Just by listening really well, I can tell a lot about what's going on and where the other kids are."

Ching Lan's father thought about how much his daughter enjoyed playing ball, and he recalled that lately she had been asking him more often to "throw a grounder." It occurred to him now that she had been learning to use her hearing to locate the ball. He wondered whether they would be able to enjoy games of catch when she had no vision, and he thought sadly that they might not. But he remembered all the other things that Ching Lan enjoyed outdoors. She had joined a girl's track team during the summer, and she should be able to run with a guide or to follow a sound ahead of her. He wondered whether she could ever keep up with her schoolwork and whether she might need to attend a special school away from home, but Ching Lan seemed confident about the changes she would have to make.

"I think you should go and talk to my teacher," she said to her parents. "He says I may still read print for a long time. I can use a magnifier to make the letters bigger, and later I can learn to use that television—it's called a closed circuit television—to help me see more letters at a time. Besides, when I can't see well enough to read any more, my teacher's going to let me start reading with my fingers like Peter Stevens does. My teacher says that when I learn braille, I can read with my eyes until they get tired and then read braille to rest them. And you know what? When I close my eyes and pick things up, I can already tell what they are."

Her parents were relieved that Ching Lan understood so much more than they realized. They told Ching Lan that she had explained a great deal about her schoolwork that they had not understood. They reminded her that there would be times when she would need to ask other people to help her, and that she should be much more careful about crossing streets and doing a lot of things that she was accustomed to doing quite easily. Ching Lan mentioned the mobility instructor who came to the school to work with some of the other students. She told her parents that the instructor might teach her how to listen carefully for sounds around her and to use a cane so that she would be safer and would know when there was something ahead of her. "Maybe when I get older, I could even get a dog guide!" she suggested eagerly. Her mother smiled, "I'm just getting adjusted to the cat you brought home last year. Let's take a little time to think about a dog!"

Later that evening when they were alone, Ching Lan's parents were able to think rationally. They realized that Ching Lan had never been like other children as far as her vision was concerned. She used the sight she had and apparently did not worry about what she did not have. Adjusting to a gradual loss in vision was not the same for her as it would have been for them. If she could take this in stride and modify her thinking in such a positive way, they would stop feeling sad for her. She was fortunate to have a quick mind and a keen sense of curiosity, which would help her continue to enjoy learning in new ways; they knew that not all children with visual impairments were able to learn as easily.

SUMMARY

These word pictures of five children who are visually disabled illustrate the range of feelings, learning, and functioning associated with different characteristics and conditions. Some children may be born totally blind and never feel the need for vision (Carlos); others may have very little vision, which they must learn to use (Lucy); quite a few have severe impairments in addition to vision (Sharon); some have mild neurological problems in addition to the visual impairment, which make learning inconsistent and unpredictable (Michael); and a few may have adequate but impaired vision and suddenly begin to lose it (Ching Lan).

Medical people are often matter-of-fact about the condition of the eyes and their functioning, and are either unable or not inclined to make helpful suggestions to parents as to how they can help their children. Unfortunately, some medical personnel are unaware of the educational and other types of intervention available to help parents and their children with visual impairments. Except for their visual impairments, these children may have few other qualities in common with each other in relation to their social, emotional, mental, or personal development. Each child's individual potential for learning to function optimally within the family, school, or the broader social environment may be fostered or inhibited by the attitudes of the people and the factors within those settings.

Carlos's behavior, for example, was similar in many ways to that of any totally blind 3-year-old who had learned to function with the resources he had and was oblivious to what he did not have. He had learned to use his other senses in his own way. Carlos's mother adjusted her interactions and relations to his patterns of learning. She obviously included him in her activities in the home and patiently explained things to him. It also was evident that she managed him and corrected him as she would any child. When he wanted to help, she let him; therefore, he learned to recognize household objects and the sounds and feelings associated with them. Although her expectations of him were never beyond what he was capable of doing, he had been included in her everyday life.

However, their life had not always been smooth and optimistic. At first, Carlos had cried frequently and had been very active. His parents soon understood his need for more attention and tried to include him in their activities. Because of their encouragement and attentions, he was able to organize his world as he experienced and understood it, and to achieve a feeling of comfort within it. As Carlos gained greater control over his actions and some knowledge about what he wanted to do, he was able to find his own ways to solve problems. Carlos could not miss what he never had (vision), but did require frequent interpretation through verbal explanation to help him sort out his experiences and use this information to expand his repertoire of behavioral responses and to structure his knowledge about the world.

During his early development, Carlos was dependent on others for reinforcement to help him gain confidence in himself, but by the time he entered school, he had acquired enough knowledge of his environment to be able to function comfortably with considerable independence. The attitudes he developed about himself and his relationships with others were determined largely by the attitudes of his parents toward him and their acceptance of him as he was. At first they were anguished, insecure, and sometimes sad—normal feelings under the circumstances. But determination, love for their son, and confidence in their ability to meet life's problems enabled them to learn the meaning of accepting realities that they could not change. They read everything available about blind children and adjusted their lives and interactions with Carlos as his needs seemed to indicate. There would always need to be special arrangements for him to learn some things, and throughout his life he would require time and greater effort to learn certain functional skills.

Carlos's parents were very grateful that such excellent help and services were available to parents of children with visual handicaps. Without the support and suggestions of the counselors and teachers, Carlos might have been delayed in his development and learning simply because they did not know how to help him learn.

In contrast, Lucy was thought of as a seeing child, since her parents hoped and looked for evidence of her ability to see. There were some commonalities between Carlos and Lucy in that both were functioning in relation to the resources they had, never having known the sight they should or could have had. Lucy's parents learned to make minor adjustments to help her clarify the distortions and confusions that arose constantly. The many contradictions in her vision presented conflicting evidence about the nature of her vision, but such inconsistencies exist in many children with low vision. Few definitive predictions can be made about such children's potential for learning and development, and none about how efficiently they will be able to use vision in the future.

People around Lucy came to be observant and perceptive of her efforts to use her vision and encouraged her continually to use the vision she had. For Lucy this stimulated an interest in searching for clarification of a distorted and sometimes bewildering world, a world in which she needed to learn to feel comfortable and secure. Her behavior indicated that she was a seeing child and could continue to develop greater visual efficiency as modifications were made for her, and she, in turn, made the adjustments compatible with her ability. She learned also that in some situations she could not rely solely on her vision and needed to ask for assistance and/or acknowledge her visual limitations to others. She even came to understand that as she progressed in school and the work became more visually demanding, she might need to learn braille to supplement her visual reading when she became too tired.

Although Sharon's development and learning had been and will continue to be slow, she is beginning to show evidence of responding to her environment and to people with whom she is familiar. It is virtually impossible to predict very much about Sharon's future, but she will require a great deal of assistance with personal care throughout her life. Her communication and interactions with others may improve as she grows older, but total independence is probably not something ever to be anticipated.

In children who have less noticeable and serious visual impairments, such as Michael, parents and others tend to think that everything will remain stable after the initial diagnosis of progressive myopia and the prescription of glasses, forgetting that progressive means "continuing to progress." The possibility of other problems for Michael was not even considered. Although he was not as focused or able to concentrate, he was just as active but not as motorically advanced as other preschool children with whom he played. The minor differences were attributed to his vision. Even when he began kindergarten and the teacher's notes should have sent up "red flags," his mother was coping with so many other problems that she found it emotionally difficult to attend to the teacher's concerns. When the vision specialist requested a thorough evaluation, the mother had to begin to face reality despite the pain she felt for herself and for Michael. She thought back to the things she had noticed but failed to acknowledge about Michael, finding it easier to pretend that everything would be all right. Michael's mother had to come to grips with her negative attitudes about the thought of her son's being in special education, thinking that it was a reflection on her parenting skills. When she was able to reason with herself and to accept the concern and help of the teachers and the psychologist, things began to be much better for Michael in school, and she developed a very positive way of thinking of special services for children who need them.

As with Michael, many children who have learning difficulties do not receive help until they begin to fail in school or have such obvious difficulties that the problems can no longer be set aside. Subtle differences in attention, lack of tolerance for certain kinds of games, and slight incoordination in motor activities are of concern in preschool children, and should be described in detail to medical or educational personnel as soon as they are noticed. Children themselves often know that they cannot do the things their playmates can do, and they find their own ways of coping with their frustrations, such as Michael's repeated fights. Many marked and obvious impairments are reported at once, but the less noticeable differences may do great damage to the child's self-esteem before help is provided.

The flexibility and tremendous capacity for adjustment inherent in all children cannot be overemphasized. Ching Lan clearly illustrates these abilities to adjust. In her case, the challenge was primarily for her parents and teachers to reinforce her positive attitudes and motivation, being careful not to interfere in her adjusting to her gradual loss of vision by stressing their concern or by imposing their adult fears on her. The gradual transition from performing as a seeing child to functioning as a child who is blind meant that she would have more time to adjust to her visual loss and could use her diminishing visual capabilities for support as she began to develop new approaches to learning. The fact that she could use remembered visual imagery to help her associate and integrate new learning patterns and skills, in addition to having been around other children who were totally blind and whom she accepted as her friends, made it easier for her to continue to consider herself as a competent person who would be able to find ways to cope satisfactorily.

Throughout the text, specific factors from each of the children's cases just described will be recalled and related to discussions, where appropriate. At times, the child (in referring to his or her impairment) may be identified by name. More frequently, the readers will be free to make their own associations and inferences.

2

Confusion in Words, Clarity in Concepts

Words are not reality, nor can they describe reality; however, words can change our understanding of reality. Words used as labels or as terms to describe persons often may assign these people to a group to which they may or may not belong, thereby ignoring other individual characteristics that may differentiate any individual from other members of the group. Labels or descriptive words used in referring to a child can sometimes imply that there is something undesirable about the child, creating a difference greater than exists in reality. The first attempts to differentiate between the terms *impairment, disability,* and *handicap* were made by persons in rehabilitation (Hamilton, 1950; Myerson, 1963; Sussman, 1969; Wright, 1960). These terms have been adopted and refined by persons in both rehabilitation and education (Scholl, 1986; Sigelman, Vengroff, & Spanhel, 1984), and may now be considered to mean the following:

- An *impairment* can be defined as an identifiable defect in the basic structure or function of an organ or a body system as diagnosable by a medical doctor or other clinician. The defect may or may not interfere with the individual's learning or functional ability.

- *Disability* has come to mean the extent to which the impairment interferes with or limits the person's functions and activities. An impairment may contribute to a disability in five areas: health, social–attitudinal, mobility, cognitive–intellectual, and communication (Sigelman et al.,

1984). Often the disabling effects of an impairment can be minimized or completely erased through medical or nonmedical intervention.

• A *handicap* results when the "individual is placed at an actual or perceived disadvantage" (Sigelman et al., 1984) in functioning because of the impairment. A disability does not have to become a handicap unless individuals accept the limitations imposed by others or impose limitations upon themselves.

HISTORICAL TERMINOLOGY

Since as far back as the early 1800s, there has been a lack of precision in the use of terms relating to those who have visual impairments or who are totally without sight. This inconsistency is apparent in the use of terms by doctors, optometrists, psychologists, rehabilitation therapists, and educators. Differences and divergent roles in each discipline have been influenced by regional attitudes, cultural practices, and clinical focus (Braley, 1962; Fonda, 1961; Hoover, 1962; Jones, 1962; Myerson, 1963). These myriad attitudes and roles reflect the confusion that has resulted from the lack of agreement in terminology, even among professionals directly associated daily with persons who are blind or have impaired vision. Table 2.1 lists terms that have appeared in the literature in the last 150 years, all describing persons with visual impairments. These terms are grouped according to their use in general and specific disciplines.

Education programs have been labeled by such names as sight saving, vision or sight conservation, sight utilization, partially seeing, braille blind, and more recently, visually handicapped. This variable terminology has confused the public, to say the least, and has been a deterrent to gathering precise information through research. The use of all these terms and inconsistencies in describing visual impairments have created many questions that have been unresolved, including the following:

How much vision is enough vision to perform certain tasks?

What constitutes a visual handicap in learning?

What critical variables influence individual visual behavior in children?

Why do some children with severe visual impairments function at markedly higher levels than others whose impairments are much less severe?

TABLE 2.1
Terms Describing Persons with Visual Impairments, by Discipline

All disciplines	*Rehabilitation*
congenitally blind	legally blind
adventitiously blind	medically blind
visually handicapped	economically blind
residual vision	vocationally blind
Clinical	*Education*
partially blind	educationally blind
visually disabled	partially seeing
subnormal vision	visually impaired
remaining vision	residual vision
visually defective	braille blind
	functionally blind
	low vision

What is the relation (if any) between impairment in component parts of the visual system and what the child can learn to see?

INTERDISCIPLINARY TERMINOLOGY

At least three major disciplines are involved in screening, diagnosis, and service delivery to those with visual impairment. Persons who fill various roles and have specialty training can be defined as follows:

- *Ophthalmologist* is a medical specialist who treats diseases and provides surgical care to the eyes. His or her primary emphasis is on diagnosis and medical and surgical treatment of the condition when possible, and in measurement (with the use of cycloplegias) of the refractive and accommodative status of the eye to determine visual acuity at a distance of 20 feet or beyond. If specifically requested, some ophthalmologists also will provide near vision acuity, especially for children.

- *Optometrist*, a specialist in physiological optics and refraction, is licensed as a nonmedical practitioner to examine eyes, prescribe and provide lenses, and sometimes perform visual therapy. His or her primary emphasis is on visual functioning at both near and far points and on describing the disorders of function, then prescribing lenses to minimize the effects of the condition.

- *Optician* is a specialist who grinds and fits lenses, and designs and manufactures optical instruments according to the prescription of the ophthalmologist and/or optometrist.

- *Vision specialist* is any medical, clinical, or educational person with knowledge and/or training in working with persons with visual impairments in order to improve functioning and efficiency.

- *Vision teacher/consultant* is a certified teacher with special training in visual impairments and individual needs for materials, devices, adaptations, and specialized services in the educational setting.

The communication and cooperation of individuals in these disciplines is important if persons with visual impairment are to receive optimal educational and clinical services. However, each of these disciplines has tended to use terminology characteristic of the specific discipline, until recent years when interdisciplinary cooperation and a greater concern for consistency has brought the various definitions into closer similarity. Classification of levels of vision has also lacked uniformity among the different professionals. In 1977, Colenbrander chaired a worldwide committee that recommended a new classification system, which was adopted by the World Health Organization and is based on the extent to which a person is disabled visually (see Table 2.2).

This classification system makes it much easier for clinical (medical and optometric) and educational personnel to communicate because the focus is more on how the individual can perform visually, and is less rigidly oriented to exact measurement criteria, which may be inappropriate to describe individual functional characteristics. Professionals from all disciplines are thinking about and working toward lessening the visual disability and the visual handicap by improving the person's abilities and/or by reducing the environmental demands for performance of visual tasks.

TRENDS IN TERMINOLOGY

An analysis of the terminology in special education general survey books published from 1983 to 1989 revealed few inconsistencies (Blackhurst & Berdine, 1985; Cartwright, Cartwright, & Ward, 1989; Gearheart

TABLE 2.2
Classification System for Persons with Visual Disabilities

CLASSIFICATION	LEVEL OF VISION	LEVEL OF DISABILITY
Normal	Normal vision Near normal vision	Can perform tasks without special aids
	Moderate	Can perform tasks near normal with special aids
Low vision	Severe	Performs visual tasks at a reduced level of speed, endurance, and precision even with aids
	Profound	Has difficulty with gross visual tasks; cannot perform most detailed visual tasks
Blind	Near blind	Vision is unreliable; relies primarily on other senses
	Blind	Totally without sight; relies exclusively on other senses

Adapted from "Dimensions of Visual Performance" by A. Colenbrander, 1977, *Archives of American Academy of Ophthalmology, 83,* 335.

& Weishahn, 1984; Hallahan & Kauffman, 1988; Haring & McCormick, 1986; Kirk & Gallagher, 1989). All the title chapters used the phrase *visual impairments,* even those written by persons outside the field. In the discussions, the term *visually handicapped* was used as a generic descriptor of the population, and in most cases *blind* and *low vision* were used as subtitles. This trend in terminology seems to have reached a rather consistent level throughout recent publications, both in general special education and in the specific field of visual impairments, when referring to school-aged children and youth.

The term visually handicapped has been accepted by educators to denote the total group of children who have impairments in the structure or functioning of the visual sense organ—the eye—irrespective of the nature and extent of the impairment. This term has gained acceptance because the impairment causes a limitation that, even with the best possible correction, interferes with incidental or normal learning through the visual sense and therefore constitutes an educational handicap. The term was adopted by the U.S. Congress as official terminology used by the Office of Special Education (1981). Hereafter in this book, visually handicapped refers to the total group of children who require special educational provisions because of visual problems. Such a definition is appropriate for educational purposes and should be encouraged to differentiate children's learning and developmental needs from those of adults, who may have additional or entirely different legal, vocational, and medical factors to consider.

For subgroups, the terms blind and low vision differentiate those persons without sight from those who can use vision. Corn (1989b) defined low vision as "a level of vision which, with standard correction, hinders an individual in the planning and/or execution of a task, but which permits enhancement of the functional vision through the use of optical or nonoptical devices, environmental modifications and/or techniques" (p. 28). In the same article, she defined *functional vision* as "visual ability sufficient for utilizing visual information in the planning and/or execution of a task which would be possible for those without visual impairment" (p. 28).

Despite the pleas of persons with impairments and disabilities, reporters in the general media still tend to to use obsolete and inappropriate terminology when discussing individuals who may have any type of impairment. Using descriptors as adjectives ("blind person" or "deaf girl") is stereotypic and infers that the whole person is incapacitated, not simply the vision or hearing. Even more offensive is the use of such terms as *invalid, defective,* or *victim* when referring to persons who may be disabled.

Perhaps through the efforts of persons with impairments and the professionals who work with them, the same sort of positive change can occur in the terminology used by the media and general public as has already taken place in the educational literature. Teachers can have some influence in bringing about such a change.

ADDITIONAL TERMS AND DEFINITIONS

Some of the terms previously discussed as well as others are defined in different ways by specialists in various disciplines. For example, in addition to the legal definition of blindness (20/200 or less in the better eye after correction, or a field of less than 10 degrees), Faye (1984) said that *blind* refers to those who have only light perception without projection, or those who are totally without the sense of vision. Educationally, blind children are those who must be educated through tactile and sensory channels other than vision (Scholl, 1986), although perception of light may be present and useful in orientation and movement.

Low vision is an especially difficult term to define. In addition to the one given by Corn above, an earlier edition of this book (Barraga, 1983) designated children with low vision as those who have limitations in distance vision but are able to see objects and materials within a few inches or at a maximum of a few feet away. Generally, most children with low vision can use their vision for many school learning activities, including visual reading, although some may need to use tactile materials and possibly even braille to supplement printed and other visual materials. For some purposes and under varying conditions relative to light, contrast, and personal characteristics, such children will always need to be made aware of what they are able to see and given assistance and encouragement in looking at educational materials and other objects (as in the case of Lucy). Even if braille is decided upon as the primary reading medium, under no circumstances should children with low vision be referred to as blind or deprived of visual materials.

Visual acuity refers to a clinical measurement of the ability to discriminate clearly the fine details of objects or symbols at a specified distance. To date, no relationship between acuity measurements and functional use of vision has been established. Persons with very low clinical acuity measurements may function visually at a very high level, whereas some persons with much higher levels of visual acuity may behave as if they had no vision.

Visual impairment denotes any optically or medically diagnosable condition of the eye(s) or visual system that affects the structure or functioning of the tissues so that less than normal vision is the result. Impairments may be of a rather minor nature, may even be correctable, or may be quite severe and uncorrectable with lenses or treatment. The impairment may be in the central part of the eye, such as the lens or the area around the macula, in which case the person could have very good peripheral vision but have trouble seeing fine detail. Conversely, the impairment might be in the outer retina in the periphery and cause what is known as tunnel vision, and the person may have very clear central vision at a specific point of focus, but not see to either side. The impairment also might be in the optic disk or nerve, which would interfere with the transmission of the retinal stimulation to the brain.

Visual perception means the ability to interpret what is seen, that is, to understand and interpret meaningfully all information received through the visual sense. Visual perception involves examining an object, distinguishing the essential features, understanding the relationship between the elements, and integrating the information into a meaningful whole. Visual perception is a decision process related more to the child's learning opportunities and capabilities than to the condition of the eyes. Even in cases of impairment and poor acuity, the brain receives visual impressions and is able to interpret them quite accurately. Faye (1970) wrote,

> It is not the poor vision that causes poor learning, but it is what the brain does with the visual data. It must be intact in order to make sense of various stimuli, to store up experience, and to see symbols and know what they mean, to remember and associate printed letters and words. The eye does not have to be intact, but the associative areas of the brain must be. (p. 137)

Visual functioning, which was defined earlier in this section, is simply the extent to which people use whatever vision they may have. Some children have extremely limited visual capability, but use the vision they have so effectively that their functioning appears to be totally visually oriented. Others having similar visual potential are not aware of, or are not responsive to, visual stimuli and behave as if they are unable to see at all. Some children have probably been taught that they are blind, and therefore function accordingly. Visual functioning is related in part to the condition of the eye; more explicitly, however, it is determined by the experiences, motivations, needs, and expectations of each individual in relation to whatever visual capacity is available to satisfy curiosity and accomplish activities for personal satisfaction.

Visual efficiency, the most inclusive of all terms relating to vision, is contingent on many personal and environmental variables. Visual acuity at a distance and at near range, control of eye movements, accommodative and adaptive capabilities of the visual mechanism, speed and filtering abilities of the transmitting channels, and speed and quality of the processing ability of the brain are all related to visual efficiency. Corn (1989b) presented a theoretical model to explain the development of efficient visual function. For educational purposes, visual efficiency is the most important consideration (Barraga, 1973), because it determines the degree to which the student can perform specific visual tasks with ease, comfort, and minimum time. Visual efficiency is unique to each individual and cannot be measured or predicted clinically with any accuracy by medical, psychological, or educational personnel.

SUMMARY

To label as blind children who are able to see many things is to imply that they are not expected to see, and in a short time they will begin to function as blind and perceive themselves as incapable visually. When a person ceases to look, the ability to see is lost. Such ambiguous terms as partially seeing or partially blind seem to suggest a relationship between quantity of an attribute and quality of functioning in the individual—a totally false inference.

However, to disregard all descriptive words would be foolish and possibly detrimental to children's safety and to their special learning needs. The words used should relate to development and learning in children, as well as the potential for more efficient visual functioning in all individuals with low vision. Using the terms blind and low vision appropriately is a realistic cue to teachers and to the general society in knowing what to expect of students.

From the list of terms given in Table 2.1, only those that have educational significance have been selected for use in this book. The following educational definition is presented in a further attempt to encourage educators to "say what they mean and mean what they say":

A child with a visual handicap is one whose visual impairment interferes with optimal learning and achievement, unless adaptations are made in the methods of presenting learning experiences, in the nature of the materials and devices used, and/or in the learning environment.

3

Early Encounters and Interactions

The knowledge explosion regarding development and learning in infancy and early childhood indicates that this crucial period may have tremendous influence throughout people's lives. Certainly, the interest in and study of infants and young children, especially those most vulnerable to developmental and learning problems, have emphasized the potential of early intervention as a preventive measure to lessen the impact of sensory, motor, endocrinological, and/or mental impairments.

Physical impairments, such as hearing or vision problems, structural or motor problems, or dysfunctional body organs, may or may not directly interfere with the physical development of the body, but may influence the maturational aspects by limiting the natural use of the body that is essential for organization and function. Likewise, a negative impact on learning and functional behavior may or may not occur as a direct result of the physical impairment, but the quality and scope of learning may be limited by reduction in environmental interactions of both a physical and a social nature. In some physical impairments, the actual structure of the body and its capacity to develop may be inhibited to some degree, if not totally. Sensory impairments immediately place a limitation on the capacity to learn incidentally without intervention or assistance. Although there is validity in making some distinction between the terms *development* and *learning,* a strong relationship exists between them and most agree that they are mutually interdependent. The human growth cycle encompasses both physiological maturation and learned behavior, and the ideal for each child is that these two dimensions be in balanced concert as the child seeks to become emotionally secure and able to function socially, physically, and mentally. Without a stabilizing emotional environment, children may experience interruptions and gaps in both physical and mental development.

GENERAL CONCEPTS OF DEVELOPMENT AND LEARNING

The process of development and learning in all children begins at birth and is related to and, to some extent, dependent on the mutually satisfying interactions between infant and caregiver, infant and environment, and infant and other children in play (Shaffer, 1977). The critical variables in interpersonal interactions and encounters as foundations for development and learning involve what happens to the child within the family. Affective development, as well as social and cognitive development, is contingent for the most part on the family's attitudes and personal involvement with the child, who is constantly striving to become a complete human being. Barraga (1973) wrote,

> With his first breath at the moment of birth, an infant has the capacity to become a receiving, participating, interacting human being who enjoys a reciprocally satisfying relationship with his immediate environment, and eventually a fulfilling involvement with an ever expanding world. (p. 117)

Studies have shown that the duration and variety of vocal, tactile, and kinesthetic stimulation provided by caretakers are related to overall development and that the mother's level and quality of preverbal interaction with her baby relates to the child's later linguistic competence (Rowland, 1984).

Attachment or bonding to another human being has long been considered basic to future feelings about oneself and others. The mutuality of the interplay between an infant and caregiver establishes a bond of communication in which each initiates an action and waits for the response, and either repeats the action or expands it to elicit a different response. Eventually, a pattern emerges in which a rhythm of interaction, alternation of initiators, and maintenance of particular actions occurs for shorter or longer time periods (Field, Goldberg, Stern, & Sostek, 1980). The bonding and attachment process may be observed during feeding (especially nursing), reciprocal gazing, gentle holding and mutual touching, and vocalizations. These interchanges provide evidence of spatial relationships between individuals, smooth or awkward body movements, strength of the initiator, and the feelings related to the action (Tronick, Als, & Brazelton, 1980).

The early reflexive movements that appear to be generated from within the infant's body soon become integrated with responses generated by external stimulation from the caregiver. Some experts theorize that early movement in infants is motivated by a need to reduce tension. If this is true, and bonding and attachment are of critical concern, then the parent's primary role is to create a feeling of comfort and mutual communication by touching, patting, stroking, manipulating, and talking to the infant during interaction. A continuation of this cuddling provides a basis for establishing trust and security, and may supply the framework from which the infant organizes responses into a "cognitive map" of self in relation to someone else and knowledge that there is a larger environment (Murphy, 1972). Cohen and Beckwith (1979) found evidence that a mutually reinforcing relationship between caregiver and infant can have an effect on the infant's performance at 9 months of age, and can be related significantly to performance at 2 years of age. The mutual activity stimulates curiosity and language acquisition and provides motivation to explore further. Increased exploration permits the infant to gain some control over body movements and to refine actions.

An infant's responses to nurturance and play have a strong influence on the quality and nature of the interaction. Because babies who are blind cannot maintain eye contact or see facial expressions or other positive indications of adult satisfactions, they are less likely to interact in ways that are motivating to parents. Passivity or lack of expected responses could lead parents to think their baby is not enjoying the cuddling and play. Parents must learn to look for other indicators of pleasure in infants who are blind and search for different ways to generate responses other than those related to visual interactions. There needs to be an alternating vocalizing and listening time. Parents must respond vocally to infants' vocal utterances, but never interrupt them (Rowland, 1984).

More touching and handling of the baby who is blind is necessary to help the infant feel the interaction rather than see it. Without eye contact, parents may feel estranged at first. It is important to learn to read these vocal and tactile responses, which may convey even stronger feelings of attachment than visual responses. If an infant who is blind fails to develop strong affectional ties and pleasure in human contact, emotional development may stall at a primitive level, creating a need to seek and exploit alternative sources of comfort to relieve separation anxiety.

In the baby who is visually handicapped, body play or manipulation helps the infant learn new patterns of body movement and minimizes the need for stereotyped and rigid tension-reducing movements (e.g., such undesirable motions as aimless waving of arms, rocking the body back and forth, poking the fists into the eyes, or shaking the head), which become resistant to change after several months. According to Eichel (1979), such mannerisms are the result of the lack of appropriate stimulation. Children usually do not exhibit them when engaged in active play. Emotional security, meaningful activity, and lessened anxiety seem to eliminate the need for these movements and the frequency of their occurrence. The common labeling of such behaviors as "blindisms" is erroneous, because the same actions may be observed in sighted babies who have been deprived of emotional needs and adequate nurturance caused by isolation from caring adults for long periods of time.

If babies begin to feel that they cannot influence their own world or have some control over what happens, they are likely to begin to retreat from the world and those within it. A certain cognitive satisfaction relates to the development of a strong self involved in making things happen and in mastering the environment, to say nothing of the mediating effect it may have on later cognitive development. Piaget (1966, 1973) suggested that feelings supply the energy necessary for action and for specifying goals for behavior; these "feeling-oriented" actions may be related to the emergence of conscious thought much earlier than one would think. In time, the infant, the toddler, and eventually all young children learn that they can do many things. They discover readily that they can function in their own way, at a chosen pace, exploring individual interests for selected purposes (Weber, 1971). Having achieved this level of affective development, children are well on the way to knowing who they are, what they are about, and how to use feelings, actions, and thoughts to direct future learning. A strong self-concept helps a child recognize abilities, accept weaknesses, and feel self-satisfaction and pride in each new learning experience (Cook-Clampert, 1981).

EARLY DEVELOPMENT AND LEARNING IN THE CHILD
WITH A VISUAL HANDICAP

The emergence of a strong identity of self may take longer and be achieved through different means when a child has a visual impairment. Parents are naturally distressed when they learn their child is blind or has a serious visual impairment. Although most parents experience similar feelings, they often feel guilty about acknowledging their disappointment, even to themselves or each other. This anxiety and insecurity of not knowing how to accept this unexpected (and unasked for) "different" baby, may cause them to overemphasize the diagnosis of the impairment and forget, momentarily at least, that this is a real, live baby who needs them and their love in the same way that any baby would. Not knowing exactly what to do and being afraid of doing something wrong, parents may have a tendency to leave the infant alone, providing only basic physical care while struggling with their own feelings. This abandonment of sorts defeats the child's need to achieve the bond and human attachment so vital to development. The following sections discuss some factors that appear to be most crucial to the early development and learning of children with visual handicaps.

Body Manipulation

With the infant who has a visual impairment, body play must replace eye contact to communicate parental concern and love—the facilitators of developing a self-concept. More than the usual amount of time should be spent cuddling, holding, touching, stroking, and handling the baby. At the same time, soothing, comforting sounds and words from the parents will help establish love bonds through a "tactile, auditory language" (Fraiberg, Smith, & Adelson, 1969) instead of the usual attachment stabilized through eye contact. Parents who resolve their ambivalent feelings early have more energy available to devote to establishing an infant–parent feedback system. Although a "self-righting" tendency in the developmental process appears to be evident, the negotiation proceedings between the infant who is visually impaired and the caregiver can be observed to be more explicit, repetitive, and amplified. As suggested by Rowland (1984), communication between parents and infants is bidirectional and can express pleasure and/or displeasure. A parent needs to be sensitive to infant reactions so as to be the follower as well as the leader in the dialogue. It takes longer to reach a heightened stage of mutual exchange, but the end goal is achieved when the infant reaches out for the parent and the objects or sounds that are offered. Human interactions provide the basis for the infant's future learning; therefore, a reciprocation of signals and responses between the baby and the parents is essential. If the child who is visually handicapped does not experience this interaction, personal security in relating to others and eventually to the outside world is impaired.

Sound Stimulation

Parents of the infant who is visually handicapped may have to find new ways of expressing their own feelings of pleasure when interacting with their child. In a few short months, as parents satisfy their hunger for cuddling, holding, touching, and handling, the baby will begin to respond and show feelings of pleasure and comfort. In addition, the infant learns to make an association between the human voice and the tactual intimacy. Once this association has been made, the human voice from a distance and without physical touching begins to unite the child with the world, forming a basis for experiencing feelings from voices and environmental sounds. Parents can continue to talk about every sound that is heard and every movement that is made so that sounds and actions begin to have meaning to the blind child comparable to those acquired incidentally through vision to the child who can see.

Language and Communication in Early Childhood

Development of appropriate language can depend on the child's ability to make connections with people, events, and relationships in the environment; therefore, the young child with a visual impairment may be at risk for delayed or different language development. A baby first understands the "turn-taking"aspects of communication when reciprocal communication with the parent is mastered. At the earliest stage, this depends on gaze and eye contact; each partner orients toward the other when conversing, and long before the infant understands oral speech sounds, he or she can participate in this communicative exchange.

For the child with a visual impairment, the absence or diminution of vision may interfere with this process. The child's attending signals, such as quieting vocalization or ceasing physical activity, may be misinterpreted by the parent, who then decreases or simplifies speech in hopes of receiving an active signal from the child. In the absence of a responding eye gaze, the parent chooses language, which offers the best possibility of a response.

Many caregivers tend to use declarative sentences ("Eat your carrots") or questions ("Are you eating your fruit?") in talking to young children with visual impairments. Adults also may label objects and repeat these labels to reassure themselves that the child understands what is being said (Kekelis & Andersen, 1984). This may be one reason why many young children with visual impairments use different language patterns when they begin to speak. They may use larger numbers of commands and questions, and they may more often repeat words and phrases (echolalia) during speech. Also, they may be less spontaneous than sighted children in using referential words and gestures for objects out of reach (Urwin, 1983).

Parents and caregivers may be concerned about the distinctive features of the language of the child with a visual impairment, and they may attempt to correct the spoken language. However, this can result in the child's decreased willingness to use language freely to interact with others. The primary goal in language development for the young child is to increase the use of meaningful language; conversation that relates to events and people in the environment and that enables the child to interact success-fully with others helps to develop stable relationships and fosters this goal.

The child with visual handicaps who has strong human attachments and has heard meaningful language is better equipped to cope with the world of mysterious objects encountered, often accidentally. Things seem to come "out of nowhere and disappear into nothingness" once contact with them is interrupted (Fraiberg et al., 1969). Sustained by a feeling of security and encouraged by supportive others, the world becomes a friendly rather than a fearful place, and toddlers are ready to explore, to learn to control, and to act on the world beyond their own bodies. Feelings and desires in all children are related closely to movement and action, and because sound and tactile sensations do not have the same arousing and motivating effects as do visual sensations, without consistent interaction and stimulation, the child who does not see well may become passive. Inactivity, occasioned by no one to talk with and nothing meaningful to touch, creates the child's need to perform the undesirable repetitive and stereotyped movements referred to earlier. Interestingly enough, none of these stereotyped behaviors is noticed in blind children in Africa, where mothers carry their infants on the back all day, talk to them, and include them constantly as part of the complete world of family life. You may recall that none of these behaviors was observed in Carlos, who was apparently emotionally secure and trusted himself and others. Conversely, for Michael, who was quite insecure in his interactions with others, aggressive behavior was his typical response to peers.

Social-Emotional Need

Infants and toddlers with visual handicaps may have feelings of rejection or of living in a world void of stimuli if left alone for prolonged periods with no tactual or auditory contacts, even if they receive warm and accepting feelings most of the time. The immobile baby who does not have a visual impairment can satisfy this need for sensory input by looking at things, learning to focus the eyes, and trying to reach out and touch; during these periods, the baby is learning eye–hand coordination. Not equipped with this ability, the child with a severe visual impairment relies on sustained sound contacts to keep in touch with the distant world. When vision begins to diminish (Ching Lan), transferring from the use of sight to reliance on other sensory stimuli takes time to adjust mentally to interpreting the meaning of sounds, odors, and tactile encounters. The learning process is not totally unlike that of the developmental pattern in young children.

During the first 18 months, toys should have a strong tactual appeal, with a variety of pleasant textures; rougher surfaces are more desirable than smoother ones (Zimmerman, 1985). Later, when the baby is more active, toys capable of making sounds may be added to encourage the child to follow the sound with the hand, and later to move toward the sound. This ear–hand and ear–movement coordination becomes critical in later months, when sound localization and spatial orientation are important for purposeful movement. Carlos, at age 3, used sound and spatial cues very effectively as he located his toys and moved about the house and even outside. Remember, however, that he also sought verbal and/or tactual reassurance frequently to feel continued security and to maintain contact with others.

In Ching Lan's case, sounds quickly became auditory cues, and attention to them provided a frame of reference for interpretation of actions. Touch becomes the means of verification and clarification of more definitive information than sound can provide. Attention and practice hasten the learning process, as do personal security and emotional acceptance of the world perceived through different senses, so aptly demonstrated by Ching Lan.

Parents and siblings form the basic psychological (social–emotional) climate for the development of positive behaviors through emotional interactions. Close relationships with loving others enable a child to satisfy the need to be loved. The resulting inner satisfaction makes it possible to cope with personal feelings and to respond to feelings elicited by others (Lowenfeld, 1981). Carlos had strong social and emotional interactions in his first years, which prepared him to reach out and interact with other people, and to involve himself actively with his entire environment. No doubt, the speed with which Lucy was able to integrate herself with her sighted nursery and kindergarten friends could be attributed to the time and attention given to her by her parents in the first years of her life.

It would be misleading, however, to suggest that either Carlos's or Lucy's emotional development was complete or would ever be fully realized. Psychosocial development must be fostered and expanded throughout life to maintain one's mental health. Although stresses and frustrations are a natural part of life for everyone, for the child with a visual impairment, the alternatives available for coping with stresses and for reducing tension and anxiety may be restricted by environmental conditions and societal attitudes and expectations. Consequently, chances for developing and maintaining a flexible, adaptable self-concept are strengthened when the child's early years in the family and in school have provided stable patterns of interaction. The same is true for older children who lose their sight through accidents or progressive eye conditions, or who have learning problems in addition to visual impairments. Family and friends can impede or hasten personal adjustment and acceptance, a fact evident in Michael's behavior once he received the assistance he needed.

Need for Early Intervention

Support systems for parents and young children with visual impairments are still very limited in some areas, although federal legislation mentioned earlier is an attempt to address this need. A team approach—involving a teacher, physical therapist, occupational therapist, pediatrician, ophthalmologist, psychologist, social worker, and/or others—seems to be the most desirable means of providing services to parents and young children (S. Moore, 1984). Moore suggested a home program for the first 2 or 3 years. Parents can be taught early stimulation techniques and strategies (such as was done for Carlos's mother), and they gain confidence in their abilities, as well as cope more easily with their own negative feelings. However, the effectiveness of such a plan is contingent on the home teachers. Many teacher education programs are beginning to recognize the need for courses for teachers in working with parents so that they understand the principles for an early intervention teacher. Teachers must think of themselves as guests in the home, and parents need to think of themselves as the primary learners. Teachers are the primary source of information for parents and can become the synthesizer of information from clinical and social services professionals. As they work with parents in the home, teachers can demonstrate how to utilize everyday materials under natural conditions, and emphasize the value of these over toys and unrealistic approaches. Team members may rotate visits as long as they are in close communication with each other so that they may act as liaison and advocate between the parents and other team members.

The child is the focus, but the parents are the learners, and through such a system, the parents gain increasing confidence in their ability to be the child's best teachers.

Without this early intervention, infants and young children may develop very slowly socially and emotionally because their parents may not realize the importance of attention to these concerns. Some of the possible effects of depriving children with severe visual disabilities of constant interaction with others need to be given careful attention. To begin with, lack of communication (both preverbal and verbal) may have a retarding effect on all dimensions of development, but especially on social communication through speech and language. Passively exposing a child with a severe visual impairment to an auditory environment, such as family conversation, household noises, radio, or television, without personalized interpretation may have negative consequences. For example, echolalic (i.e., repetitive) speech develops frequently in children who are blind and left to listen without reciprocal verbal interaction. This imitative speech pattern may be exhibited by verbatim repetition of jingles or commercial tunes. However, oral imitation of sounds or words without understanding them neither indicates language acquisition, nor fosters sequential development in higher cognitive levels.

The sounds and words heard and repeated from passive exposure never become important as a means of social communication with another person. Interpersonal communication through language is one of the strong forces in the socialization process, because feelings are both expressed and received more vividly through verbal interaction. For the child who cannot see facial expressions, gestures, and other subtleties conveyed through body language, the feelings communicated vocally are most meaningful.

Without the bonding and attachment to loving, caring people, children may develop bizarre behavior patterns as a means of getting attention and attempting to satisfy their unmet nurturing needs. In fact, later in life, some children are able to manipulate adults so adroitly that they exercise almost complete control over their environment, although the attention they receive is not the type that helps them develop socially. Could it be that these children feel they are puppets maneuvered through life without understanding how or why?

SUMMARY

Failure to recognize the importance of bonding, attachment, and communicative interaction in the personal and social development of a child who is visually handicapped may have lasting inhibitory consequences on the person's psychosocial aspects of personality throughout life. When children share feelings and thoughts with an adult and that adult responds in an accepting manner, children realize that thoughts and feelings can be accepted by others and are significant to them. This does not mean that the adult should bombard the child verbally, talking about things without appropriate tactile or visual contact, but rather that the adult should listen as the child reveals personal impressions and should talk only to verify or to correct inaccuracies in the child's perception. Experiencing frequent communicative interaction helps children learn that they can acquire information on their own and are considered of value and worth to another person.

Satisfaction in human relationships frees children to recognize that they possess a self independent from another person. They can search actively to encounter and relate to the world of concrete objects and even begin to exercise some control over it. As movement and activity increase in the preschool years, more and more independence fosters development in another dimension—sensory–motor—the topic for the next chapter.

Movement, Exploration, and Spatial Awareness

Chapter 3 focused on the necessity of bonding and human attachment for the development of feelings of security and trust in the infant and young child. Once established, a sense of security provides a stable basis for the desire and motivation to "reach out" and extend beyond the self into the world of objects. Chapter 3 also suggested that rhythmic involuntary movements seem to be related to the infant's neurological and/or physiological need to relieve internal tensions through involvement with external stimulation. Both reflexive and intentional movements at an early age may permit motor patterns to be internalized kinesthetically (Furth, 1969; Hebb, 1949), and assist in "programming the central nervous system to seek and search" (Foulke, 1981).

EARLY MOVEMENT

Although unintentional at first, reflexive movements in infancy provide body contact with the environment. Later the baby becomes aware of the object world as a basis for self-initiated, goal-directed movement. These early movements begin to have meaning when infants internalize them and are able to structure and control future movements of their bodies. Functional exchange between the moving infant and the environment provides the sensorimotor integration that is essential for the development of mental images from which perceptual development ensues (Ayres, 1981; Furth, 1969). Movement helps to define, integrate, and understand the body as a source of information gathering since "action learning is considered a vital component in the cognitive development of visually handicapped children" (Stephens, 1972). Unless they experience the world through their bodies, true concepts elude them and the words they hear have no referents (Hall, 1981).

After patterns of movement have begun to be established, and the infant has become aware of the surrounding world, motor activities may become goal oriented. There is a purpose for the child's movement, such as to make contact with a person or object, or to change the position of the body or of a single body part. These primitive actions form the groundwork for later coordinated movements of manipulation, locomotion, and skill development. The concept of body and objects as a factor in movement begins before 2 years of age according to some specialists (Hill, Dodson-Burk, & Smith, 1989).

Movement and Vision

When vision is present, it is the first sense to make contact with the environment beyond the body itself. From the time an infant with sight opens the eyes, light is all around, and stimulation of the visual sense from this point on is virtually constant. As early as the first weeks of life, infants attempt to focus on and respond to patterns and colors. It has been theorized that visual stimulation excites the infant, and indeed, babies do tend to engage in very active movement when looking at unusual visual patterns in both black and white and in color.

The extent to which vision is actually a stimulating and facilitating factor in perceptual and cognitive development is not known precisely. Whether vision promotes movement or whether movement promotes visual search and control is not yet determined; however, there are many indications that sensorimotor development proceeds with greater rapidity when the reciprocal action between vision and movement is optimal. Clearly, movement toward an object is more likely to happen when the object can be seen, and certainly the child's movement through space is more likely to happen when there is something of interest in the immediate distance toward which to move.

Vision, even without movement, offers opportunities for looking at the world and provides a wide variety of vicarious experiences that become part of the child's knowledge of the world. Vision not only extends the quality of information available, but also provides unique sensory data that are never quite as accurate when gathered through another sense. Specific details of form, color, and spatial relationships between objects can be perceived only through vision. In addition, vision provides an instant concept of the totality of what one sees and is thought by many to be the prime unifier of all other sensory information acquired during the early months and years. Visual images held in the brain provide a constant reference system for recall, even after the actual objects are no longer visible. An impression of the constancy of the world and the objects in it is achieved readily through the visual sense, but remains variable when perceived only through other senses. Vision permits children to learn to imitate actions very early, thereby enabling them to refine the coordination of the body by repetition of observed movements.

Movement with Impaired Vision

If there is a strong interrelationship between movement and learning, then for children who are blind or who have low vision, movement may be the most accurate replacement for vision in clarifying information about the world. For all children who are visually handicapped, external visual stimulation for spontaneous movement, exploration, and spatial awareness will be greatly diminished or totally lacking from birth. The manner in which they organize perceptions and learn through other senses will be different (although not necessarily inferior) to those of the child who has vision. In fact, a movement program designed specifically for infants and young children with visual impairments may strengthen the connection of body movement to the "scheme of things in their world" and provide a greater variety of perceptions (Palazesi, 1986). Because the needs and problems of the child who is totally blind differ somewhat from those of the child with low vision, we discuss the two separately. We first discuss the child who is totally blind, using Carlos as an example. For the aspects of movement and exploration unique to the child who has low vision, we refer to Lucy.

BODY AND MOVEMENT IN CHILDREN WHO ARE BLIND

The body in action defines space and organizes it into a perception of personal space even without the advantage of "visual spatial perception" (Van Weelden, 1967). Some suggest that space exists for people who are blind only to the extent that the body or some part of it has moved through space. Movement involves both the proprioceptive and the muscular systems; the action stimulates the proprioceptive sense, which is essential to the development of muscle tone—the foundation of coordinated movement. Movement also creates a kinesthetic awareness, or a "feel" that is perceived and internalized. Knowledge of this nature may be referred to as "muscle sense." The responsibility for parents, who are the first educators, is to foster as much as possible this internalization of kinesthetic information—by moving the baby's arms and legs in up, down, and circular motions to imitate reaching, turning, and stepping— for use in later exploration and independent movement. The role of the parents or caregivers is very important early on because they are the mediators who determine the child's access to the environment from which exploration follows, and without which no meaningful interpretation of the world is possible for the child without vision (Davidson & Simmons, 1984). Studies have indicated that selective use of such electronic devices as the sonic guide at a very early age may assist in environmental awareness of objects and in directing movement in children without vision (Baird, 1977; Ferrell, 1980b; Harris, Humphrey, Muir, & Dodwell, 1985; Strelow, Kay, & Kay, 1978).

Body Image

Cratty (1971) first emphasized the need for developing "body image" in children who were blind, because, he said, the body is the "center platform" from which all knowledge of movement and space is acquired. Persons who are blind must know about their own bodies, the movements possible, the potential for exerting control over movement, and the body's relationship to other objects and persons in space.

In the infant who is blind, the first awareness of body parts comes through movement of the extremities (hands and feet) to touch another body part or something in the environment. Any movement of the body promotes the development of "motor patterns." If this structured manipulation is not done for the infant by adults, primitive, involuntary motor behaviors may persist into childhood as purposeless mannerisms, a subject discussed in the previous chapter.

Using the hands to find the head, feet, shoulders, and other body parts stabilizes the infant's orientation in "near space," which is critical to freedom of body movement through "extended space." The hands become finely developed instruments of investigation, essential for tactual exploration and the manipulation skills required in later learning. The feel of motion helps to replace the inability to see motion. The parent's constant use of words to identify the part of the body being touched is necessary to develop an awareness in the child that there are names for different body areas. This use of words helps to establish a kinesthetic image of the body as a related and constant whole capable of being regulated at will. In advocating a motor development program for preschoolers with visual impairment, Palazesi (1986) suggested daily 20-minute movement sessions with a patterned sequence of activities from early in life.

The tactual–kinesthetic awareness and stabilization of the object world is the next hurdle in the beginning of motor development of the child who is blind. The parents should make available every small and large object that is safe to touch or to explore and manipulate, as the child begins to show interest in both inanimate and living things. Removing objects from the house for the sake of protecting the objects from falling or breaking creates a sterile environment from which no information is available. Confining a child who cannot see to a crib or playpen after being allowed to crawl or toddle about creates a further obstacle to learning. Encouragement and freedom to explore and move about are indispensable for providing a range and variety of experiences necessary for all facets of development and for future success in academic endeavors.

Permitting the child who is blind to encounter the same bumps, bruises, falls, and other natural consequences of independent actions that all children experience is difficult for some parents. The common inclination is to protect such a "helpless" child from a seemingly hostile world, but to do so communicates feelings of inadequacy and incompetence and makes the child needlessly dependent.

Two important skills can be developed through freedom to move about the house: the use of the total body as it moves through space to encounter stationary (and usually larger) objects, and the use of the hands to explore objects that are either stable or that move with contact. Parents can help by verbally describing body actions and objects to assist in interpreting the nature of things and the body functions required to control the movements among them.

Without the ability to see and imitate the body movements of others, the child without vision must experience movement in the muscles before a specific action can be perceived or verbal instructions from others understood. Hearing actions described has no meaning to young children who do not see unless they are simultaneously performing the action with their bodies (Duehl, 1979).

Many of the postural deviations and infantile patterns of movement observed in numerous children who are blind can be prevented by the use of simple instructions, such as "head up," "shoulders back," "long steps," and "swinging arms." There are specific exercises designed to accentuate body image in stationary positions as well as in locomotion. For example, *Movement and Fundamental Motor Skills for Sensory Deprived Children* (Kratz, Tutt, & Black, 1987) contains a variety of suggestions for physical activities, dances, and games for children with visual handicaps.

Thinking back to Carlos and how easily and with specific purpose he was able to move around the house and outside, one may infer that his parents taught him about his body and its use from early infancy. They may have done this by moving his body in all possible ways, turning it in every position, moving individual limbs and parts through space to develop his kinesthetic sense, and by stroking and touching his body with different textures to stimulate awareness of the multitude of possible sensations and perceptions. Carlos's parents worked to teach him to hold his head up to gain muscular control of the head and neck, since a child without vision has no reason to hold the head in an upright position in to see. In addition, his parents probably played many hand and finger and other body part games with him, which enabled him to learn to position his body in relation to theirs. Perhaps the very early services Carlos received may have included a specialist who used a sonic guide with Carlos beginning in the early months, because it has been observed that children who are blind hold their heads more erect when wearing it (Ferrell, 1984). Children wearing sonic guides also have been observed to move around people, reach out to an object before touching it, and in general show greater confidence in movement (Harris et al., 1985).

By the time Carlos was 4 or 5 months old, his parents were probably propping him in a sitting position and playing with him on their laps to promote the strengthening of head, neck, and trunk muscles, as well as helping him expand his world by hearing sounds from different distances and locations and by learning to manipulate objects with his own body. When he was able to sit alone, by 6 or 8 months of age, he was probably given a "controlled space" (Fraiberg, 1977) in which he could find many interesting objects. According to Fraiberg's studies, babies who are blind exhibit exploration and recognition qualities through handling and manipulating objects as early as 8 months. From observing Carlos, it seems apparent that he was given much guidance and frequent demonstration of how to use objects, in addition to explanations of the effects of his actions on them. For children without vision, nursery rhymes that use body manipulation substitute for picture books. Again, if he had not been encouraged to search and find objects or received adequate body manipulation, he might have become inactive and passive and sought stimulation through his own body, which would have caused him to exhibit the meaningless movements described earlier.

The objects offered the child for play in the first year or so should be simple in form and shape, varied in texture and weight, and capable of some auditory feedback to encourage the child to develop ear–hand–brain coordination as a substitute for eye–hand–brain coordination developed by children with normal vision. If children are encouraged to use hand and finger movements to lift and press and move toys and objects that change form, they gain perceptions that are necessary for more refined tactual discrimination and recognition, which are discussed later in this chapter. Such structured play gave Carlos the knowledge necessary to organize and reorganize mentally the objects in relation to himself and his ability to act on them, and also taught him a reality and a constancy similar to that acquired by children who are able to view the objects visually.

Having gained some control of his body, a perception of space from movement through it, and a perception of objects in relation to himself, Carlos developed at a normal rate the muscular coordination and strength to hold his body in an upright position (for the most part) and to walk and move in purposeful directions. As he began to move, he was evidently able to perceive the position of his body in relation to echoes bouncing off walls and near and far objects, enabling him to avoid them as he moved. At first, of course, Carlos was given much guidance, encouragement, and physical contact. His parents may even have stood him on their feet and walked with him to give him the feel of movement of his body through space. Familiar toys that make a sound were probably used to get him to move toward those toys to touch and manipulate them. Because of previous experiences in having his body moved and in learning to move it himself, his kinesthetic memory developed, giving him the ability to determine his position and to use selected external cues from the things he encountered, and permitting him to begin to move on his own.

Spatial Orientation

According to Hill, Rosen, Correa, and Langley (1984), "orientation is the process of utilizing sensory information to establish and maintain one's position in the environment" (p. 58). With practice, the child who is blind learns to assimilate these signals into a meaningful conceptual model of space. Lydon and McGraw (1973) suggested that four aspects of spatial concepts form the basis for concept development in children who are blind: (1) *action space* with the body as a fixed point from which to anchor movements; (2) *body space* in which short distances can be measured in relation to body movement; (3) *object space* as the area within which awareness and location of objects can be perceived without actual contact; and (4) *map space,* which is the mental organization of certain spatial areas in relation to the body. In one study of the development of space concepts in children who are blind, Birns (1986) investigated the age at which topological and projective space concepts were achieved. Topological space was defined as "spatial relations that remain constant whatever changes there may be in size, shape, proximity, or order of figures" (p. 577), and projective space "included concepts of rotation and perspective—or the projection of how an object will appear from another viewpoint" (p. 577). Birns concluded that children who are blind achieve topological space at about the same time as sighted children, but that 50% of those studied had trouble making the transition to projective space.

With the help of very early intervention, Carlos completed a cognitive map of himself and his surrounding world and was beginning to develop a style of learning that was unique for him. If he had lacked the opportunity to form these perceptions from birth and throughout the early learning years, Carlos would most likely not have acquired freedom of movement and purposeful manipulative skills that were evident from his behavior. He had learned to move and function efficiently without vision.

Because of the recent infant and preschool federal legislation, the role of the orientation and mobility specialist is expanding. No in-depth curriculum has been accepted as yet, but the emphasis is far broader than simply cane travel; the focus now is toward basic skills (rather than pre-mobility skills) used with or without a cane (Pogrund & Rosen, 1989). For very young children (toddlers), push toys, miniature grocery carts, hula hoops, and beach balls may be the first tools for independent movement. The possible benefits of this early teaching of independent movement are enormous: better postural patterns, whole body muscle tone, vestibular stimulation for balance, and an increase in the awareness of textures and objects in the environment. For this concept to be most effective, there is a need to include parents, early childhood teachers, and all therapists who work with young children. For youngsters with low vision, there is some evidence that they may feel more comfortable in using their vision for near and distant landmarks than for looking at their feet to see where they are going (Hill et al., 1984).

When a child who is blind enters a more structured school learning situation lacking the early movement and manipulative skills more easily acquired before 5 or 6 years of age, the retarding effects are likely to be long lasting and possibly permanent. In such cases, achieving ease and efficiency in independent travel may never be possible, and the negative influence on developing abstract cognitive skills may be noticeable throughout life (Gerhardt, 1982; Hall, 1981).

Assuming that Carlos had taken walks with his parents and accompanied them on shopping tours, he would have developed numerous perceptions of the vast world of space and the information available for use in later learning. If his parents described to him such landmarks as lampposts, mailboxes, buildings, curbs, and gutters, then he would have learned how the environment was constructed, "how to manipulate it, and how to move freely in it" (Hill et al., 1984, p. 62). Ability to relate spatial layout of structures in the environment has been linked to more effective use of the cane for independent travel. Talking about the differences in the textures of grass, gravel, cement, or sand while walking through them would help develop a vocabulary necessary to progress in academic subjects. Unless such words as *inclines, slants, hills,* and *valleys* are "felt" through body awareness, they have no meaning to children who cannot see. Expanding knowledge through using the body, combined with verbal interpretation, is the key to continuous refinement in motor skills for children who are blind throughout their lives. Many frustrating problems could be avoided through greater focus on use of the body with freedom and confidence.

USING LOW VISION OR VISUAL IMAGERY FOR MOVEMENT

Warren (1974) postulated that, "having vision simultaneously with the motor function allows registration of the motor function and its effects in a visual framework" (p. 161). In a later publication (1984), he concluded that "it may be documented that the child with some visual function is at least potentially at an advantage over the totally blind child" (p. 78). Being able to realize that potential, however, requires early, concentrated attention to learning how to use the impaired vision. One can see from the descriptions of Lucy and Carlos that there are obvious differences in the potential for motor development of a child who has limited visual capacity and a child who is blind. Despite the discrepancies in Lucy's behavior in relation to her use of vision and the confusions in her movement patterns, the fact that she moved her body when she was visually aware that objects were present indicates that she was using the functional vision available to her to guide movement. Her spontaneous awareness of visual space was, and could continue to be, limited to very small areas surrounding her body, but the fact that she was able to see objects and movement within this space permitted her to develop an awareness that there was something beyond her body.

The more her parents encouraged and enticed her to continue to move and explore, the more accurate she became in her movements and the greater curiosity she had about the blurred world she saw and toward which she could move to gain a clearer impression. Crawling or toddling toward a wall mirror may have contributed to body awareness and body image. In this movement, she learned to gauge distance, even though she could not actually acquire a clear visual picture of what was in the distance. Although she knocked over, bumped into, and stumbled over objects she could not see clearly, she was learning to correct herself without assistance. This behavior forged motor patterns into her nervous system, which would be key factors in developing increasing independence in movement.

Lucy, never having had normal vision, saw the world as "clear," rather than the blurred image by which those with normal vision may tend to describe her perspective. Of course, Lucy's parents were concerned and exercised some cautions, with good reason. Because of the lack of detail in her distance vision and the blurred nature of the environment she was experiencing, Lucy's safety was an important consideration. Perhaps her parents suggested that she listen to help clarify what she could not see, and that she learn to anticipate possible dangers so that her movements would be cautious without being fearful. Her orientation in and relationship with the environment was a more easily acquired ability for Lucy than for Carlos. Her limited vision permitted her to stabilize her concepts of both near and extended space into integrated visual and motor patterns. Her visual–motor organization may have been fostered by games such as rolling, bouncing, or hitting balls; crawling and walking up and down flights of stairs with and without assistance; and others requiring her to use vision for accuracy in spatial position or prediction of spatial distances.

Selecting playthings for nursery-aged children with low vision is a matter for careful consideration. Attention to texture and shape is as important as for children who are blind, but the color and light-reflecting qualities are equally important; in fact, toys that have highly visible differences are often preferred over those that make noise.

Even children who have close-range vision do not see well enough at a distance to recognize toys or to imitate the use other children make of them. They seem to interact differently with objects, try few manipulations with them, and require assistance in determining their functional use (Gerhardt, 1982; Olson, 1982; A. A. Parsons, 1982). In a definitive scientific study by S. Parsons (1986), qualitative differences between sighted and low vision preschool children in play patterns were identified. The children who had low vision spent much more playtime involved in stereotypical behaviors (mouthing and banging) and less time in functional play (the use of toys for their intended purpose). Other differences noted were in styles of play, ability to play independently, and the capacity to stay focused on the functional use of toys.

Studies of children, youth, and adults blinded at different ages suggest that a relationship exists between the length of time vision was present in early life and the subsequent ability to perform increasingly complex tasks requiring spatial awareness and manipulative skills (Valvo, 1971; Warren, 1984). Differences also have been recorded in the knowledge of positional concepts, as well as success in orientation and independent movement in mobility and in making judgments of spatial distances (Fletcher, 1981a; S. E. Miller, 1982; Overbury, Goodrich, Quillman, & Faubert, 1989). Personal observations indicate an observable difference in movement patterns between children who are congenitally blind and those who had vision for as limited a period as 18 months to 2 years, which lends validity to Piaget's idea of an internalized sensorimotor integration through early movement experiences.

Because Ching Lan had limited but adequate vision during her developmental years, it is reasonable to assume that her movement and exploratory patterns were well established before she began to lose her vision rapidly. She had good visual imagery of space, understood the relationship of her body within space, had seen her body in various positions and knew what she could do, and had developed stable motor patterns and skills. The primary concern for Ching Lan would be to adapt to the use of other senses to alert herself about the world and to guide her in movements, as she recalled her visual perception of spatial relations. In fact, she indicated that she was already doing that as she became aware that she was losing vision. She would continue to update her perceptual cues and use a variety of "computational strategies" to travel from place to place (Reiser, Guth, & Hill, 1982).

Provided that her parents and teachers encourage her to continue independent movement, her complete self-confidence should return with some ease, even after her vision is totally gone. However, if she should develop anxiety and fear because of restriction and overprotection imposed by them, her adaptation to the use of her other senses would be much slower, and some of her motivation for adaptation might be lost. Calling on previously established visual imagery and associating this imagery with new patterns of tactual and auditory information, things will soon begin to feel or sound like they looked, and a modified picture of the world will soon emerge.

Because Ching Lan already knew the names of the parts of her body and had the language associated with body position within her repertoire, she was especially attuned to following verbal instructions in relation to her new exploration and movement and could interpret and associate the descriptive language of others in relation to her remembered visual imagery. Continuing recall of visual imagery in the case of those who have lost all their vision is crucial. The more visual recall required of the person, the longer and more vivid the visual images will remain. Like any other facet of thought, unused memories soon lose their clarity. During the adaptive period, it is especially important that verbal instructions be used to assist Ching Lan in her movements and that her parents, peers, and teachers refrain from physically moving or guiding her except when she requests assistance or her safety is threatened. Independence and self-confidence are much more easily acquired if children who lose all vision are assumed to be able to follow instructions and are permitted to move independently, according to instructions. Applying the notion that success promotes success, the more that youth move and travel independently, the more rapidly confidence and efficiency will become a reality.

Although Michael had visual impairment of a moderate nature, he was very like Ching Lan in his early years as far as using vision in relation to movement. His problem was more of a perceptual than a visual problem, which may have affected his ability to always know how to interpret what he was able to see, and to develop stable visual imagery. Michael's needs related to encouraging him to give full visual attention to whatever he was doing, and to giving him a great deal of support to strengthen his self-confidence and increase his self-esteem. Many of the suggestions about Ching Lan can apply to Michael, especially if his near-sighted condition begins to progress more rapidly, remembering that he needs to have more time to process information and to interpret sensory information.

DIFFERENTIAL PROGRAM PLANNING

Children who are congenitally blind and whose early experiences have been similar to Carlos's can enter physical education activities with sighted children with minimal assistance and encouragement when given the opportunity to participate. As soon as they learn stationary landmarks and are shown the routes to follow, children blind from birth will learn to travel alone within the classroom, around the building, and on the playground with efficiency and confidence. Given the assistance of an orientation and mobility instructor, they will be ready to begin some independent travel within the neighborhood and to and from school on foot or by public transportation by the time they complete elementary school or sooner. With travel instruction in high school, blind youth with good motor development have the potential for efficient independent travel in unfamiliar areas.

However, not all children who are blind enter school with established patterns of motor development. Those who have been restricted because of parental fear that they will hurt themselves or parents' lack of knowledge about how to raise a child who is blind, may know little about their own bodies and even less about the realities of the environment. Such underdeveloped children may require as long as 2 or more years of physical therapy, intensive exercise, daily excursions in the out-of-doors, and regular field trips, in addition to a concentrated program of concrete learning experiences in language and developmental concepts (Dodds, Howarth, & Carter, 1982; Hill et al., 1984; Palazesi, 1986). Many children progress rapidly and are able to grasp formal abstract concepts almost as readily as those whose early development was less delayed. Others may have multiple disabilites in addition to blindness, which may limit learning potential (a topic to be addressed in the next chapter).

Unlike Lucy, some children with low vision may enter school having no awareness of their visual potential and may behave as if they were unable to see anything. Their parents, having been told the child was blind (using medical–legal criteria based on acuity and/or restricted field), have made no effort to stimulate the child visually or to encourage the use of low vision. For children with low vision such as these, a program similar to that proposed for underdeveloped blind children, with special emphasis on visual development in relation to movement, would be advantageous. In every experience and activity, the child would be encouraged to "look" so as to learn to coordinate visual and motor systems and to begin to bring increased clarity and order to a world that may have been confusing. Although not all children with low vision will become primarily "visual learners," increased visual efficiency will enhance their movement patterns, motor coordination, and conceptual development (Barraga, 1980c; Dodds & Davis, 1989; Hall & Bailey, 1989)

Because Ching Lan and Michael both had vision in their preschool and early school years, their movement patterns developed normally as a matter of course. However, because of some lag in his motor development, Michael began to encounter some difficulty in speed of movement as he grew older. Not only will Ching Lan retain a mental picture of the world of objects and space, but she will unconsciously use the movement patterns internalized within her body, even when she no longer has sight. The primary focus in teaching such children will not be their learning how to move, but instead will concentrate attention on the feel of movement and visual recall of spatial concepts, while adapting to using ear–brain coordination (rather than the eyes) to orient themselves within space and to guide and direct movement.

SUMMARY

There are obvious differences in freedom of movement, mobility within limited environments, and future independent travel among children who are congenitally totally blind, those with low vision, those who lose vision after having good vision, and those who have learning problems in addition to visual impairment. These differences must be considered in relation to the learning process and the teaching technique for which appropriate adaptations must be made. Spatial orientation and concept formation require a long and tedious learning process for children who are totally congenitally blind. They will learn to use other senses, but must be constantly encouraged and supported by adults who carefully plan sequential experiences as the children gradually acquire skills. The concepts acquired will necessarily be different from those acquired through the use of vision. The potential for independent travel at a later age is directly proportional to the early learning experiences provided by parents and teachers and to the extent to which the children are encouraged to reach out and be independent and knowledgeable in movement from the very beginning.

The child who has limited visual impairment will be able to enhance knowledge of the world and patterns of exploration more easily. Independence in movement will come with less effort and greater efficiency as opportunities for practice are provided. As with the child who is blind from birth, independence in travel is closely related to the appropriate learning experiences and encouragement provided in the early years.

Children who lose some or all of their vision after having established their concepts of the world and their movement patterns must learn to adapt these patterns through using other senses. The process of adapting may be slow in the beginning and is related to psychological factors within the children and those around them. Independence in travel can be maintained through appropriate teaching procedures directed toward stressing the acquisition of different skills for movement and travel. Mobility training programs must be designed for each individual specifically in relation to previous development and learning. No doubt, increasing use will be made of electronic travel aids in the near future (Ferrell, 1984; Harris et al., 1985).

The trend in the field of orientation and mobility is to begin to work with children in the preschool years, and to begin teaching the use of the cane at earlier ages than was thought appropriate a few years ago. Experimentation and research with younger children and multihandicapped individuals is increasing, and the validity of this approach is likely to be substantiated in the next few years.

5

Children with Visual Impairment and Multiple Disabilities

Like increasing numbers of children, Sharon (described in Chapter 1) experiences several disabilities that affect her development and learning. Although children with both visual handicaps and impairments in other body systems are not a new subject, in the past few years they have received greater attention. As early as 1969 (Lowenfeld, 1969), surveys indicated that a growing percentage of children who were visually impaired had other medical or physiological conditions not related to the functional or developmental ones discussed in previous chapters. During the 1970s, increasing evidence indicated that half or more of school-aged children with visual handicaps had clinically and medically diagnosed impairments in one or more body systems other than the visual system (Kirchner & Peterson, 1980; Kirchner, Peterson, & Suhr, 1979; Organization for Social and Technical Innovation, 1971). Gates (1985) attributed the increasing numbers of children with visual and other disabilities to three factors: etiological causes such as retinopathy of prematurity and maternal rubella; medical advances that have saved the lives of children, but in the attempt, may have created other problems including visual impairment; and current trends in service to previously unserved children.

Most children with visual impairments described as multiply handicapped who received educational services before the early 1970s were in fact able to learn to care for their own needs such as toileting and feeding (Erin, Daugherty, Dignan, & Pearson, 1990). Not until after the passage of PL 94-142 were children such as Sharon, who have severe multiple disabilities that may prevent them from caring for themselves as adults, included among those served in educational settings. Before that landmark legislation, these children may have been ignored by educators as "hopeless" and therefore not entitled to inclusion in educational settings; they may have been institutionalized at birth; or they may simply have been kept at home, given total care, and considered to be incapable of learning. The rubella (German measles) epidemic of 1963–1964, which resulted in a population of several thousand deaf–blind children, and the passage of PL 94-142 have provided the strongest impetus for alternative thinking and adapting service delivery systems to accommodate children with personal and educational needs not encountered heretofore in the residential or public schools.

TYPES AND CAUSES

A variety of conditions can result in a visual impairment with other disabilities. These conditions may be genetic, may be caused by prenatal or perinatal factors, or may result from trauma after birth. Medical technology has provided a future for many children who may not have survived at all 20 years ago. It is up to families and professionals to ensure that these children, regardless of the severity of their handicaps, are provided with the opportunity to reach their potential.

Many children with multiple disabilities are affected by cerebral palsy. Of children who have cerebral palsy, 25–50% have visual impairments that may affect their educational process (Hardy, 1983). Children with cerebral palsy have experienced damage to or dysfunction of the brain that causes them to process motor signals differently from other children. This may mean that their physical tone is too high (hypertonic) or too low (hypotonic), or that it alternates between too high and too low. It may be virtually impossible for children with cerebral palsy to control certain muscle groups, and they may have difficulty with gross motor skills such as walking, sitting, or rolling, as well as with fine motor skills such as handling a pencil or picking up coins.

Children with cerebral palsy most commonly have two types of visual differences. One is a strabismus, or a muscle imbalance of the eyes. This lack of the ability to fuse the images from both eyes may result in a condition known as amblyopia, in which the child relies on the vision from only one eye, or uses each eye for different distances. For the child with cerebral palsy and strabismus, careful observation is important to determine the best physical position to permit the child to see tasks well and to have maximum physical control over use of materials.

The second type of visual impairment common with cerebral palsy is neurological in nature and is related to the brain's role in interpreting visual information. There is some brain dysfunction, usually in the area of the visual cortex in the lower back part of the brain. Children with this condition may show a puzzling combination of behaviors: Their vision may fluctuate from one minute to the next; they may turn or look away from objects toward which they are reaching; and they do not normally show nystagmus or visual mannerisms (Jan, Groenveld, Sykanda, & Hoyt, 1987). According to Ferrell (1987), cortical visual impairment is the leading cause of visual disability in children with multiple handicaps.

Some children with visual impairment are considered multiply disabled because they exhibit major developmental delays that persist, sometimes in spite of high quality intervention. These children may lag behind in language, with echolalia and meaningless or irrelevant speech dominating their spoken output. They may show asocial characteristics that cause some to be described as "autistic-like"; these characteristics include limited initiations of interactions with others, rigidity in following certain routines, stereotypic behaviors, and preference for repetition in environmental stimulation. Such children are often diagnosed as mentally retarded by the educational systems that serve them. Although they clearly function within the ranges of retardation according to clinical definitions, their unique patterns of behavior suggest a more complex problem imposed by the combined effects of visual deprivation and a cognitive inability to process and interpret their environment.

Children who were formerly called deaf–blind are now being described as dually sensory impaired by some professionals (Goetz, Guess, & Stremel-Campbell, 1987). The largest group of children with both hearing and vision losses in the 1960s and 1970s were those affected by maternal rubella; now most of these people have reached adulthood, and their primary needs are for appropriate living and occupational arrangements. Of the students who are currently described as dually sensory impaired, many have pervasive neurological impairments caused by conditions such as cytomegalovirus (CMV), anoxia, toxoplasmosis, meningitis, maternal rubella, or a recently identified condition known as CHARGE association. CHARGE is a grouping of anomalies that may include colobomas, heart conditions, and hearing loss, not all of which appear in every child. In addition, a few children experience hearing and visual impairments without additional disabilities, often related to conditions such as Usher's syndrome or to traumatic injury.

A few children who need educational services sometimes have complex health problems that may limit their life span and their level of physical activity. Children affected by acquired immune deficiency syndrome (AIDS) are vulnerable to infection of any kind and need flexibility in programming according to their day-to-day comfort and capacity. The visual effects of this condition may include viruses such as CMV, a common virus that may settle in the retina and destroy vision in the affected areas.

Additional disabilities may have various functional effects on children. Although it is helpful to know about the impact that specific conditions may have, there is no way to predict function based on etiology alone. Each child is an individual, and many factors influence what he or she can do.

THE IMPACT OF A VISUAL IMPAIRMENT

Peter was 3 years old, and his mother was becoming more concerned. Even though the doctor said that there was no problem except for blindness, Peter's mother knew that he was not like other children in his preschool class for students with visual handicaps. At playtime, Peter would sit in his favorite rocking chair and hit a block against the arm of the chair; he would rock back and forth, smiling and making nonsense sounds. When a teacher encouraged him to play with the other children, Peter would scream, "No playtime!" and would throw the block angrily. At home, he often wanted to be left alone; when his mother called him to dinner or to get ready for bed, he would cry and sometimes bang his head.

The teachers at school used words like "developmentally delayed" when they talked about Peter's progress. His mother wondered secretly whether he might be retarded, even though no one had used that word. She had tried to follow all the suggestions in the books she had read, and she encouraged Peter to play with other children and to become curious about the world around him; however, his preference for repetition and his dislike of other people was making it more difficult as he grew older. Perhaps his difficulty was not only blindness—or was it? Some children may have developmental and learning differences that cannot be associated with diagnosable medical or physiological conditions. The sensory deprivation, along with isolation from natural experiences and human interactions, can result in behavioral deviations and influence normal psychological development.

The presence of a visual impairment with additional disabilities imposes several difficulties that may affect learning. Some of these are rooted in the concept of sensory deprivation, the idea that the failure to use and receive input from the senses will eventually result in a long-term inability to use that learning channel. A child with multiple disabilities may not only lack experiences that are primarily visual, but also may not have the ability to confirm or replicate experiences through movement, through hearing and speech, or through recalling similar experiences.

A classic experiment by Held and Hein (1963) illustrates the problem experienced by many children with multiple disabilities. They studied the effects of visual deprivation in kittens by raising two kittens in the dark for the first few weeks of life. After the kittens were exposed to light, they placed them in baskets at opposite ends of an arm on a small structure like a merry-go-round. One kitten was moved passively while the other one was active in using his legs to move both his basket and that of the other kitten. The active kitten developed visual perception, whereas the passive one remained virtually blind. This is further evidence of the probable relationship between the motor and visual systems in perceptual development, an idea suggested in Chapter 3.

The experience of the passive kitten is similar to the experiences of children who, because of a physical disability, cannot interact freely with their environment by moving within it. They may learn to experience the world as an event unrelated to them, and they do not learn that they can have an effect on the environment. As they grow older, their motivation and their ability to interact may diminish. It is critical that the learning experiences for children with multiple disabilities involve plenty of opportunities for them to act on the environment and get results. A smile and a hug from a parent when they vocalize or a piece of wanted food when they request it with a sign or gesture are examples of results that can convey the message, "You did it!"

The intensity of stimulation in the environment can be another area of concern as a child develops. All people vary in their toleration for various levels of activity around them, but children with neurological differences often show greater ranges of toleration (Rogow, 1988; Smith & Cote, 1982). Some children are hypersensitive to stimuli and dislike tasting new foods, touching sticky or moist substances, changing activities, or being lightly touched by others, even in an affectionate manner.

Other children seem to tolerate any type of stimulation to the point that they do not have preferences or attempt to alter the environment to their liking. The child who listens placidly to the radio at the highest volume, who does not show excitement even at a party or an event when excitement would be appropriate, who does not laugh when tickled, and who does not complain about pain or discomfort is a child who may need to learn to notice even gross differences in the activities and stimuli around him or her.

The absence of vision may increase the intensity of these reactions. The child may have no way of predicting when a new stimulus is presented and may become hypersensitive or passive as a defense against the lack of control over external events. Again, the critical objective is to provide a means by which the child can act successfully on the environment in a satisfying manner. This takes much patience, and may require consistent long-term conditioning for it to become a reality.

Some children with visual impairments show repetitive or stereotyped behaviors, such as head bobbing, eye poking, light flicking, or rocking. These are more common among children with multiple disabilities, who are often more frustrating to discourage because they sometimes lack social awareness. Scholl (1986) suggested a variety of causes for these movements: the need for sensory stimulation, the effect of movement limitations, lack of social experiences, inadequate relationships with adults, and lack of knowledge about appropriate behaviors. Huebner (1986) suggested consideration of the causes and effects of the behavior when planning interventions; she emphasized the importance of providing a variety of opportunities for activity to the young child as a preventive measure.

The interaction of vision loss with other disabilities can also affect the appropriate development of language. Among some children who are blind, inappropriate speech patterns can become predominant. Many children demonstrate echolalia (repeated speech), including delayed echolalia (repeating something heard in the past) and mitigated echolalia (using shorter rote phrases within original speech units) (Rasmussen, 1985). Other children who are blind demonstrate a low frequency of utterances, which may indicate a lack of understanding that they can have an effect on the world through communication; still others do not develop speech, but may learn to use other forms of communication such as sign and gesture. A few will continue to communicate at a prelanguage level, through vocalization, intonation, and movement.

It is important that language be considered primarily as a means of communication and expression, and that language intervention not be merely an attempt to shape the formal processes of speech production. For the child with multiple disabilities, language is a critical connector to other people; the important message to be conveyed is that language is a means of building social relationships. Rogow (1978, 1988) recommended the use of social routines and play activities such as nursery rhymes to establish early communication. By associating movement and action to these routines, the child learns to expect and share a social interaction even though his or her expressive language may be limited.

The presence of additional disabilities may also affect a child's ability to use any functional vision effectively. Some children who are physically handicapped have to exert effort to attain their best visual position and to maintain head control in order to fixate on an image. Children with cognitive or learning difficulties may experience problems in interpreting visual information, particularly if their acuity is poor and they have no previous experience with the shape or configuration of an object. Many children with neurological differences experience perceptual confusion: They may not understand constancy of depth, shape, and size, and may not be able to select important information from a busy background. These children may respond best to simple, high contrast visual stimuli in a setting that will allow them to experience the same stimulus frequently. Later, when the image is familiar and meaningful, more complex visual situations can be introduced.

A visual impairment can multiply the limitations imposed by other disabilities. Such children are at risk of becoming passive observers to the world around them. To prevent this, we must evaluate carefully to identify capabilities and set goals that will promote interaction with the environment for each of them.

ASSESSMENT

Valid assessment of the child with multiple impairments requires the skill of many individuals. Assessment is a particular challenge because the team must gather information that provides a representative picture of the child's abilities and yet must maintain the integrity of the whole child without presenting a fragmented perspective.

Although it is generally accepted that the team is the foundation for effective programming and assessment, the composition and structure of the team may vary. A *multidisciplinary* team includes specialists who work individually with a child on goals specific to the special skill area; this structure closely approximates a medical model of service delivery. On an *interdisciplinary* team, each member works individually with a child, but also maintains regular communication with other team members through meetings and documentation. A *transdisciplinary* team, more recently preferred in infant and early childhood programs, provides services directly through one or two primary team members and the parents; others act as consultants on this team (Campbell, 1987; Silberman, 1986).

Assessment of the young child with multiple disabilities may involve the use of a developmental instrument or scale. This approach provides information about the child's attainment of skills in comparison with the age at which a child usually achieves them. Very few of these are standardized for use with a child having both visual and multiple impairments. The *Callier–Azusa Scale* (Stillman,1979) has been developed for children who are multiply disabled or deaf–blind; it includes an inventory of items from six areas, and is intended to be completed by someone who is observing the child regularly over a period of time.

In using a developmental scale in assessing the child with multiple disabilities, the professional should be aware of its disadvantages as well as the information that can be gained. As a child with disabilities grows older, physical change is less rapid and learning becomes more greatly influenced by environmental factors. It cannot be assumed that a child will acquire skills listed on a developmental scale in the exact order in which they are listed, especially if it is a scale not intended for children with visual limitations. Differences in priorities, experiences, motivation, and capabilities will determine what a child achieves. The older a child becomes, the less helpful a developmental instrument will be in determining goals.

Assessment of children with severe disabilities has recently broadened from a focus on the use of specific instrumentation to regard environmental influences on the child's learning and behavior. Known as an *ecological* approach, this perspective itemizes the skills a child needs to function in the immediate and in the next environment (Netupski & Hamre-Netupski, 1989). It provides guidelines for the development of objectives that can be easily translated into program activities. For the child with a visual impairment and additional disabilities, it provides a highly individualized approach to assessment that will help the team to identify what the child can accomplish in the immediate environment, such as reaching for a toy.

The accurate assessment of vision in the child with multiple disabilities is a particular challenge. Standard screening instruments and procedures often are not appropriate, particularly if a child cannot indicate preference or make a choice. Although some newer clinical procedures, such as preferential looking and the *Parsons Visual Acuity Test* (Cress et al., 1981), offer response options that are appropriate for the child with multiple impairments, careful observation will continue to be the best indicator of a child's visual abilities. Responses such as blinking, turning the head, or brightening toward a visible object may be the only evidence that a child is aware of changes in the visible environment. Observations across time, in various settings, and with different caregivers will provide a more representative picture of the child's functional vision. Only a few resources exist that assist the professional in assessment of vision in the child with multiple disabilities; among these are *Look at Me* (Smith & Cote, 1982) and the *Functional Vision Screening Inventory for the Child with Severe Handicaps* (Langley, 1980).

Assessment of the child with multiple disabilities involves collaboration among families and professionals in order to gather information about a child's function. In most cases, use of a standardized instrument is inappropriate because of the highly individual patterns of development demonstrated by children with multiple disabilities. Criterion-referenced instruments and skill inventories will provide information that is more easily translated into program objectives than will items on a standardized instrument. To ensure the development of skills that will allow that child to function in the immediate environment, the ecological approach will encourage maximum flexibility in developing an appropriate plan for each student.

INTERVENTION AND PROGRAMMING

Recent trends in programming for the child with multiple impairments emphasize integrated approaches that teach skills to help the child be a functional member of his or her community. The concept of the team as the core of program planning acknowledges that the child with multiple disabilities requires the specialized knowledge of a variety of individuals; however, in some settings, a transdisciplinary team is preferred because it involves only one or two professionals along with the family as primary implementors of the child's program; other professionals act in support roles (Silberman, 1986).

Early intervention is vital for the infant with multiple disabilities; the effectiveness of this intervention depends strongly on the family's involvement. Mori and Olive (1978) described the importance of encouraging families to interact with their infants and to allow the infants to participate in normal family activities, including being cuddled and played with by friends and family members. Sensory stimulation can be planned to encourage children to respond to the world around them: Use of varied textures, odors, and sound effects in the environment can generate awareness of differences in their world, even before they are ready to initiate cause–effect actions. *Reach Out and Teach* (Ferrell, 1985) provides direction for parents and professionals in planning activities for the preschool child with visual and multiple disabilities. The handbook and manual clearly convey the challenges that confront a child with a visual disability, as well as the satisfactions of meeting those challenges; through the use of illustrations and step-by-step activities, families and caregivers can encourage active learning.

As the child grows older, the emphasis is on the mastery of functional skills, that is, the skills that will enable an individual to meet the demands of his or her immediate setting and the requirements of future settings. Priorities are set according to these specifications, as well as student strengths and interests, family preference, and age appropriateness.

Although goals may be specific to designated skill areas or domains, integrated programming is the key to mastery and application of skills for most students. Instead of scheduling a single time of day in which a child will work on a skill, adults must provide opportunities to practice a skill throughout the day. For example, if a goal for Mary is to perfect a pincer grasp (grasping with the thumb and index finger), the teaching strategy can be applied at group time when she places a sticker on a chart; at snack time when she picks up a raisin; later in the day when she is given a penny to place into her bank; and at the end of the day when she helps to clean up paper clips from the work table. Practice on one skill for extended periods of time usually is not as productive as frequent work on the same skill, for short periods within tasks that are meaningful at different moments.

It is also important that the students experience an activity at the time of day when it would naturally occur, and in a setting as much like the actual setting as possible. Because many children who are blind or have low vision are not aware of incidental events in their world, instructors cannot assume that they will associate details from a simulated situation with a real one. Although a classroom store may be a motivating way of reinforcing a child's completion of work tasks, a visit to a real store is a more accurate learning experience and provides opportunities for finding out new information: "Do you know that their cash register talks?" "How did you know you were getting close to the frozen foods?" "How much money will you need to buy those raisins?"

Time awareness is an important feature of learning to organize the world for the child with multiple disabilities. Because children have no understanding of clock time, they may operate in a world in which random events seem to happen in unpredictable order. Not only is it vital to establish a routine and follow it consistently in programming, but it is also important to include antecedent activities that will give children clues about what will happen next. This can be as simple as letting a child carry a placemat to the lunchroom, or as complex as giving a child a braille list of events planned for that day.

The *Prelanguage Curriculum,* based on a program developed by Van Dijk (1965), emphasizes communicating to the student about time through the use of a calendar box. Using this strategy, the student begins by associating a related object to an event that will take place, and by wearing or carrying that object during the duration of the event. The student moves from that level of recognition of routine through the complex use of calendars to establish a sense of past, present, and future. This curriculum, which emphasizes the teaching of language through movement, moves a child from the stage of relating to an adult through the spontaneous use of language.

The Van Dijk curriculum is only one approach that has been used with children who are deaf and blind, who usually require highly specialized educational programming. Children who are deaf and blind, also described as having dual sensory impairments, often have usable vision, hearing, or both. Programming goals emphasize communication and socialization because of the isolating effects of a dual sensory loss, which is combined with neurological differences in some children. Many children who are deaf and blind show autistic-like characteristics and are not motivated by human contact and approval; therefore, one of the greatest challenges for the educator is to create motivating and functional learning activities that encourage the child to make contact with others.

Communication methods used by individuals who are deaf and blind vary according to several factors. The child's functional ability, motivation, and the previous or current existence of hearing and vision all have an impact on the communication modes used by those with both vision and hearing impairments. For many children, a total communication approach will provide the most intensive information about the meaning and structure of communication; this includes the use of speech, sign, gesture, facial expression, and any other modality that conveys information and ideas.

Vocal communication may be an option for those who are highly motivated or who have usable hearing. This may be taught using some variation of the Tadoma method (Kates & Schein, 1980), in which the individual learns speech by touching the throat and lips of the speaker. Alternative manual systems include the one- or two-hand manual alphabets; use of

American Sign Language with the hand of the receiver lightly covering the hand of the signer; printing on the palm of the hand; and the use of communication boards or augmentative systems that may utilize braille or tactile systems. Technological advances have increased the options for this population: The Tellatouch, in which the sender types a message that is conveyed to the receiver through a braille cell, and the recently available mechanical hand developed at Stanford University for Smith–Kettlewell, provide a broader array of options for the individual who requires an alternative form of communication.

For the child who is not able to use a complex language system, there are approaches that can make the immediate environment more understandable and predictable. The use of anticipatory cues, particularly touch cues for children with little vision, can make them aware that they will be touched or moved. The shaping of natural gestures, devised by children themselves, can enforce the relationship of a body or hand movement to a predictable event. The establishment of a routine and the presentation of choices within that routine will build the foundation for the development of communication and language.

Like children who are deaf and blind, children with other multiple disabilities will require highly individualized educational programming. Prepared curricula for young children with visual disabilities may serve as a supplemental resource in developing a program that will differ from child to child according to family preference, service availability, age, and functional level. *Growing Up* (Robinson, 1982) and the *Oregon Project* (Brown, Simmons, & Methvin, 1978) are intended primarily for the child who is visually impaired without additional disabilities, but both specify activities and milestones that can help in program planning for the child with multiple disabilities.

Some children with multiple disabilities will be able to develop academic skills, often with the use of adapted materials or methods. Braille reading may be introduced as a functional skill for the blind student who may not have the cognitive ability to master higher order reading skills; the association of "sight" words in braille with significant objects and possessions reinforces the concept of braille as a means of communication, and braille can be used to identify responses on an augmentative communication device for some students. The use of braille should not be ruled out as a part of the total communication system simply because a child does not appear to have the cognitive capacity to read complex materials.

Programming for the child with multiple disabilities and a visual impairment must also include assessment and programming in orientation and mobility to encourage self-initiation and independence in movement and travel. Although some people may not learn to plan complex outdoor routes or to use public transportation, the ability to travel efficiently within familiar environments will enhance an individual's ability to manage the daily routine. Children whose physical disabilities prevent independent locomotion may still gain the skill to communicate choices regarding where and how they are to be moved. They can comprehend directionality, learn safety measures, give accurate instructions to others, make choices, and learn concepts that support the understanding of their own body movement.

A variety of adapted techniques and devices have been applied to encourage greater control in moving through the environment for the individual who is severely disabled (Coleman & Weinstock, 1984; Del Frari, 1978; Uslan, Malone, & De L'Aune, 1983). Harley, Wood, and Merbler (1981) also emphasized the use of flexible teaching approaches in working with individuals who have severe impairments. Uslan et al. (1983) especially encouraged consideration of the cane as a travel device for many such individuals, and they cautioned that a lack of physical activity can be of particular concern with this population. In developing independence within the environment, the multiply disabled individual with a visual impairment may be disadvantaged by overprotective caregivers, a lack of experience in initiating activity, and the inability to recall locations that are not visible or immediately available to other senses. It is important that a qualified instructor be involved in the assessment and planning of orientation and mobility programming for the individual with severe disabilities.

Children with multiple disabilities who have useful vision should be encouraged to use vision contingently to affect the environment (Utley, Duncan, Strain, & Scanlon, 1983). This can be most effectively done in functional activities, in which the child is required to use vision to complete the task (e.g., hanging a coat on a hook or stacking cups) (Goetz & Gee, 1987). To be applied meaningfully, goals in functional use of vision, as in other program areas, must be integrated into daily routines and generalized across settings, people, and materials. If the functional use of vision is not encouraged, the child with multiple disabilities is at risk of increased isolation from the environment and a decreased sense of control over the events around him or her.

SUMMARY

The population of students with multiple disabilities and visual impairments is becoming more diverse and complex. Educational programming must provide the opportunity for children to learn that they can have an effect on the world around them. The selection of functional goals, the

6

Tactual, Auditory, and Visual Development and Learning

In Chapter 3, we discussed that emotional–social development and children's feelings about themselves and others are related directly to the quality and extent of human interaction. In Chapter 4, we developed the idea that motor development and learning are facilitated by exploration, movement, and knowing how to control one's body in order to respond purposefully in relationship to the environment and objects within it. In Chapter 5, children with a myriad of additional handicapping conditions were described, along with some notions for assessment and programming for the development and learning problems they exhibit. In this chapter, we present a comprehensive discussion of learning and cognitive development through the senses.

INTRODUCTION TO SENSORY LEARNING

The development of cognitive ability—that is, knowing and thinking—involves the use of the senses, because the mind cannot perceive anything that has not first been received through the senses (Arnheim, 1969). What a child feels, hears, sees, tastes, and smells is internalized and stored as a model corresponding to the environment, and determines what is known about the world and one's relationship to it (Bruner, 1966).

Information coming through the senses must be received, interpreted, combined, and stored in the brain. The acquisition of language facilitates the integration of discrete sensory impressions to permit the learner to bring order to the material stored. Language also acts as a medium of exchange with others for clarifying and verifying sensory receptions. The ability to note the likenesses and differences between touch sensations, sights, sounds, tastes, and smells determines the relationships later developed between ideas. Integrating the diverse bits of concrete information received through the senses into a unified group of concepts about people and things provides the functional knowledge for thinking and talking about abstract ideas. The process of sorting, coding, and organizing sensory data and concepts to make all the characteristics and operational functions fit together is a complex mental task. Each child learns this process in a unique manner, which Piaget (1973) called "a cognitive style of learning."

Seeking, selecting, ordering, and programming information evolves as a consistent, individual pattern that each child uses in learning. The notion of unique learning patterns emphasizes the need for individualized instruction for maximal learning. Given this concept, parents and teachers should understand and accept each child's preferred learning strategies as appropriate (Keogh, 1973). Some theorists hypothesize that cognitive style may be well established by the age of 3, but that it is amenable to alteration or modification for many years. Numerous studies have demonstrated that style affects learning success and achievement. In fact, studies of youth and adults who lost their vision indicate that after vision loss, adaptation to the use of alternative senses can be achieved more readily when sensory training exercises are focused specifically on individual senses. Those who could utilize this approach in performance of tasks in their own homes and daily lives were able to make the mental adjustments with greater ease (Behar & Zucker, 1976).

Learning Progression

Before trying to understand the specific problems in cognitive learning experienced by the child with a visual handicap, we must first distinguish between the terms used to discuss sensory learning and the type and quality of information received through the various senses. Irrespective of the sense used to gather information, the term *discrimination* is used to refer to the ability to note the differences or likenesses within and/or among tastes, smells, sounds, touches, and visible objects or materials. In the baby, discriminations are gross in that there is attention to only a fraction of the available features at any time. With more and more sensory input, discriminations become increasingly refined. *Recognition* is an indication that what is sensed has been encountered previously. Memories and discriminations are being stored and recalled, which is one of the first indications that learning is taking place (Barraga, 1986).

Discriminations and recognitions enable children to develop perceptions about what they see, hear, touch, smell, or taste; that is, when they are able to give meaning to, understand, and interpret incoming information through the senses, they are perceiving that information and are able to use it. Perception is an active process in that the learner is constantly seeking, attending to, and accepting information that is needed or desired and is ignoring sensory input that is useless or unnecessary (Foulke, 1968). Bower (1977) suggested that the sensory and perceptual systems may be coordinated rather than differentiated in the early months, but both systems seem to register modality specifics after perceptions become organized. Perceptual selection is determined by whether the received information fits with previously sorted data to give a different type or level of new understanding. Piaget referred to this process as "cognitive accommodation and assimilation." At this stage, the child has the capacity to seek and accept stimulation of one specific sense to the exclusion of other sensory input.

A minimum level of stimulation (threshold) is required in each sensory system before the impulses can cross the connecting nerves and be directed to the appropriate receiving station in the brain. For example, stimulation of retinal cells by light rays leads to the transmission of impulses through the optic nerve directly to the occipital lobe of the brain. Sound waves arouse no activity in the retinal cells, but are directed through the auditory nerve to the nerve endings in the inner ear and on to the auditory reception center. It should be understood, however, that the intensity of the stimulation in any sense is not necessarily related to the strength of the sensation received in the brain. Physiological maturation and the consistent flowing of stimulation across the nerve fibers seem to affect the quality of sensory reception. For this reason, it is difficult (if not impossible) to determine accurate acuity measurements in any sense organ in the early years. Hence, acuity measurements alone do not give valid information about the usefulness of a particular sense for learning.

Tactual–Kinesthetic Sense

The tactual–kinesthetic (touch and movement) senses are often referred to as the "skin" senses and may be given less significance than they deserve. Active involvement with the environment and with the objects in it is dependent on effective use of the tactual–kinesthetic sense, which is stimulated by mechanical, thermal, electrical, and chemical stimuli. The hands and other parts of the body can push, press, grasp, rub, and lift to get information. The fingertips, however, provide the most distinct impressions with a degree of accuracy exceeding even that of visual impressions (Fieandt, 1966). Measurement of the acuities of the skin senses is an almost impossible task; touch sensitivity varies over the body surface because different parts of the body have fewer or greater numbers of receptors. There is no way to separate kinesthetic information from touch information, which is why we use the term tactual–kinesthetic sense. Knowlton (1987) suggested that teachers can make students aware of efficient methods of acquiring tactual information by presenting simple learning tasks at first, and gradually proceeding to those requiring finer and more complex discriminations, a concept already emphasized in pre-braille reading materials. When one is unable to use the visual sense or when vision is severely impaired, information gained through the tactual–kinesthetic senses provide the individual with the most complete and reliable information. "Getting my hands on it" may be thought of as analogous to "seeing it with my own eyes." Some theorists suggest that there is a developmental trend in the ability to use proprioceptive and tactual–kinesthetic senses throughout the learning years (Gipsman, 1981).

Auditory Sense

The auditory sense functions through nerve endings that are deeply imbedded within the inner ear and surrounded by fluid. Stimulation through the sense of hearing is more difficult during the early months of life because the reception area for hearing is located deep within the center of the brain. Probably little usable information is available through the sense of hearing before 3–6 months of life (Fraiberg, Smith, & Adelson, 1969). Although the infant may show involuntary responses to sound, actual discrimination and recognition of sounds are not possible until several months after birth. Hearing acuity is related to the vibration of receptor cells in the cochlea caused by the intensity of the sound waves traveling through air and fluid, the frequency of vibrations, and the masking effects of the environment. There can be no fixed unchanging level of sensitivity of the auditory system to any single sound or groups of sounds (Ludel, 1978). When the human voice at very close range provides pleasurable auditory sounds, infants may begin to note other sounds. Soon they begin to imitate sounds, especially the human voice when encouraged by vocal play with adults. This imitation is an important process because information fed to the brain through the auditory sense forms the basis for future sound repertoires necessary for speech production and language development.

Visual Sense

Because the visual sense provides a greater quantity and a more refined quality of information in a shorter period of time than does any other sense, vision is often thought to be the mediator between all other sensory input and is sometimes attributed with stabilizing the child's interaction with his or her world (Barraga, 1973). Most of what young children learn incidentally (without direction) is learned through the visual sense. For this reason, the most efficient use of any existing visual capacity is critically important for children with visual impairment regardless of the degree of severity. When there is sufficient light to provide contrast between objects or to permit motion to be seen, there is potential for the child to use this visual information in meaningful ways. Visual acuity measurements are influenced by a wide variety of factors, such as the type of stimulus target, the light surrounding it, the distance from it, and the time needed to bring the target to focus and to respond. Unless these conditions are optimal, and the target is appropriate to the developmental level of the child, the acuity measurement may be irrelevant when considering children with impairments in the visual system. The role of vision was summarized by Sonksen (1983) as "guardian of the personality, tutor of the senses, monitor of movement, and builder of concepts" (p. 92).

Olfactory and Gustatory Senses

The olfactory and gustatory senses react more readily to environmental chemical qualities, of which little is known; thus, thresholds and acuities cannot be estimated at this time. The information received through the sense of smell may be very different from the information received through the sense of taste, even in response to the same stimulus. Thus, these two senses may give conflicting and confusing information, especially when they are involved simultaneously. The gustatory sense (without the use of olfaction) provides little specific information about flavor, but gives a wide range of information about texture, contour, and size through the tip of the tongue and the sides of the mouth. The tip of the tongue is thought to have the most sensitive of all nerve endings in the body. In fact, persons have been able to read braille quite efficiently with the tip of the tongue. For teachers, the overriding consideration is not the sensitivity or acuity measurement of any sense, but whether the child can respond to selected sensory stimulation and receive and interpret its meaning for use in learning and functioning.

The senses probably do not provide isolated bits of data, but the extent and manner in which information received through a single sense might be transferred to another sense have not yet been determined. Some research indicates that attempting to use two senses simultaneously is inhibitory because of the interaction between them. Anater (1980) found that auditory information presented simultaneously with haptic information (through touch) did not interfere with storage or recall of the information acquired through touch. Apparently, haptic information is processed independently of auditory interference. Possibly, children can translate information through one sensory channel into another modality for storing and thinking (Buktenica, 1968), but do not need to in order to remember it. Regardless of the unsettled controversies about multisensory learning and intermodal transposition of information, there is little question that every available sense needs to be used by children who have impairments in one or more of the other senses. If the available senses are not developed, learning is likely to be fragmented and inaccurate.

TACTUAL LEARNING

The progression of sequential learning is similar for all the senses. In children with visual handicaps, however, greater attention may need to be given to a task-analyzed approach to presentation of the skills in smaller increments and in an orderly progression. Early studies suggested that children's development in tactual discrimination followed a pattern of using large-to-fine hand movements (whole hand to fingertips); from the early use of active touch to later use of passive touch; and from simple to more complex. Later studies have provided more definitive information about the tactual (sense of touch), kinesthetic (sense of movement), and haptic (the act of touching) systems and their effectiveness in making discrete discriminations and recognitions of objects and materials with different characteristics.

When studying 20 blind children at each of three grade levels from kindergarten through second grade, Kershman (1976) was able to identify the hierarchical order in which tactual skills were acquired by this group:

1. Large solid geometric shapes

2. Flat figures (puzzle pieces) smaller than geometric shapes

3. Embossed-dot geometric figures smaller than flat figures

4. Raised-dot line figures

5. Braille figures

Heller (1989) found that people who had never had vision were as efficient in tactile pattern perception as were those who had been blinded, leading him to conclude that visual experience might not be necessary for tactile perception. Familiarity with braille did not seem to guarantee good performance with tactile pictures, although tactile skills and tactual perceptual experience did have some effect. He had concluded earlier (1985) that simultaneous use of vision and touch by persons with low vision seemed to enhance recognition of embossed patterns; he suggested that persons with severe low vision use their vision to guide their tactual exploration.

When discussing the intelligent hand, haptics was defined by Klatzky and Lederman (1988) as a "perceptual system incorporating inputs from multiple sensory systems" (p. 122). They postulated that both tactile and kinesthetic systems were involved, including skin, muscles, and joints. They considered haptics as an encoding device in its own right and not simply a poor substitute for vision. In an earlier study (Klatzky, Lederman, & Reed, 1987), they found that haptics were able to identify specific characteristics of objects in this order: shape, hardness, texture, and size. Klatzky, Lederman, and Metzger (1985) called touch an "expert system," compared with a sensory substitution system for the deaf, citing the Tadoma method of understanding speech (mentioned in Chapter 5) as evidence that tactual systems can process complex spatiotemporal patterns at rates close to those of auditory speech perception.

Millar (1985) was concerned about the perception of complex patterns by touch, especially for those who would be reading braille. She concluded that perception of global outlines was not the basis of fast perception of dot patterns by touch (braille). The production or perception of outline shapes did not seem to be related in any way to reading efficiency in terms of rate of reading. One possibility might be that the important features of touch perception are not "shape features," but rather depend on dot density relations, an idea suggested by some of the very early braille recognition studies.

Let us use Carlos as an example as we discuss some of the above conclusions in light of what is known to be the sequence of development in tactual learning. This approach may be useful to teachers as they plan prereading programs for blind children.

Awareness and Attention

Tactual–kinesthetic development begins with awareness and attention to differences in shapes, hardness, texture, and size, as well as temperatures, vibrating surfaces, and materials of various consistencies. As Carlos holds objects in his hands, pressing and lifting them, he becomes aware that most of them are shaped differently, that some are rough and some are smooth, that some are heavy and others are light, and that he can mash a few of them, but many are hard to the touch. When he plays with such materials as clay and dough, he begins to understand that there are different consistencies. Putting his hands and body in water of varying temperatures and moving himself and objects in water or in sand make him aware that substances are not all alike and do not all behave in the same way. It can be said that he is attending to the quality of the tactual information (Griffin & Gerber, 1982). With students who are blind, the preference for specific textures (which is shown very early in life) seems to influence the accuracy of their discrimination (Hanninen, 1976; Zimmerman, 1985).

As they touch objects that vibrate and those that do not, they learn that some give off stimulation and others do not. Children who are blind learn that they receive information from objects, and at the same time, are able to alter and adapt some objects through tactual–kinesthetic handling, whereas they are unable to change others in any way. This beginning level of tactual learning is especially important for children with multiple impairments to assist them in learning safety and survival skills necessary for their daily living.

Structure and Shape

The second level of tactual–kinesthetic understanding relates to knowledge of the basic structure and shape of objects encountered. By moving his hand across objects, grasping and holding many shapes, and manipulating objects of various sizes, Carlos acquires information about protrusions and indentations, as well as general contour and the variations in size and weight. Interaction for maximum learning during this stage is best achieved through well-known objects that are part of his daily life, such as bars of soap, cups, plates, glasses, shoes, and socks. As Carlos discriminates objects, it becomes appropriate to introduce language to teach recognition of specific things. Cupping his hands around something gives him a bit of gross information about it; moving his hands around and tracing the shape of the object gives him successive information about the variations to enhance recognition by name. This early handling and exploring may help isolate distinctive components of objects, discriminate likeness and differences, and "provide a means for mental reconstruction of the objects" (Simpkins, 1979b).

The Relation of Parts to the Whole

Once Carlos is able to recognize simple, everyday objects by name, the next level of tactual–kinesthetic perception is possible. Whole objects that can be taken apart and put back together will help him learn the relationship of parts to the whole. At this point, it is important that he manipulate actual, three-dimensional objects, such as toy cars that can be taken apart and put together, blocks that fit together, and household objects that have parts to be assembled, such as a mixer or a food processor. Putting lids on pans, keys in locks, and screwdrivers into heads of screws are examples of object manipulation relating parts to wholes. These activities also foster concepts of mental space, because "spatial concepts are internalized ideas based on actions" (Simpkins, 1979a).

Grouping objects according to texture is another appropriate skill to learn. For example, Carlos's mother may present to him only clothes that have the same texture, all silverware that is alike, blocks of the same texture, and buttons that feel alike. Learning would focus on differences in size, length, and weight of objects, and the uses to be made of them. Such activities increase skill in using the hands in manual inspection to detect specific cues for identification. Concurrently, Carlos becomes aware that he can exercise control over objects and make them work in desired ways. Through this handling, he begins to form concepts of groups and categories. Practice in making finer and finer discriminations and maintaining the ability to recognize parts and wholes of objects prepares the child who is blind for more complex tactual–kinesthetic learning related to academic work.

More complex manipulative experiences permit the child to develop "tactual strategies" for fitting parts to each other and into a recognized whole. Carlos developed such strategies because he was able to fit blocks together to complete a unified structure, such as a house. Synthesizing tactual and haptic impressions permits the child to make accommodations to new elements touched and to assimilate these rapidly in relation to the information already stored. Such concepts of physical characteristics are not easily perceived without vision. For students who have multiple impairments, this may be the highest level of tactual–kinesthetic information possible, because they are less likely to be able to understand the more abstract concepts required to interpret graphic representations.

Graphic Representations

Presenting two-dimensional objects in graphic representation is the next stage in tactual–kinesthetic development. Such representations may be made with string or wire, or by using a tracing wheel or stylus on foil, plastic, or paper. The graphic representation of a real object may bear little tactual resemblance to the actual thing, and what is perceived may not fit with previously stored information. The spatial arrangement in a graphic representation is often quite unlike the spatial perspectives gained by handling the three-dimensional object. For this reason, it is useless and confusing to present any two-dimensional replications unless the real three-dimensional object is well known and has been handled many times. Even then, it may be necessary to accompany the graphic representation with the actual object at the first exposure to graphic forms. Approaching the presentations in this manner may help to minimize missed or distorted concepts. Selecting simple structural patterns, such as geometric forms, that can be handled by the children while examining the two-dimensional graphics, permits children to gain successive tactual impressions gradually. As fingertips and muscles move in certain patterns, they learn to associate the real object and the flat representation. For example, once a child recognizes round objects or forms easily, then various sizes of roundness may be presented graphically for the child to examine. Carlos has not yet reached this stage, but gradually increasing his experiences to include many shapes and structural forms will provide the basic experiences necessary for later learning (Barraga, Dorward, & Ford, 1973).

Such graphic replications as raised lines, curves, simple geometric forms, and object outlines of very well-known objects should be introduced slowly. It is important to provide only one piece of information at a time and to assure that the concept is not confused by focusing on a less important aspect of the object (e.g., the hole rather than the doughnut itself).

As that basic information is interpreted, then each additional element may be added in successive graphic representations. For example, if one is going to prepare material for a child to perceive the human figure tactually, the first step would be to present a straight line and seek the child's understanding of the relationship of the line to the straight postural position of the human body. Adding a circle for the head would be the next step; then adding lines (both straight and angular) to represent arms and legs, emphasizing the contrast between the straight lines of the body and the roundness of the head. Adding lines to represent fingers and toes would complete the figure. In contrast, if the child were given the entire graphic of the body at one time, it could be very confusing—what has been termed as "tactual noise" (Hammill & Crandell, 1969).

Also appropriate at this time is to teach children to make their own graphic drawings. As they make a line with a tracing wheel or with a tool on a piece of heavy aluminum foil or on a raised-line drawing board (heavy plastic on a hard rubber mat), children begin to realize how the hand and arm moves to make certain lines or forms. Becoming aware that they are making pictures that they can feel with their own hands is exciting and provides motivation to examine everything on paper or in books that is tactually perceivable. This desire and skill prepares them for understanding abstract tactual representations, such as maps of floor plans or room arrangements or even maps for mobility (Bentzen & Peck, 1979; Easton & Bentzen, 1980; Fletcher, 1981a).

Braille Symbols

The highest level of tactual–kinesthetic development is discrimination and recognition of symbols in the form of braille characters that denote letters, words, and eventually stories of the child's own experiences. Symbol recognition through the visual sense requires a high level of visual coding and association, but the tactual discrimination and recognition of symbols in the form of braille characters is an even more abstract level of perceptual–cognitive association. Children who are totally blind not only must recognize the symbols tactually (which in itself is a high-order task), but must interpret their meanings in relation to other surrounding braille characters and in the context of the material being read. Each braille symbol is temporal in nature and can be perceived only when the finger tip is touching it. This places a burden on tactual–kinesthetic memory and requires the child to make immediate decisions in relation to recognition, memory, association, and interpretation (Harley, Henderson, & Truan, 1979).

If Carlos's early preschool experiences continue to provide a wide variety of tactual–kinesthetic exposure and manipulation, then his readiness for academic learning through reading will be more advanced than that of a child who did not have preschool activities that provide the appropriate development in learning through touch. If the child who is blind has not reached a high level of tactual–kinesthetic perception before entering prereading programs, the teacher's role may be quite different from that normally expected in a school setting, because braille reading would need to be deferred. The appropriate experiences for developing perceptual skills to the refined stage of symbol recognition would need to become part of the child's readiness curriculum, and in some rare instances, could require several years before the child would be ready to begin more formal types of academic skills, such as reading. However, with the new federal mandates for preschool programs, the likelihood of this occurring should be eliminated in the near future.

Such mechanical skills as hand movement, finger positions, finger dexterity, wrist flexibility, light finger touch, and tactile perception and discrimination have been identified as precursors to efficient braille reading (Mangold, 1977, 1978; Olson, 1981). Although learning to read braille is much more mental than physical (Mangold, 1978), the mechanics of tracking and the lightness of touch are important skills for the child to develop.

The tactual reading process is more complex than the visual reading process because of the numerous braille characters (63 possible combinations in the six-dot cell) and because of the contractions used in embossed material in the abbreviated Grade 2 braille found in school texts, magazines, and other materials. Many braille symbols have multiple uses, and the interpretation of their meaning depends on their relationship to other characters; their position in the cell; and the initial, medial, or final position within the word or sentence. Braille symbols representing the same letter or word may be different within a single sentence; hence, decision making in braille reading requires a high level of ability in cognitive abstraction. Only those children who have achieved the mental flexibility and processing necessary for this task can be efficient in tactual reading as a primary means of learning (Harley et al., 1979). Children who are functioning below average mentally may learn to recognize letters and safety or single-object words, but may not be very good readers of running text unless special materials are prepared. The braille symbols should be introduced gradually. At first, only those standing for a single letter are appropriate; later, symbols representing whole words could be incorporated. Thorough understanding and recognition of each group of symbols is imperative before adding a more complex group. There is little evidence to suggest that discrete tactual symbols are useful with children who have multiple disabilities.

Fortunately, *Patterns*, the only beginning reading series designed and written specifically for braille readers, is now available from the American Printing House for the Blind (APH) (Caton, Bradley, & Pester, 1982). Research on the braille reading efficiency of students who began at the readiness level with this series shows promise of the series' value to both students and teachers, although some disadvantages of this series have been reported by teachers. Ongoing research is leading to refinement of this series, with additional worksheets becoming available on a continuing basis. Work is being completed on a series for adventitiously blinded children, youth, and adults.

Children with severe and profound low vision, such as Lucy, also need tactual–kinesthetic learning. Even though Lucy has some visual capacity, and she has begun to use it early in life, her development of touch still needs to be given the same attention as was necessary for Carlos. Touching and feeling objects will help to clarify and support the unclear images she receives visually. Maximum haptic development in the child with low vision will unify all sensory input and enable the child to form more stable concepts.

Decisions about reading media for children who have low vision need careful consideration. Some children who, unlike Lucy, do not indicate by their behavior that they are truly visual learners, may need to have the opportunity to learn to read using both inkprint and braille (Mangold & Mangold, 1989; Mangold & Roessing, 1982; Rex, 1989). After learning to read both inkprint and braille, some learners with low vision will show a definite preference for one medium, whereas others may continue to use both media throughout their school years, depending on lighting, availability of material, and fatigue factors. In fact, reading both inkprint and braille could increase overall learning efficiency for some students; teachers have observed that average and above average learners utilize both media with little difficulty (Barraga, 1980c). Below average learners and most students with multiple impairments who have usable vision will do better concentrating on visual reading (when possible) because of the abstract nature of the braille code. Decisions must be made on an individual basis according to the physical and mental characteristics of each student, the age and grade level, and the stability or instability of the eye condition. Students who need ultra-high magnification to read any visual material must use braille for primary learning, but continue to read inkprint when the devices are available to them. Some guidelines and assessment procedures to assist in making objective decisions regarding reading media have been developed by APH and can be obtained upon request.

In the case of Ching Lan, who was losing her vision rapidly, previous visual learning and her understanding of visual images made the transition to loss of vision less traumatic for her. She did have to learn when she could continue to rely on vision or when she needed to supplement her available vision with auditory and/or tactual cues.

Although Michael showed himself to be a completely visual child, his learning difficulties posed some of the same problems for him as severe low vision might for another child. He could see at close range, but had problems understanding what he was seeing, especially if it was not known to him or was of a complex nature. Even with his moderate low vision, he seemed to use touch as a means of confirming what he was seeing. The speed of his visual processing might be likened to that of a child who had much poorer vision and was slow because of trying to see more clearly or to integrate the fragments into a meaningful whole.

AUDITORY DEVELOPMENT AND LEARNING

Some have suggested that the ears of a blind person are comparable to the eyes of a sighted person for providing information. There is some truth to this, but one must exercise caution in accepting this idea without qualification. Because of the nature of the auditory sense and the continuous presence of inescapable sound in the environment, the human being has little physical control over auditory input, but instead must learn to exercise mental control—selective perception. This "masking" of sound occurs through a process that is at first unconscious, and later becomes conscious attending to sound according to its meaningfulness to an individual. The mere presence of sound does not necessarily mean that everyone listens to or hears the same sound.

Although sound and auditory input are a primary source of contact with and orientation in the environment for children who lack the ability to see in the distance, excessive auditory stimulation of meaningless sounds may evoke verbal repetition or echolalic responses to sound, and may actually inhibit the use of meaningful auditory input as a means of learning. Auditory stimulation for the sake of producing noise must not be confused with meaningful auditory input translatable into learning experiences; for example, having constant sound from a radio or television so that the house will not be so quiet, may interfere with auditory development in children with severe visual impairment who are not engaged visually with objects or people in the environment. Parents and teachers should direct specific attention to the sequence in auditory development, the use of hearing as a primary learning medium, the promotion of efficient listening skills, and the relation of auditory learning to language development as instruments for thinking.

The sequential pattern for the formation of auditory perceptions and concepts (Gleason, 1984) is similar to that of tactual–kinesthetic and visual development, although the appropriate application of these sequential ideas to the child with visual handicaps is clearly different for hearing than for touch or seeing.

Environmental Sounds

The first level of learning through the sense of hearing is the awareness of sound at the reflexive level; responses are unintentional and cannot be taught. This is soon followed by the attention and alerting level to specific sounds. The infant may be both soothed and startled by some sounds, whereas other noises appear to have little effect. Part of the explanation for this is that only sounds of great intensity, in either volume or pitch, penetrate through the infant's auditory receptive system, which is actually a built-in protective device because the infant has not yet learned to mask disturbing or confusing sounds.

To bring soothing sound into awareness, the child with visual impairment should have the opportunity to hear many pleasing and comforting sounds, such as soothing music and a soft human voice. These sounds create an unconscious awareness and attachment to the environment, in addition to conveying affective feelings of warmth and comfort. Even in a young infant, before attention is given to specific sounds, the human voice is a sound that provides a feeling of communication and attachment, probably substituting for facial expressions and gestures, which do not exist for children who are blind. Without exposure to the human voice in the first few months of life, children who are blind may feel as if they are living in total isolation (Fraiberg et al., 1969). Continuous and appropriate vocal stimulation in the early months may help children who are blind learn to use this auditory contact in much the same way that sighted children use eye movements to follow the actions of those around them. Placing bells or other pleasant sound producers on objects the infant touches or on a person helps to stabilize the idea that there are many sounds within the environment. In the early months, it is appropriate to urge the infant to listen to specific pleasant sounds when being moved about by someone else.

Specific Sounds

Although the infant who is blind may show awareness of sound and attend to a few specific sounds, the second level of development—response to and localization of specific sounds—probably does not occur before approximately 4–6 months of age (Fraiberg et al., 1969). Responses to specific sounds may be in the form of smiling, turning the head, listening intently and silently, and later attempting to imitate vocally. This behavior suggests that the child is beginning to maintain contact with specific sounds and localize the source of the sound. Turning the head in response to specific sounds indicates that "listening to hear" (Piaget, 1973) is the intent. Also, at this stage, ear–hand coordination (again, comparable to eye–hand coordination in the sighted child) is possible. This can be taught by use of sound toys, music, speech, and distinct environmental sounds. The manipulation of objects simply to hear sound may be observed, indicating the beginning of recognition that a certain hand action may produce a particular sound. Knowledge that sound can be associated with an object implies that the baby can be taught to reach for sound, such as in searching for a toy or moving toward an appealing sound, which occurs at around 1 year of age.

Sound Discrimination

Discrimination between familiar household and outdoor sounds, voices, and musical tones is the next level in auditory development for the child with visual handicaps. By this time, babies may move in relation to household sounds to find their source. Parents should encourage this activity and permit the child to explore sources by attending, localizing, and moving toward the sound until tactual contact is made. This enables them to note the variations in frequency, intensity, rhythm, and duration of auditory signals. Attention can be focused on relevant sounds, such as the telephone or doorbell, or even the washing machine or dishwasher.

At this discrimination level, it is appropriate also to name the sources of sounds to establish the knowledge that sounds come from different things in the home and to permit children to associate sounds with things they will hear every day and can touch. By noting the differences in environmental sounds and voices, children are learning to connect their own actions, and those of others, with particular sounds. As these associations become more frequent and refined, they may be able to make discoveries for themselves by attending to sounds as orientation cues for movement, a skill necessary for independent travel in the ensuing years.

It is important that parents/caregivers name the source of the sound and encourage vocal mimicking. Such guidance in auditory development permits children to organize their behavior as it relates to a specific goal or purposeful movement in relation to sounds. For example, children with severe visual handicaps may begin to recognize people by the differences in their voices or their footsteps and may actually associate the footsteps or voices with anticipation of an event. For example, one child with profound low vision, upon hearing her father's footsteps, learned to say her first connected words, "go–car," associating the footsteps with the anticipation of going for a ride.

In this discrimination stage, sound begins to replace vision for perceiving distance relationships and may also serve as a primary motivation for movement as children are learning to walk. Movement, in relation to sound, may also provide (unconsciously perhaps) incidental development in the use of sound echoes to indicate the presence of objects. The level of sound as children approach an object becomes a referent for distance in addition to guiding direction in movement. The greater the range and variety of sound sources toward which children can move and also touch, the more rapidly discrimination and familiarity of sound will proceed, and the more stable the base for interpreting sound sources.

Sound Recognition and Association

As words begin to have meaning to children, the next level of auditory development—recognition of sounds related to specific words and connected speech—is possible. As children are learning that objects have names, they may learn also that sounds and their own actions have words to describe them. To assist in this process of recognition and association, parents should talk about their child's movements and actions, interpret in words what is happening when there is response to certain "noise-makers," and clearly differentiate between the sounds of words. Children may soon respond to the tonal variations by smiling when they hear happy words and praises and by sobering when scolded. There is some indication that imitative speech (when hearing words and jingles) comes about more rapidly in children with visual handicaps than in sighted children. This may be related to the fact that, without the full use of the visual sense, attending to auditory input develops acuity and a greater sensitivity to sound. There is no indication that children with impaired vision have any greater capacity for auditory perception than do sighted children, but their constant use and heavy reliance on the auditory sense permits development to proceed rapidly.

During this vocal period, children with visual impairments are developing linguistic strategies that will be the basis for their speech and language development during the school years. Mistakes in the use of personal pronouns, confusion in the use of "I," and lack of the use of the verb "see" have been noted in some children with little or no vision (McGinnis, 1981). Adverbs of location and prepositions are used with less frequency. Adults need to exercise care in the construction of their verbal explanations so as to minimize imitative errors.

It is important when children respond to sound that parents/caregivers give them the opportunity to listen carefully without interruption and to touch the sound source whenever possible. If touching is not possible, parents/caregivers should provide verbal interpretation of the object. Talking to children with visual handicaps as they move and play is more important than talking to sighted children, because the only way the former children have to interpret their own actions is by having others talk to them about what they are doing. As mentioned earlier, passive auditory stimulation from radio or television without meaningful verbal discourse with adults often results in echolalic speech, or verbalizations that have no real meaning and do not contribute to cognitive development. Playing word games, reading nursery rhymes, and singing action songs while holding or moving children can strengthen sound association and memory.

Comprehension and Interpretation of Verbal Instructions

The next stage of auditory perceptual development involves an understanding of words and phrases so that children respond to commands of increasing complexity and length from one-part commands to two- and three-part directions that are related. They then learn to respond to instructions of actions that are unrelated (e.g., "Please close the door, then sit down," or "Put your toy on the shelf and hand me a tissue please"). During this period, selective listening may be taught most easily by focusing children's attention to the action they are being asked to perform. When they have achieved the ability to mask out irrelevant or meaningless sounds, and to attend to musical themes and to speech that provides directions and instructions, children may begin to formulate their own speech for feedback to themselves and to others. Adults will recognize discrepancies in meaning, as well as inaccuracies that have occurred because children hear without being able to verify by looking. For example, adults can play games that focus on identifying voices of specific people by questioning, "Who is that?" Adults also can make tape recordings of environmental and household sounds and ask children to talk about what is being heard.

Translating vocal instructions into purposeful actions is one of the highest levels of auditory perceptual processing, and is a critical skill if children with visual handicaps are to work in groups with sighted children in preschool, as well as a major determinant of academic success if they expect to be a part of the regular class in a school setting. Given the proper opportunity to develop through previously mentioned stages, children with visual handicaps should be able to respond and carry out actions according to instructions given to them. Young children who are unable to do this should be given greater attention to determine whether they understand the meanings of the words they hear in relation to their own movement and actions. Children with poor body image and inability to understand how to control body actions may have greater hesitance in acting on instructions. Unless children can translate auditory input into meaningful options or associations that can be used immediately, there is little indication that auditory input is being related to mental processing. For children with visual impairment, the cognitive translation of auditory language provides mental stimulation that may be equivalent to sighted children's motivation through visual perceptual skills. Children form images in relation to spoken language. This imagery creates a basis for recall and for higher level abstract thinking when the words are no longer heard. For example, when instructions are given to move the body to a specific position or to walk in a particular pattern, children have to think about what was heard and translate this into body actions. Later, when the same or similar instructions are heard, movement patterns associated with the words are remembered. Michael gave evidence of some problems in this area by his slow actions; fortunately for him, he had enough vision to help him to confirm what he was hearing or to imitate what he could see. Hall (1981) said that children with visual disabilities often form fewer and less detailed images of their environment, unless they have experienced actions with their own bodies. Words that represent things that can be heard, felt, or experienced are concrete words and can be used as referents. Practice in translating what is heard into personal meaning may stimulate searching for meaning in other spoken messages.

Auditory Skills and Listening in Learning

Once children with visual impairments enter regular classrooms, one of their primary channels for learning is hearing; consequently, achieving the highest level of auditory processing and listening efficiency is essential for further cognitive development. Paying attention to the outlined sequence in auditory development and perception will help adults avoid the mistaken assumption that simply because the child can hear, he or she is able to use listening efficiently for academic learning. Processing through the auditory sense without the preparatory perceptual skills is almost impossible.

Teaching listening skills is sometimes considered an important part of the educational program for students with visual handicaps. For this training to be useful, students must be taught to listen to something (Cobb, 1977; Gleason, 1984). How material is presented on tape or records is of crucial concern if aural learning is to be effective for students who must rely on it for the bulk of their information input, especially in high school and for vocational purposes.

Acquiring information tactually through reading braille is a slow process. As students progress through school, they may find that auditory input is more efficient, especially for literature and history courses. How material is presented on tape is a factor in long periods of listening; for example, too slow a rate may cause the brain to "go to sleep," and the listener may lose attention more rapidly than when the reading rate is faster than normal. Attention wanders and processing is fragmentary when reading rate is either too slow or too fast for some learners; the use of technology with variable speed adjustments has been of help. Research in aural study systems (Nolan & Morris, 1973) and the perfection of reading machines with vocal output are changing the availability of printed material for students and those whose careers require constant reading.

VISUAL DEVELOPMENT AND LEARNING

Developing maximum visual perceptual ability in children with visual handicaps is of major importance because more than three-fourths of all school-aged students with visual handicaps, even those who have other impairments, have some usable vision. The past tendency to equate the extent of visual impairment with the limitation in seeing imposed on the individual has been found to have no basis in reality. Nor does the assumption that visual acuity has any relationship to the capacity for visual development or for actual visual functioning (Faye, 1984; Jose, 1983).

Another erroneous assumption is that children with impaired vision should be protected from eye strain and that using the eyes might in some way damage the vision present. Faye (1984) suggested that whatever vision a child has should be used to maximum capacity, which from a perceptual and learning point of view, means that the more children look and use their vision, the more efficient they will be in functioning visually.

Vision not only is related to the structure and function of the eyes, but involves many parts of the visual system and brain, as well as other body systems. Figure 6.1 identifies the components of the total visual system and the particular function of each in relation to the entire process of visual interpretation. The physiological structures in the eye, such as the pupil and lens, facilitate or impede the rays of light from reaching the sensitive retinal cells. The location and spread of the activated cells help determine the strength of the burst of energy sent along the optic nerve to the brain, where the person receives the electrical charges as fragments of visual information, organizes them into a visual image, and relates the image to messages received from the other senses for full interpretation.

In recent years, the patterns of visual development in children have been studied extensively, and findings indicate that visual acuity, visual skills, and visual perception may progress at a faster rate than was previously thought. From a comprehensive review of literature in vision (Barraga, Collins, & Hollis, 1977; Hall & Bailey, 1989) and recent research

light	cells in		nerve		in
enters	RETINA		fibers		BRAIN
EYE	where	and	in	reception	where
refracts focus on	neural	transmitted	OPTIC	area	visual
rays that	energy	along	NERVE		information
	is		in		is
	generated				interpreted

FIGURE 6.1. Components of the visual system (capitalized words) and their functions in visual interpretation.

(Corn, 1989a; Hall, Kekelis, & Bailey, 1986; Heersema & Hof-Van Duin, 1990), a model of visual development can be proposed that begins with optical control, which leads to visual stimulation, which prepares for actual visual learning (see Figure 6.2). In addition, this model suggests the periods of optical and visual perceptual development; concept development and maximum organization of visual imagery; and storage and recall of visual information. The model also incorporates aspects of concept development and periods of growth spurts in the brain. This model is derived from recent research that has studied the functioning of the visual system before birth and throughout life. This model permits the teacher, clinician, and rehabilitation person to approximate the visual developmental age of the person with a visual impairment as it relates to the pattern of optical training; the nature of the function in visual stimulation; and the behaviors indicative of actual visual learning from which visual imagery and memory can be evaluated.

How to promote the continuing development of the visual system and functional behaviors has been the concern of some investigations. For example, Hall et al. (1986) found that visual behaviors could be taught most effectively by concentrating on (1) visual attending behaviors, which would include the refinement of optical skills using the eyes to focus in a variety of spatial areas; (2) visual examining behaviors, which would be the equivalent of stimulating the use of vision with an array of objects, colors, shapes, and eventually pictures of the same things; and (3) visually guided behaviors involving the motor system in reaching, grasping, manipulating, marking, assembling, and finally making choices from a selection of visual materials. These behaviors prepare the person to use vision for learning and making decisions about the appropriate responses to the multitude of visual stimuli encountered in the environment. Bell (1986) postulated that programs to ensure the stimulation of visual pathways led to the development of anatomically based compensatory neural mechanisms that foster the maximum development of the visual system. The sequence of visual behaviors and functions may be assumed to develop in a similar pattern for all children; however, the model shown in Table 6.1 uses *visual age* rather than the usual chronological age, because this denotes the maturity of the visual system itself in regard to its functional control and the cognitive maturity needed to use the system for purposes of learning. Without stimulation, optical control and subsequent learning through vision cannot be accomplished.

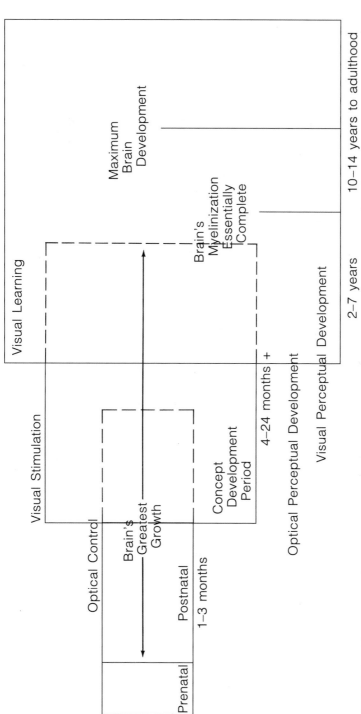

FIGURE 6.2. Model of visual development. This model permits the teacher, clinician, and rehabilitation person to approximate the visual developmental age of the person with a visual impairment as it relates to the pattern of optical training; the nature of the function in visual stimulation; and behaviors indicative of actual visual learning from which visual imagery and memory can be evaluated.

VISUAL HANDICAPS AND LEARNING

TABLE 6.1
Developmental Sequence of Visual Age Behaviors

VISUAL AGE	OPTICAL	STIMULATION	LEARNING

1–3 months	• Focusing
	• Fixating
	• Tracking
	• Convergence
		• Colored lights, glass
		• Complex patterns
		• Moving objects
		• Close to distant
		  movements
			• Discriminates faces,
			  colors

3–7 months	• Smoother movements • Exploring • Sharpened acuity • Shifting of eyes • Eye–hand coordination	• Small objects to reach • Changes in facial expressions • Suspended objects • Face pictures • Peek-a-boo • Actions to imitate	• Grasps, looks • Imitates faces • Manipulates • Chooses • Places objects • Chooses face • Anticipates action • Makes faces
8–12 months		• Finger paints • Looking and hiding games • Expanded games • Hidden objects	• Makes marks • Plays games • Searches • Initiates play • Gives to other
1–2 years		• More objects • Picture books	• Uses objects • Matches objects • Stacks blocks • Scribbles • Imitates actions

2–4 years		• Geometric forms, colors
		• Simple puzzles and
		  shapes
		• Crayons
		• Pictures of forms
		• Picture puzzles
		• Magazines
			• Matches colors and
			  forms
			• Matches shape and
			  place
			• Draws circle
			• Matches form to picture
			• Selects by name

5–7 years		• Action pictures
		• Complex scenes
		• Abstract shapes
		• Letters and words
		
		• Signs, books in different
		  styles
		• Word games
		• Chalk and pencil
			• Sequences
			• Arranges objects
			  spatially
			• Copies
			• Associates with pictures
			• Names shapes of letter
			• Perceives sameness
			• Matches words
			• Writes, letters, words in
			  all styles

Visual Skills

Such optical skills as fixation, tracking, focus, accommodation, and convergence are achieved by the majority of children with normal vision in their day-to-day functioning when they have a visually stimulating environment. However, the child with a visual impairment may have difficulty in developing these skills if the impairment is severe enough to interfere with normal visual scanning. When very little light can enter the eye or reach the nerve centers in the retina, muscular control may be difficult, especially when no image can be formed from the blur. Studies (Barraga, 1980a; Bell, 1986; Downing & Bailey, 1990; Hall & Bailey, 1989) have concluded that use of impaired vision can be taught, even in children with multiple disabilities. The earlier this stimulation and training is begun, the greater the likelihood that efficiency in use of vision will continue to improve for many years and facilitate overall mental development.

Several programs are available that present a step-by-step process to be followed from the earliest months of life to the time when the child with low vision (or adult who begins to lose vision) can function visually at the highest possible level for the particular individual (Barraga, 1980a; Bell, 1986; Downing & Bailey, 1990; Erhardt, 1987; Goetz & Gee, 1987; L. Harrell & Akeson, 1986). Each program has some differences, but they all include a variety of stimulating materials for use in numerous environments, focusing on a multitude of visual responses, initiated behaviors, and visual–motor activities beginning with the very simple and gradually becoming more complex.

Although skillful use of the eyes may not, by itself, enhance visual learning, it certainly increases the possibility of perceptual development through the visual sense. Of course, actual seeing cannot occur until messages transmitted through the eyes are received in the brain and interpreted. Even when visual information is blurred, distorted, or incomplete, as long as the brain is able to combine the images with auditory and other sensory information, the person can use vision as a contributing sense in cognitive development. Medical specialists and educational researchers have shown that poor vision does not necessarily cause poor learning—what the brain is able to do with the visual information it receives determines how well the person will be able to function visually (Barraga, 1964; Bateman & Weatherall, 1967; Faye, 1984).

Visual Perceptual Development in Students with Low Vision

The extent to which the impaired visual system will enhance the capacity for perceptual–cognitive development in individuals is virtually impossible to predict because an infant or young child may have "a recorded visual acuity of light perception and later show some useful vision" (Seidenberg, 1975). For example, Lucy's only visual response at first was to bright light, but she later gave evidence of having vision, although limited at a distance and in some circumstances.

Barraga et al. (1977) and Rogers and Puchalski (1988) assumed that from the evidence available, learning through an impaired system occurs slowly, but follows the same sequential pattern as visual development in a normal system. However, the visual skills and perceptual organization is seldom, if ever, spontaneous or automatic in a system with an impairment other than a refractive error. The sequence of perceptual development may emerge quite unevenly and is influenced by such factors as type and extent of impairment, mental capacity, stimulation and encouragement to look, and numerous environmental factors, some of which may be adaptable whereas others are not within control of the individual (Corn, 1985a). A broad base of visual stimulation and a wide variety of looking skills are the keys to the refinement of more discrete skills as visual development is integrated with perceptual and cognitive learning.

Barraga and Collins (1979) presented a rationale for a program of visual development and learning for students with low vision. They identified in detail all the visual functions and skills necessary for maximum efficiency, specified the types of tasks compatible with the progression of perceptual–cognitive development, and discussed the pertinent considerations in visual environments. This rationale became an integral part of the design for instruction in a *Program to Develop Efficiency in Visual Functioning* (Barraga & Morris, 1980). Since that time, others have adapted the ideas and applied them to specific children, detailed them in smaller learning increments, and designed sequences especially for children with multiple impairments, an increasing challenge that is now being addressed with greater frequency (Bell, 1986; Corn, 1989b; Hall et al., 1986; Smith & Cote, 1982).

Teachers must remind themselves constantly that learning through the visual sense can never exceed the overall level of the individual's perceptual–cognitive development, always a concern in working with multiply disabled students of any age. Although it is difficult to think of visual and mental age rather than chronological age when working with this population, if we do not, we tend to expect higher levels of visual functioning and present materials and activities far too complex for the level of mental understanding. Another factor to consider when working with students and youth with low vision is that they may have usable vision, but they may not have had the concentrated visual learning activities needed at an early age to enable them to use their vision effectively. If this is the case, regardless of chronological age, we must concentrate on visual age, and begin with activities at the lowest level so that visual images of form, objects, pictures, and finally symbols, as outlined previously, can be learned in sequence.

When children with visual impairments, especially those with very low vision, enter school, they may need to spend a long period of time in visual perceptual development as a part of their readiness before attempting visual reading material. With the increase in infant and preschool programs, as well as earlier identification of impairments, this may not occur as frequently as in the past, but still deserves sensitive consideration. Visual–motor and eye–hand coordination seems to be an area in which some children with low vision have tended to function less efficiently. In fact, an item analysis of the performance of 112 students with low vision aged 5–20 revealed that the most frequently missed items on the *Diagnostic Assessment Procedure* (Barraga, 1980b) were those requiring motor skills (Berla, Rankin, & Willis, 1980). The use of the visual sense in students with severe visual disabilities was long neglected, but more than 20 years of intensive research and development have resulted in more and more programs and activities to enhance visual perceptual development in children, youth, and adults with low vision.

Lucy, whose parents were told it was impossible to tell at her young age to what extent her visual capabilities might improve, is an example of a child with low vision who will probably need a longer period of readiness in visual activities designed specifically to acquaint her with print symbols and enable her to relate these to visual concepts she may have experienced in her preschool years. Consequently, the program will need to be stabilized and associated very gradually as she learns to use her vision for acquiring information in school and in responding by writing, typing, and/or using the computer. This may well be the case for Michael also, because his learning difficulties, along with his moderate visual impairment, indicate he will need smaller increments and more time to understand and process symbols.

Because Ching Lan is gradually losing her vision, she will need help and guidance in continuing to retain her visual imagery and in recognizing things that she can no longer see clearly, although she has retained visual memories of many objects. Children who are losing their vision will retain functioning for a much longer period if they are encouraged to use their vision and are helped to interpret and make decisions about the unclear visual information they receive. If the vision loss is gradual, monoculars for distant viewing, and other optical devices such as magnifiers for near use, may be of assistance, but the time may come eventually when even these become of little value.

Children seem to use different senses in varying degrees and for their own purposes, even when all senses are intact. Some children with rather good vision look very little, whereas others with very limited vision look quite intently. Nevertheless, cognitive development follows a more stable pattern when a child has use of all available senses; only when all senses are used to their maximum capability can learning and cognitive development reach the optimum for each person. Whether the individual is totally blind, has very low vision, or has only moderately impaired vision, there is need for opportunity to explore the use of all senses and to develop a unique style of learning that gives the greatest quantity and the highest quality of usable information for cognitive development. For example, the use of optical devices may give a person with low vision the ability to exercise greater control over the visual environment by modifying the visual perspective, and to receive a higher quality of information to process cognitively.

COGNITIVE DEVELOPMENT

Piaget (1973) suggested that there are many object classes that children who are blind cannot act on perceptually (through vision or hearing or muscular motion) and must simply know in terms of the symbolic auditory language. This may be a factor in a problem referred to earlier as verbalism, that is, using words without understanding their meanings. Studies of cognitive development in children who are blind (Anderson & Fisher, 1986; Dodds, 1983; Gottesman, 1976; Hall, 1983; Higgins, 1973; Stephens & Grube, 1982; Wan-Lin & Tait, 1987; Witkin, Oltman, Chase, & Friedman, 1971) have indicated some lag in various aspects of abstract thinking, such as conservation, mental rotation, and reasoning. Problems also have been identified in the areas of spatial concepts and nominal realism, possibly because of the relatively limited manner by which students who are blind can experience the world, which influences their understanding of objects, spatial features, and language expressing their mental imagery (Anderson, 1984; Pereira, 1990). Boldt (1969) found that cognitive development of children who are blind proceeded along similar lines to that of sighted children; however, the ability of children who are blind to process complex auditory material suffered a tremendous lag until about the age of 16 or 18, which is several years behind that of sighted students. This finding exemplifies the fact that hearing and verbalizing appropriate words does not mean necessarily that the words are completely understood cognitively. Numerous studies have found that children who are blind are less able to define the meaning of vocabulary words on intelligence tests than are their sighted peers of comparable age and intellectual ability. A broad generalization suggests that children who are blind may know and use a word, but are unable to express a cause–effect relationship, possibly because of the lack of a clear mental image to use as a referent (Stephens, Simpkins, & Wexler, 1976).

Some have suggested that children who are blind and some of those with severe visual impairment operate from a different "data base," depending on experiences and verbal explanations offered by others. An anecdotal interview with a gifted blind person reported by Whitmore and Maker (1985), included the following statement: "The teachers paid more attention to teaching how to use equipment than how to think about the process, particularly in math; computation skills took precedence over the concepts involved" (pp. 83–84). The suggestion followed that students who are blind need to learn underlying principles first, followed by the individual skills and strategies to apply them in meaningful ways.

There needs to be clarification between academic knowledge (e.g., of how to spell or calculate square root, of the names of presidents, or of the theory of relativity) and practical knowledge (e.g., of how to balance a checkbook, of how to read a help wanted advertisement, of what "RSVP" means, or of how to make hotel reservations) when discussing learning (Corn & Bishop, 1984). These authors emphasized that practical knowledge is what enables an adult to live successfully in society. Using the *Test of Practical Knowledge* (TPK) (Wiederholt & Larsen, 1983), Corn and Bishop found that adolescents with visual impairments in their small sample of 116 students performed poorly when compared with sighted norms in areas of personal, social, and occupational skills and knowledge. Interestingly enough, the students with low vision (those who were legally but not totally blind) seemed to have more difficulty in acquiring the knowledge than did their peers who were totally blind (Corn & Bishop, 1984). This may have been related to factors other than the amount of vision, but perhaps teachers spend more time making sure that students who are blind have skills and knowledge they think important in "daily living skills," and make the unwarranted assumption that students with low vision need less direct teaching because they learn by using their limited vision. Corn and Bishop concluded that a new test designed specifically for students with visual handicaps needs to be developed to complement the TPK, and that further research in this area is indicated.

It appears that children without vision, or with very little vision, cannot fully develop many concepts unless carefully planned teaching strategies counterbalance the perceptive privation. Because of limited visual input, students with visual handicaps construct reality differently from sighted students, although not necessarily with a deficit (Sanctin & Simmons, 1977). Obviously, this difference will affect the problem-solving and reasoning strategies. However, lessons designed to teach logical reasoning can be very helpful and should be a part of the specialized curriculum for students with visual handicaps (Sicilian, 1988; Stephens & Grube, 1982). This logical reasoning approach might help to minimize some of these deficits in practical knowledge by the high school years.

CONCEPTS APPLIED TO CHILDREN

A few studies have shown that blind youth have superior ability to sustain attention and to process material auditorially with ease. However, no general conclusions would be applicable to all students who are blind; the individual characteristics of each must be considered in relation to previous background and experience. The evidence presented in the word picture of Carlos suggests that his auditory perceptual abilities were in keeping with his level of development, as demonstrated by his awareness of footsteps indicating someone's arrival, his ability to understand verbal instructions and to act accordingly, and his efficiency in localizing sound sources to use in easy movement in familiar surroundings. When Carlos reaches school age, there is good reason to believe that his auditory perceptual abilities and listening skills will have developed to a level that will permit him to expand and refine them for use in mobility training and as one of his primary means of learning and interacting.

Lucy, who has questionable visual ability, will need as careful attention to auditory perceptual development as to tactual–kinesthetic and visual development. Because of the probability of limited vision throughout her school years, she will need to use auditory learning as a supplemental, if not her primary, sense for academic and environmental learning. Auditory perception and careful listening may assist her in clarifying the incomplete or blurred visual impressions she receives. Obviously, her low vision will limit or preclude the use of vision as a sense, and Lucy will be required to rely on audition as the distance sense. Sound localization will be her major safety clue in movement and travel outside her home.

Ching Lan, because of her spontaneous adjustment to the gradual loss of sight, has no doubt already begun to use sound as a key referent in her environmental interactions. As visual loss continues, her parents and teachers should direct her toward refining auditory localization and listening skills to help her bridge the transfer from visual learning to tactual and auditory learning. She must be taught to use some caution in movement so that she may learn to be sensitive to her own safety.

Efficient braille reading will develop slowly for Ching Lan, during which time she will rely heavily on listening and auditory learning as she perfects her tactile skills. In her educational program, she will probably use both tactual and auditory learning to complement each other and enable her to continue her achievements in schoolwork and related activities.

Michael may find it difficult to attend to and process all sensory stimuli because of his learning problems, but as he matures and teachers and family are constantly sensitive to the need for orderly, small increments of new learning, he can be expected to improve his attention span and find it easier to process sensory information with additional speed. Time and patience on the part of adults, as well as Michael himself, may facilitate his understanding of his own style of learning, and eventually enable him to organize his world for his best interest so as to reduce the possible confusion he might experience with uncontrolled stimuli bombarding him through all senses.

SUMMARY

In recent years, more attention is given to the role of the senses in learning and cognitive development for all children, and especially for children who are visually handicapped. Every child with a visual impairment needs to be encouraged in the early years and perhaps through school years and adult life to support and confirm information being received and to search out additional information through the use of all other senses. The tactual sense keeps a person in direct contact with the concrete world and provides a variety of information that is not available visually and that lacks clarity and precision when experienced only through the sense of hearing.

All children with even moderate to severe visual impairment, and certainly those who are totally blind, learn to rely heavily on auditory input as a primary means of alerting them to what may be seen or of keeping them in contact with distance information that will never be available to them visually. For persons who are congenitally totally blind, auditory information will be the primary guide to movement, even in familiar environments, and will provide cues for safe movement in new environments and eventually in independent travel. Similarly, individuals who have lost vision after having used vision as the primary learning and functioning sense, will need to develop auditory sensitivities to be alerted to every sound emanating from the environment and to use sound clues as a valuable means of associating previously seen information with what now can only be heard.

Teachers and others may find it valuable to give greater attention to reasoning activities related to the academic facts and computations so that maximum cognitive development is fostered in all students with visual impairment. In an ever-changing and highly sophisticated workplace and living environment, persons with visual impairments need the knowledge and skills of sighted peers if they are to live productive and satisfying lives as truly integrated citizens.

7

Educational Settings and Services

Questions about where education should take place and who should provide that education have generated many different answers as long as formal education has existed for children who are blind and visually handicapped. The inception of established educational programming took place in France in the late 1700s, when Valentin Haüy began his school for blind children; this was followed rapidly by the creation of residential schools in other European countries (Roberts, 1986). Even during this era, when the concept of a separate residential school implied a higher quality education for any child, professionals had begun to debate the viability of providing an education in a setting beyond the child's own community. Lowenfeld (1981) translated a paper by Jakob Wilhelm Klein, an early Austrian educator of children who were blind and visually handicapped, in which Klein stated in 1845,

> Everybody will agree that children in their tender years, especially blind children who are so much in need of help, are best cared for in their parental homes under motherly care; and if the regular schools suffice for their education, why should they be removed from their homes and placed in costly institutions that accommodate scarcely the sixtieth part of those who are in need of education? (p. 165)

The first educational institutions in the United States for children who were blind and visually handicapped were segregated settings in the strictest sense of the word. From the opening of Perkins School for the

Blind in Boston in 1829 to the establishment of 48 other residential schools by the early 1900s (Roberts, 1986), most of these schools educated children of normal intelligence whose only disability was a visual impairment. Black students were educated separately, sometimes on other campuses. Children with additional disabilities often were institutionalized or kept at home with no education except that which the family could provide. The enrollment standards for the Texas School for the Blind cited in the 1869–1870 Annual Report described the populations included in the early schools for children with visual handicaps: The school would enroll no students who were "incapacitated by age, physical infirmity, mental debility, or moral obliquity," and all students had to be of "sound health, good mental capacity, good moral character . . . [and] free from spasmodic and eruptive diseases."

During the early 1900s, some innovative public school programs began to serve students who were blind and visually handicapped. Chicago began a public school program in 1900 at the urging of Frank H. Hall (Roberts, 1986), and a few large cities developed and operated their own public school programs from the early 1900s. However, as a result of the births of large numbers of children who were visually impaired from retinopathy of prematurity, then called retrolental fibroplasia, the focus shifted to individual learning characteristics of the children themselves and to new and more creative ways for those children to acquire the same information available to children with better vision.

Educators have since come to realize that there is no single answer that prescribes the way all children should be taught; the setting and educational needs of children with visual impairments vary, and a continuum of services and settings must be available to meet the needs of the students optimally. This recognition has been the primary impetus for innovative educational planning and programming during recent years.

LEGISLATIVE INFLUENCES

In more recent years, federal legislation has provided the mandate for educational opportunities that in the past existed only in some areas. PL 94-142, The Education of All Handicapped Children Act, was passed in 1975; as a result, children with visual handicaps were served in a wider variety of settings than previously. By mandate, public schools are required to make available an appropriate educational program for all children. If the schools are unable to offer such a program, they must secure and pay for that program to be delivered in another setting.

Although the federal laws dictate the requirements for states in providing appropriate educational programming, it is the states' responsibility to identify eligible students; to establish, implement, and monitor programs; and to interpret the federal mandates with regard to each state's educational system. Therefore, questions of student eligibility, teacher qualification, and alternative settings may vary greatly from state to state according to interpretation.

Under the original law, services were to be provided to children with disabilities 3 years of age or older unless this was contrary to state law. In 1986, the original law was amended through PL 99-457, Disabled Infants and Toddlers Act, to require that all states provide services to children aged 3-5. States that chose to apply for special funding to serve children from birth through 2 years of age could also serve that group of disabled and at-risk students, and most states that were not already doing so chose to provide these services.

These new amendments require that an individual program be written for the families of children in the 0-2 age range. This plan, known as the Individual Family Service Plan (IFSP), recognizes that family members are the primary teachers during the early years and that professionals support the family's interaction with children in helping them to respond to the environment.

The value of complete parental involvement in any early education program cannot be overemphasized. Under PL 94-142, parents must be included as part of the educational team in designing experiences, being a part of the instruction, and evaluating the child's progress. Teachers and counselors provide information, guidance, and support to parents. In addition, interaction and participation with other parents of children with visual handicaps can have unlimited benefit for some parents. This can take place through informal local groups or through branches of national groups, such as The National Association for Parents of the Visually Impaired (NAPVI).

The passage of legislation requiring an appropriate education for children with disabilities and extending that education to all children aged 0-21 has guaranteed an appropriate education for all children, regardless of disabling condition. To qualify a student for specialized services because of a visual impairment, medical and educational professionals must collaborate to determine the extent and implications of an identified visual difference.

Recent laws have been enacted to assure the continuation of the rights of the adult with a visual impairment even beyond the educational years. Among the most important of these are Section 504 of the Rehabilitation Act in 1986, which ensures that people with disabilities can have building accessibility and job opportunities in government-supported agencies. The recently enacted Americans with Disabilities Act in 1990 provides a legal foundation for the rights of people with disabilities in regard to equal access to public facilities, including transportation and job opportunities. The legal mandate for equal opportunity now extends throughout life for people with disabilities.

IDENTIFICATION AND ELIGIBILITY

When an infant has a severe visual impairment, this fact usually is recognized by parents, caregivers, and/or medical personnel early in the first year. A child's father may notice that his son does not smile and turn toward him when the father quietly enters the room; a grandmother may notice that her granddaughter does not try to reach for her shiny earrings as her other grandchildren did at that age. Such observations may not be confirmed for some time by medical evaluation, and this can result in delays in diagnosis and in important early intervention services. For example, if Lucy's parents had not been concerned by her erratic visual behavior and sought a specialist's opinion, she might never have received the early visual stimulation so vital for maximum development of the vision she was able to use.

Children with less severe visual impairments may remain undiagnosed for years, sometimes until they reach school age. Many infants and pre-schoolers have never been examined to determine what the clarity of their vision is at near and far distances or whether they see equally well with both eyes. A promising trend in recent years has been to stress the need for screening of all young children to detect visual problems much earlier.

A few states have passed mandatory screening for vision and hearing problems of all children. Trained regional teams make preschool screening available in shopping centers, day care centers, private schools, and community centers. Often the state health services are involved, sometimes a ladies' medical auxiliary, and frequently the Society for the Prevention of Blindness (SPB). SPB has developed a home kit with instructions for parents to check their children's vision. Such techniques as visually evoked responses and preferential looking (a technique in which the child turns toward a patterned stimulus) can be used by clinicians to screen high risk infants and children with severe disabilities who are unable to respond to symbol charts, such as the widely used Snellen chart.

Among children with less severe visual handicaps, the majority of near-sighted children can be identified easily during the preschool years by the standard Snellen eye chart with E symbols printed in various sizes and arranged in different positions. SPB sponsors screening programs throughout the country. Strabismus (a muscle imbalance that results in eyes that are turned outward or inward) often can be recognized easily and should receive immediate attention from a specialist. If it is not treated before the age of 3 or 4 years by patching of the better eye or the prescription of glasses, the child may develop amblyopia or lazy eye, in which one eye loses its sharpness of vision because of disuse.

Other problems such as farsightedness (hypermetropia) and astigmatism (irregularity of the cornea) are less easily detected and may not interfere with visual function until the child begins close work in school. Although the use of vision for every type of activity may be one means of recognizing minor visual limitations, it is not necessarily the most critical. Cellular changes in general growth patterns may alter visual function. The eyeball and its internal structures grow rapidly until about age 7, and continue their physiological growth into adolescence. This growth process alters the refractive components as well as the accommodative mechanisms so that a child may experience visual problems for the first time in mid-elementary school or even the teen years.

Without well-planned and regularly conducted visual screening programs during the preschool and the early school years, many children and youth with limited vision are never identified. The tragedy is that they may be labeled academic failures, or even mentally retarded, because their learning and achievement have been limited by an undetected visual problem.

Occasionally, it may be difficult to determine when a child requires special educational services because of a visual impairment. PL 94-142 describes a visually handicapped child as one who cannot benefit fully from education because of the visual difference (Office of Special Education, 1981). Each state sets its own criterion for determining whether a child qualifies as visually handicapped. Although a few states still rely on a clinical criterion such as legal blindness (20/200 acuity or less in the better eye or a field of less than 10 degrees) for deciding whether a child is eligible for special educational services, many now consider the functional use of vision as a primary criterion for providing services. Along with the eye specialist's report indicating a serious vision loss, many states also require a written observation by a teacher of children who are visually handicapped or by an orientation and mobility instructor. This document, a functional vision assessment, is considered by the team that determines whether a child experiences disadvantages in learning due to a visual impairment.

Once a child is identified as needing specialized services because of the visual impairment, a team—which includes the child's family, teacher, the child when appropriate, an administrative representative, and other professionals as needed—determines what services are desirable and how often they should be provided. This team may be known as an IEP team (Individualized Education Program), an ARD team (Admissions, Review, and Dismissal), or a multidisciplinary or transdisciplinary team. The team is responsible for determining the specialized program goals for each child, as well as identifying the least restrictive environmental setting in which these goals can be met appropriately plus the related services that are needed to facilitate a child's attainment of the specified goals. For the child with a visual impairment, effective decisions about the appropriate organizational plan and setting are based on the assumption that a continuum of placement options is available.

ORGANIZATIONAL PLANS AND EDUCATIONAL SERVICES

Organizational programs and services may differ from community to community and from state to state. Ideally, program patterns should be determined by the needs of the children to be served, but that is not always possible, and unfortunately, often is not the primary consideration. Organizational patterns may be based on availability of personnel, the attitudes of individual school districts, financial resources, and/or administrative expediency, rather than on an objective appraisal of the needs of the children to be served.

Service delivery approaches in public schools have not changed dramatically since a survey by Jones and Collins (1966), who identified five basic types of organizational patterns: itinerant, resource room, special class, cooperative special class, and teacher consultant. The major differences are in services to preschool children, in those at the postsecondary level, and in those in rural areas. Generally, organizational plans in public schools include some variation of those mentioned in the next few pages.

Infants aged 0–3 years are usually served in home programs under the supervision of transdisciplinary specialists with periodic evaluations and parent instruction in the school setting. Preschoolers aged 3–5 years are in school programs, either in self-contained classrooms or with other children with disabilities or in regular head-start or kindergarten classes.

Under PL 99-457 (the early childhood amendments), many infants and preschoolers with visual impairments have expanded options for intervention. Community nursery schools continue to serve children with visual impairments who are able to function with little or no assistance in a group of sighted children. Children with moderate and severe low vision may adapt well to such a setting, although fewer children who are totally blind may be ready for this experience. Socialization and development of many emotional characteristics that contribute to a child's personal and social development can be gained through association with normally seeing children, especially when teachers and children include them in all the regular activities.

Special nursery schools, either private or sponsored by community agencies, may be more desirable for children with severe visual handicaps who seem to be slower in their development. Most children who are totally blind need highly specialized attention and can learn to function more easily in a group of children who function primarily through the senses of touch and hearing. Some children who are severely visually handicapped and totally blind develop rapidly and may be included in nursery programs with sighted children when their movement skills and self-directed learning strategies permit them to participate with the total group. Very few residential programs are available to children under the age of 4 or 5 years, although many residential schools operate outreach programs that provide home-based services or parent training for families of infants and preschoolers.

The current emphasis on kindergarten and early childhood education for all children, and especially the legislative provisions for early childhood education programs for the disabled, have opened the way for many children and their families to participate in preschool activities that would not previously have been available because of geographic location or lack of funds for establishing such programs. Preschool programs for children with disabilities are found in community agencies, and more often as a part of public school programs (Felix & Spungin, 1978). Outreach programs are being developed by state regional centers and some residential schools to serve children and parents in rural areas. When residential schools are too far from the child's home, parents are reluctant to consider such a program even though no specialized services are available to them nearby. Some states have developed outreach teams to serve parents and children within a radius of 100 miles or so. Largely rural states in the United States and provinces in Canada have been very successful in giving support to parents and in guiding home teaching until the children are old enough for public schools or until specialized services can be made available.

The objectives for most of these programs are to provide information and support to parents, and to evaluate consistently the development and learning in infants and young children. Parents do most of the teaching, with suggestions from specially qualified personnel in visually handicapped as well as support personnel in other disciplines. Some programs are located in hospital settings, where qualified persons from many disciplines are available to assess both clinical and educational needs. Other programs, which utilize the services of trained personnel from related disciplines, emanate from regional education service centers or from intermediate units within certain states in combination with various state agencies serving children. Children with visual impairments and multiple disabilities, whose progress may be slow or who have extensive medical and developmental problems, may require total care facilities when families are unable to assume responsibility and no other program is designed to meet their numerous needs. The objective of many programs is to assist children in developing learning readiness to enter either public school academic programs or modified academic and vocational programs.

Children like Carlos and Lucy will probably develop the necessary learning skills to move into regular school programs with little difficulty. Some studies (Hull & McCarthy, 1973) have indicated that when children with low vision are given special instruction in visual development at nursery and kindergarten levels, they are able to move into regular school programs and to perform as competently as their normally seeing peers. Although this may not be true for all children with low vision, the idea is worth considering. It also will not be true for all children who are totally blind such as Carlos, but because of his parents and teachers at the preschool years, he is learning and developing similar to any 4-year-old, and can function within a group with only minor modifications. All children with severe visual impairments need to be given the opportunity to experience the specialized learning experiences available through early childhood educational programs designed for their specific needs.

For children who make steady progress in development and learning during the preschool years, the options for services expand during school years. Hazekamp and Huebner (1989) described five minimum options that should be included among the range available to students with visual impairments: (1) specialized instruction provided by an itinerant teacher, who may travel among several schools to serve students individually; (2) a resource room, in which students spend some portion of their day in a separate classroom equipped with needed equipment and materials with a specially trained teacher; (3) a self-contained classroom, in which students spend the majority of their school day in a separate classroom; (4) a special school, in which only students with a disability such as a visual impairment or developmental delays are in attendance; and (5) a nonpublic school setting, in which there is no publicly funded agency that can provide appropriately for the child.

The question should be not which plan is best for any school district to adopt, but instead, through which programming patterns can children in that area be served most appropriately and effectively. Some districts have formed cooperative plans with one or more nearby districts where only small numbers of children with visual impairment live in each district. It is imperative that children who are totally blind or have low vision have the assistance of an individual specially trained to teach children with visual handicaps. These specialists must be familiar with special materials, basic learning concepts, difficulties that are related or unrelated to the visual impairment, and the difference in learning-to-read and learning-to-write processes for children with visual handicaps. The decision regarding where to place a child needs to take these factors into consideration and not rely solely on the concept of the "least restrictive" environment (Curry & Hatlen, 1988).

For many years, the general policy in local schools and in a few residential schools was to separate for instructional purposes children who were blind from those who were then called "partially seeing." This practice may have originated when there were very few teacher education programs, and the majority of them focused on the concept of "sight saving" or "sight conservation" for partially seeing children. All the teacher education programs that were available had separate training programs for teachers of the blind and teachers of the partially seeing. At present, teachers are educated as specialists to serve all children and youth with visual handicaps. There is no longer a controversy about integrating children who are blind with those who have low vision, whether the delivery system is a special class, a resource room, or itinerant consultation (Jones & Collins, 1966). Terms such as partially seeing and legally blind are used infrequently in the professional literature, because clinical measurements are no longer the criterion for determining need for educational services in most states. In special education, we have moved from the medical model to the functional model, at least for children and youth with visual handicaps.

Although no data on the achievement of readers who use braille or print, when instructed together, have been reported in the United States, one study done in England (McLaughlin, 1974) recorded no differences between braille readers and print readers in integrated instruction programs. The similarity in learning ability is a more important factor than the nature or extent of the visual impairment. Children who find achievement difficult or who are not yet ready to develop such academic skills as reading, writing, or computation, may need a special class placement for a long time. In fact, the current population of children with visual handicaps, many of whom have other problems interfering with their development, has required local school districts to create or reinstate self-contained and/or resource room programs to serve these children more effectively and to try to prevent the almost inevitable cumulative lag in educational progress that occurs when the regular teacher tries to assume responsibilities for which he or she has received no training.

As a result of PL 94-142, with the mandate for public schools to provide services to all children, and with the cost of materials and specialist teachers (even when available) to small districts, more and more children are being served on an itinerant basis with limited visits by the specialists in the region. In many cases, very young children, especially those who are totally blind, are being placed in regular classrooms long before they have their basic learning skills. Some are placed in "generic" special education classrooms with other disabled children whose learning needs are quite different, and with a teacher who may not have any course work related to visual handicaps. Only time will enable us to determine the appropriateness or inappropriateness of this approach. We may regret the overwhelming stress on mainstreaming when we discover in a few years that children and youth with visual handicaps have been cheated educationally because of our need for expediency and an effort to save money. There is nothing cost-effective about such service delivery if children pay the price by being unable to take their rightful places as independent, tax-paying citizens.

In some local school settings, the majority of children at the elementary level are served through the resource plan. This plan involves selection of a particular school to which all children with visual handicaps within that district are transported; it is more often available in densely populated areas where there may be groups of visually handicapped children of similar ages and functional abilities. This school contains a specially equipped classroom with a teacher who is specifically trained for work with these children. Integration into regular classes within that school for varying amounts of time during the day or week is desirable, according to each child's needs as determined by the educational team. Although this plan requires that some children be placed in settings other than their neighborhood schools, it does offer the children a readily available constellation of materials and support services. In such a situation, a child who needs more intensive assistance may spend several hours a day with the resource teacher in practicing and refining social and academic skills while other children may spend the majority of their time in regular classes with their peers, receiving only minimal help and consultative services from the resource teacher.

Itinerant services afford the opportunity for children with visual handicaps to remain in their neighborhood schools and in regular classrooms with peers, but still be served by a specially qualified teacher on a periodic basis. In this model, the education of children with visual impairments is the primary responsibility of the classroom teacher, with the consultative services of the special teacher and the provision of special equipment and materials adapted to their learning needs. For children and youth who have reached the level of being self-directive and independent in learning skills, these itinerant services would provide them with sufficient assistance. For children or youth who have not yet developed their academic learning skills or who are not as socially aware as their sighted peers, this plan may offer less than the necessary range and intensity of services actually needed.

The number of children to be served on an itinerant basis should be determined by the characteristics of each child rather than by a specific number determined by some formula. This plan also requires a great deal of teacher time spent traveling from school to school. The decision to establish such a procedure must be made on the basis of the effectiveness and efficiency of the plan for the child to be served, in addition to considering the appropriate use of the time of highly trained specialists.

Many school districts, especially large ones or those in strategic population centers, find that a combination of resource and itinerant programs best meets the needs of their districts. Ideally, when children with visual handicaps reach the academic level of junior and senior high school, they have acquired sufficient independent learning and other skills so that they can progress consistently with minimal help from itinerant special services. Many elementary level students actually need the resource plan. A few of the very young or slowly developing children need self-contained situations for some time. Therefore, in large cities or heavily populated areas, probably the most effective plan would be to provide early childhood education programs, self-contained classes, resource rooms, and itinerant programs.

Traditionally, many states have established residential schools to provide educational experiences for children with severe visual impairments. A few states have combined their residential programs with programs for children who are deaf, creating what have been known as dual schools. Formerly, most children with visual handicaps within some states were sent to the residential school established specifically for them. Since the

1950s, the general trend has been to increase the percentages of students with visual handicaps attending local public schools, and the passage of PL 94-142 not only lowered the percentage of students attending residential schools, but caused a reevaluation of the role of residential schools for the future. Spungin (1982) and others suggested that residential schools develop cooperative relationships with state and local education agencies and place capable students in local schools, which some have done with good success.

The role of the residential school is becoming increasingly specialized, according to state and regional needs. Some residential schools serve visually handicapped children with multiple disabilities who need around-the-clock consistency in programming. Some provide statewide services in the areas of diagnosing and assessing; case finding, counseling, and parent training; teaching skills of daily living, leisure time, and vocational pursuits; in-service training and continuing educational programs for all teachers; developing curricula; managing and distributing materials; serving as a research center; and providing respite care for relief of parents. Harley and English (1989) reported that residential schools are moving in the direction of providing more support services for children who are in public school programs; frequently these services include summer school programs in recreational activities and daily living skills, as well as in-service seminars for public school teachers.

There is no overall policy for residential schools or states. In some cases, the residential school services primarily children from remote, less populated areas of the state; those whose families for various reasons prefer to have them attend a residential program; or those who cannot, for whatever reason, fit into the local school program in their community. Despite the mandatory legislation for public schools, some states have been slow to enforce the legislation and develop quality public school programs. The small numbers of students and their sparse geographic distribution have influenced the delay in some areas. However, as local schools have developed programs on a widespread basis, the approach to attendance in residential schools continues to vary among states and situations. In a few states, the residential school has ceased to serve children who can progress normally in academic learning and serves only those children who, because of the mutiplicity of their disabling conditions, require a special curriculum and highly adapted program.

The variability of the nature and role of the residential school has made it difficult for policy to be established concerning the legal requirement for this option under the guidelines of PL 94-142. Silverstein (1985), who reviewed court cases regarding residential school placement, suggested that three issues have influenced policy decisions: the broad definition of the term *education* to include nonacademic skills, the fact that program issues must be addressed before the "least restrictive" requirement is followed, and the determination that some children require programming beyond the normal school day.

Many states are reevaluating their total special education programming for children with visual impairments in an effort to provide a range or continuum of educational services through a variety of educational plans. For example, some states are planning to bring all programs and services together under one agency, thereby creating a continuum of services for students with visual handicaps from birth to vocational independence. Still other states are expanding their residential programs to maintain their academic nature, while providing a broader spectrum of programs for children with multiple disabilities in diagnostic services, daily living skills, and vocational programs. This expanded arrangement places an almost impossible task on administration and is far more costly, to say nothing of the difficulties encountered in maintaining quality and diversity in the academic area.

There are no clear guidelines for placement decisions regarding children with visual handicaps. Hatlen (1990) emphasized that placement decisions should be based on each child's program needs, and placement should not be a "goal in itself but a means for meeting goals" (p. 81). In selecting appropriate placement, the team should consider what is known about the characteristics that contribute to successful mainstream situations. In a national survey of teachers, administrators, students, and parents, Bishop (1986) identified the characteristics associated with a successful public experience. The five factors ranked highest were an accepting classroom teacher, acceptance by peers, appropriate social skills, high academic achievement, and a good self-image. Ashcroft and Zambone-Ashley (1980) stated that higher academic achievement was characteristic of children in public schools with resource or itinerant support, and they emphasized the importance of student social skills and the availability of educational resources and specialized teachers as requirements for successful public school education.

The attitude adopted more than 30 years ago (Abel, 1959) advocating that no one educational setting is the most appropriate for all children with visual handicaps, and that a diversity of educational settings is desirable to meet the needs of children and their families, is still valid. The acceptance of this idea has resulted in the expansion of programs into a variety of settings during the preschool, elementary, and secondary school years (Felix & Spungin, 1978). At the present time, it is estimated that approximately 80% or more of school-aged children with visual impairments receive services within their communities and, in most cases, within public school settings.

TEAM APPROACHES AND SUPPORT SERVICES

Until recently, little attention has been given to the quality of programs in the public schools. The concerns of professional organizations, such as the Council for Exceptional Children, the Division for the Visually Handicapped of the Council for Exceptional Children, the National Accreditation for Agencies Serving the Blind and Visually Handicapped, and the American Foundation for the Blind, have led to a group of suggested guidelines and standards from birth to 21 years of age (Scholl, 1981; Spungin, 1980; Stager, 1978). In 1989, Hazekamp and Huebner published their guidelines for excellence in programming for children with visual handicaps; this document provides essential information to public school programs that serve these children, including a self-review guide that may be used by professionals to evaluate local programs.

The major responsibility for assessment and programming for children with visual handicaps rests with the educational team or IEP team. In all cases, the parent should be an active and involved member of the team and, in many cases, the child may be an active participant. An administrator from the child's school district, as well as the child's primary teacher, are important members of the team. A psychologist is usually involved in the evaluation of the child, according to state requirements, and may also contribute to the team process. In addition, support staff such as physical therapists or speech–language therapists may participate as appropriate.

The child with a visual disability usually requires the services of several professionals who work with the family to support educational progress. Decisions about who will participate in the planning and implementation of the child's program can be a difficult one: Unnecessary additional services can waste valuable learning time and fragment the child's whole educational experience, whereas insufficient involvement by specialized team members can deprive the child of necessary learning opportunities and skills.

Several professional roles are critical in effective educational programming for a child with a visual impairment. One is the role of the regular classroom teacher, who is responsible primarily for the academic curriculum of this child in a public school setting. An "accepting and flexible classroom teacher" was one of the most frequently named of 70 factors cited by respondents to Bishop's (1986) study of the factors that influence success in the mainstream. Hazekamp and Huebner (1989) described the role of the classroom teacher as including direct instruction and cooperative work with the teacher of children with visual handicaps; among the cooperative tasks they identified are providing classroom materials to the specialist teacher in a timely manner, providing times for the student to work with the specialist teacher, and modifying classroom procedures as needed for the student with a visual impairment.

Another essential member of the educational team is the teacher trained to teach students with visual handicaps. In most states, this teacher must be certified through the state education agency to teach children with visual handicaps (Huebner & Strumwasser, 1987). These teachers are required to complete a college undergraduate- or graduate-level program in teaching these children. The recent trend toward noncategorical preparation of special education teachers has influenced schools in some states to employ teachers of special education to serve children with visual impairments; this trend toward general services has raised concern among professionals about the adequacy of services when provided by those who are not specifically prepared to work with people having visual handicaps (Gallagher, 1988; R. L. Harrell & Curry, 1987).

The role of the specialist teacher for students with visual handicaps includes a wide range of activities that vary according to the ages, numbers, functional levels, educational setting, support services available (e.g., transcribers), and extent of visual impairment of the children served. Spungin (1984) described activities that may be included in this teacher's role as they relate to six major areas: assessment, the learning environment, the unique curriculum, guidance and counseling, administration and supervision, and school community relations. In the area of assessment, the teacher of students with visual handicaps performs functional vision assessments and participates in evaluation and placement decisions, among other activities. Within the learning environment, the specialist teacher promotes understanding of vision loss among the student's general education teacher and classmates; the specialized teacher also assists in the preparation and adaptation of materials and instructional methods. Spungin listed 16 areas of unique curriculum, such as braille instruction, typing, visual development and efficiency, and techniques of daily living.

The teacher of students with visual handicaps also may have varying levels of direct contact with each student, depending on each student's educational needs. Many teachers serve as consultants, supporting the child's program through work with the classroom teacher and staff rather than through regularly scheduled direct contact with the student (Erin, 1988). Others work individually with the child to teach skills that support the child's ability to function in the primary educational environment.

The unique role of the teacher of students with visual handicaps can result in a different level of morale in some situations. Teacher isolation and the acceptance of children with visual handicaps in the regular classroom are among the factors that have an impact on teacher morale. Bina (1982) surveyed 238 teachers of students with visual handicaps in 10 western states, and found higher morale among those from smaller cities (populations ranging from 10,000 to 50,000) than among those in larger cities. However, the most critical factors influencing morale were lack of supervision and democratic leadership. Teachers reported that they often had no one with whom to discuss problems or brainstorm strategies. They also were frustrated with the type of service delivery, often feeling that itinerant services did not provide appropriately for some of their students. In addition, the continuing shortage of teachers of students with visual handicaps has an impact on the workload of teachers who are serving those with individualized needs. Many geographic areas, particularly rural locations, are unable to secure or retain teachers with knowledge of visual impairment; children are often unserved or underserved in these areas, and may be placed in more restrictive environments than necessary because districts are unable to adequately staff their programs for learners with visual impairment.

Fewer than 30 colleges and universities prepare teachers of students with visual handicaps, and decreasing funding for low incidence areas is causing some of these programs to close. The fact that teachers from geographically remote areas often must travel far from their homes to acquire preparation in teaching children with visual handicaps makes the shortage problem even more acute. All these factors make it difficult to maintain a strong pool of well-prepared professionals in rural or economically disadvantaged areas, where salaries are often quite low.

Another critical member of the team for some students is the orientation and mobility specialist. This individual evaluates the child's orientation within the immediate environment and works with the team to set goals to improve the child's awareness of body image and space as well as to teach skills that lead to independence in movement and travel activities (Uslan, Hill, & Peck, 1989). For children who require the use of travel devices, such as low vision devices or the long cane, or even wheelchairs, the orientation and mobility instructor works individually with the child to teach the use of this specialized equipment during movement.

Other professionals may be involved in programming for the child as consultants or as direct service providers. These individuals provide related services, which are needed to permit the child to benefit from the educational program. These professionals may include physical therapists, who are responsible for programming to facilitate effective motor development; occupational therapists, who monitor activities to promote functional use of the child's fine motor skills; speech–language therapists, who focus on the child's communication abilities for most effective interaction; counselors and therapists, who work with the child and family to resolve emotional and/or behavioral concerns.

Parents and professionals meet at least annually, and sometimes more often, to decide on the best educational plan for the child. The decision-making process may be informal, or it may follow a more systematic model (Hupp & Rosen, 1985). However, the ultimate goal is to provide a program that will meet the child's learning and educational needs at a level that will foster maximum potential.

With respect to services and educational settings, the concept of a continuum of available options is critical, based on the fact that students with visual impairments vary widely in abilities and needs. With careful planning and frequent monitoring, an educational team can agree upon a program that meets the student's needs and still follows a sequence that enables the child to be involved in activities similar to those of sighted peers.

SUMMARY

Education for children with visual handicaps started in the United States within residential settings; however, it has evolved to provide a continuum of options for students, depending on each child's individual needs. The special educational process must begin with identification of the child's eligibility as a child with a visual handicap. The identification of an appropriate program depends on the needs of the child, parental preference, and the geographic location. Whereas some children may be educated in their neighborhood schools, others require the more specialized services of a residential setting. The multidisciplinary team may include a number of professionals, such as the teacher of the visually handicapped, the orientation and mobility instructor, and/or the occupational and physical therapists. The availability of a continuum of services and the flexibility to develop a program that meets the changing needs of each child are critical to an effective education for all children with visual handicaps.

8

Assessment and Evaluation of Individual Functioning

Throughout the field of education, the question of assessment and evaluation remains a worrisome matter because of several factors: not all states have the same policies and requirements for identification and assessment; the characteristics of the school population is constantly changing; and there seems to be a paucity of valid instruments and reliable procedures, even for the children considered normal. These concerns are especially true of psychological and educational evaluations of present functioning in students with visual handicaps for predictive purposes. Because many educators working with children with visual handicaps are not psychologists, and because many psychologists have had little opportunity to study the effects of low vision or blindness on a student's behavioral responses, communication between the various professionals and specialists and coordinated approaches to evaluating individual functioning are even more difficult to achieve.

The use of instruments designed for and standardized on sighted students to assess children with visual handicaps has been questioned through the years. The trend to compare these students' educational and psychological development and functioning with sighted peers on the basis of scores also has been controversial. In gathering information and reporting results, very little distinction has been made between those students who were totally blind and those who had usable vision. The use of contaminated samples, along with the lack of desirability of the instruments, has called into question the validity of the findings and negated the possibility of generalizing to a total population with only one characteristic in common—visual impairment.

Although children and youth with visual handicaps as a group function psychologically and educationally at levels below those of sighted peers, many of these children seem to achieve just as well or better in academic work and are able to perform at comparable or higher levels in real-life situations. Contradictory observations of this nature have led psychologists and educators not only to examine the procedures used in evaluation, but to call into question the entire approach toward assessment and evaluation as applied to students with visual handicaps. M. A. Moore and McLaughlin (in press) concluded, "Special expertise in nonstandard evaluation and clinical judgment as well as an interdisciplinary approach are necessary to yield valid and relevant conclusions from assessment."

Some of the provisions in PL 94-142 specify that assessments are to be done by persons who are qualified to assess each individual. Thus, the American Foundation for the Blind sponsored a series of workshops for psychologists and psychometrists over a 3-year period. Subsequently, a manual with a model for such workshops was made available (Jastrzembska, 1982).

Critical issues and questions raised by Bateman (1965), Weiner (1967), Chase (1972, 1975, 1986a), and Morse (1975) indicated that more careful consideration should be given to a wide variety of variables and approaches. Chase (1986a) suggested that each examiner may wish to evaluate personal attitudes toward visual impairment and blindness in order to have the fair and open-minded approach necessary, citing examiner's lack of ease as a primary impediment to effective evaluation of students with visual handicaps. Prior to any testing or assessment, the following questions deserve careful consideration:

1. For what purpose is the assessment being made? Is it to exclude the child from some program or service, or is it to prove eligibility? Is assessment for the purpose of prediction, or is it an attempt to determine present level of functioning in many areas as specified by law? Is the primary purpose to have the information necessary to plan a more realistic learning program?

2. When, if ever, are definitive norms or age-level equivalents desirable? Should assessment tools and measures designed for sighted children be utilized, or should specific measures and tools be designed for chil-

dren with visual impairment—separate ones for children with low vision and for those who are totally blind? Or perhaps, should items be adapted from those already available or should criterion-referenced items be individualized across the dimensions of behavior to be evaluated?

3. In evaluating functioning, how does one determine whether level of functioning below that which is anticipated is related to the visual impairment, resulting in a lack of experience or opportunity to learn, or whether the student is incapable of learning? Conversely, is a high level of functioning a result of an enriched background of experience, or does the person have greater learning capacity?

4. How can the examiner determine whether an inappropriate response or behavior is the result of the visual problem, or whether there is a neurological or learning problem, or whether there is an interaction between all these variables?

Substantial information about whether tactual and auditory experiences are analogous to visual experiences is lacking. Possible differences in how various sensory systems process the data received could influence learning styles and patterns; however, these differences in information processing have eluded assessment through present instruments and procedures. Despite the perplexing questions, assessing functional behavior can be valuable to the students, the teachers attempting to work with these students, and the parents. Thus, instead of rejecting the idea of evaluating children with visual handicaps because we do not agree on a process or a cadre of tools or instruments, a better approach would seem to be to suggest how the procedure could be improved and which measures and approaches are most valuable to individual children.

RANGE AND TYPE OF BEHAVIOR TO BE EVALUATED

Intelligence or Mental Development

Although attempts have been made to develop and standardize instruments specifically for assessment of cognitive development in students with visual handicaps, none have been published to date that have shown the degree of reliability desired. The Interim *Hayes–Binet* was used for years, but is now obsolete. The *Perkins–Binet Test of Intelligence for the Blind,* which followed, was recalled because of unreliability probably related to inadequate sampling, especially at the younger ages (Chase, 1986a). The most widely used scales for estimates of mental development are the Wechsler intelligence scales: the *Wechsler Preschool and Primary Scale of Intelligence* (WPPSI) (Wechsler, 1963), the *Wechsler Intelligence Scale for Children–Revised* (WISC–R) (Wechsler, 1974), and the *Wechsler Adult Intelligence Scale–Revised* (WAIS–R) (Wechsler, 1981). Although only the verbal portion is appropriate for students who are totally blind, Chase (1986b) recommended giving the performance subtests to persons with usable vision without regard for time restraints; in this case, no score would be given, but the amount of time required would be recorded. The purpose would be to evaluate whether the task could be completed, and if so, the amount of time required. Some studies have shown a positive correlation between scores on the verbal measures and future academic success in school, possibly because of the nature of the classroom learning situations.

Despite efforts through the years to develop an instrument for evaluating functional intelligence on performance tasks by students who are blind, none has yet been produced that is comparable to the Wechsler scales. The lengthy time required to develop such projects, the great expense, and the difficulty in finding sufficient numbers for standardization samples of students who are totally blind are some of the problems limiting these endeavors. A group in the Netherlands (Dekker, Drenth, Zaal, & Koole, 1990) designed an intelligence test series for blind and low vision children that is purported to be comparable to the Wechsler scales, but at the present time, the series needs further cross-validation and longitudinal studies to establish the validity and reliability on larger numbers of students.

Although not widely publicized in the psychological or psychometric disciplines, *The Blind Learning Aptitude Test* (BLAT), based on abstract symbol discrimination, recognition, seriation, and association, uses culturally neutral items to sample the psychological operations by which learning takes place (Newland, 1961, 1979). The entire procedure is process oriented, not product oriented, in that it seeks to determine how the child goes about learning. Memory and verbal adequacy are not required. The items are constructed of embossed dots presented in bas relief on heavy plastic paper. Total configurations are larger than the traditional braille cell. Minimal emphasis is placed on what the child has learned previously so that the predictive potential for future learning by touch is uncontaminated. Unfortunately, the age range for use (ages 6–16) is limited to that approximating the WISC–R (ages 5–16), and no other such measures are available for younger or older students. The BLAT is recommended as a supplement to the verbal portion of the WISC–R for children without any vision who have good tactual learning skills.

The need for assessment of psychological functioning in even younger children has been precipitated by the increasing number of programs beginning at birth, and particularly from 3 years of age. Portions of widely used preschool instruments may be valuable if used with discretion by a psychologist/psychometrist/diagnostician with specialized training or knowledge of visual handicaps. Uzgiris and Hunt's (1975) *Ordinal Scales of Psychological Development,* the *Bayley Scales for Infant Development* (Bayley, 1969), and the *Battelle Developmental Inventory* (Newborg, Stock, Wnek, Guidabaldi, & Svinicki, 1984) all have some items that may be useful even for children who are totally blind (Bradley-Johnson, 1986).

The *Reynell–Zinken Developmental Scales for Young Visually Handicapped Children* (1980) were developed in response to a clinical need for professionals to be able to work more effectively with parents (Wilhelm, 1989). They have the unique characteristic of being appropriate for use with children who have multiple disabilities. They include assessment on six subscales: social adaptation; sensorimotor understanding; exploration of environment; response to sound and verbal comprehension; vocalization and expressive language, vocabulary, and content; and communication. Many of these areas are not assessed on the previously mentioned scales. The examiner needs to have a thorough understanding of early intellectual development and how that development is different in children with visual handicaps because the focus is on intellectual processes rather than on skills or specific knowledge that has been obtained. Experienced examiners may be able to make adaptations of many items from other measures as well. Caution must be exercised in assigning global developmental ages to young children on the basis of selected or adapted items or in overinterpreting the results of the responses. These various measures of intellectual and mental evaluation may provide valuable clinical data and some pertinent information for educational planning; however, to assign intelligence test scores and use them as reliable indicators of learning potential or future academic achievement could do a great disservice to some children.

Nevertheless, teachers would like to use information from psychological/psychometric reports of mental functioning to help them plan realistically for children, and to identify critical needs to be included in the Individualized Educational Plan (IEP) as required by PL 94-142. They want to know each child's strengths and weaknesses in specific learning areas and may be unable to make such inferences based only on test or subtest scores. Diagnosticians, psychometrists, and psychologists would provide a real service to teachers and students if they would specify the mental processes evaluated in certain tasks and highlight the areas of present intellectual deficits.

In addition to, or instead of, using single measures to obtain IQ scores, selected subtests from several measures could provide useful information for educational planning. Bullard and Barraga (1971) analyzed the subtests of numerous evaluative instruments and organized them according to the type of mental tasks required in each. The following categories were identified: (1) immediate recall, (2) association, (3) logical thinking, (4) discrimination, (5) spatial relations, (6) deductive reasoning, (7) inductive reasoning, (8) imitation, (9) generalization, (10) attention span, and (11) language development. Sampling intellectual functions in such a manner would not yield scores, but could result in a profile of functional abilities and deficits useful for prescriptive planning of learning experiences. Chase (1986a) reported the use of a similar approach, adding the *McCarthy Scales of Children's Abilities* (McCarthy, 1970), the *Peabody Picture Vocabulary Test* (Dunn, 1965), and the *Goodenough–Harris Drawing Test* as valuable supplements to those already mentioned. Others have suggested that, with careful modifications, some subtests of the *Kaufman Assessment Battery for Children* (1983) may be appropriate for children with low vision (Moore & McLaughlin, in press).

Affective and Social Development

For younger children, the revised *Vineland Adaptive Behavior Scale* (Sparrow, Balla, & Cicchetti, 1984) and the *Maxfield–Buchholz Scale* (1957), adapted from the original *Vineland* and standardized on preschool blind children, can be quite useful. The items give some indication of personal, social, and functional development, including physical control of the body, eating, dressing, and communication and self-direction. Also included are items that indicate response patterns; interactive styles; relationships with family, peers, and others; frustration tolerance; and the ability to enjoy social pleasures, friendships, and intimacy. Observational scales such as the *Callier–Azusa Scale* (Stillman, 1979) and Langley's (1979) *Functional Vision Screening Inventory* have been reported as applicable, especially for preschool and multihandicapped children. Portions of other scales or instruments may also be useful in evaluating the above mentioned factors.

Achievement

Achievement testing of students with visual handicaps began in the early 1900s, and the American Printing House for the Blind (APH) has been publishing a variety of such tests both in braille and in large print for many years. Three widely used tests, the *Stanford Achievement Test* series (Morris, 1974), the *Iowa Test of Basic Skills* (Hieronymus, Hoover, & Lindquist, 1986), and the Brigance scales (1978, 1981, 1983), are available from APH. The *Stanford* has been adapted specifically for students with visual handicaps, and permits them to be ranked in relation to their sighted counterparts. This is especially important now that approximately 80–90% of students with visual handicaps attend public school programs, and many states require mandatory achievement testing for all students at several grade levels. In addition, more and more states are requiring competency testing for high school graduation. In many cases, appropriate modifications in content and format permit students with visual handicaps to take tests in a reading medium they prefer, such as braille or large type, or with an optical device, Optacon, listening, or reading machine.

Special Skills

The increasing number of infants and preschool children receiving services and the growing percentage of visually handicapped children with multiple impairments have created a need for more functional approaches to assessment of various abilities. Some of the more basic skills needed by children with visual impairments include assessment of the use of sensory abilities, especially vision, hearing, and touch; gross motor development and freedom of movement in the environment; the performance of tasks of daily living; and prevocational and occupational skills. Many, if not all, of these are best accomplished by the teacher in cooperation with the child's parents using planned observation, checklists, and selected criterion-referenced measures, especially with preschool and elementary-aged students, and with some older students for transitional purposes or for further habilitation and occupational preparation.

The *Visual Efficiency Scale* (VES) (Barraga, 1970) was designed to assess the level of visual functioning through a series of increasingly less visible and smaller items, sequenced in complexity from gross form to visual detail and finally to sentences and words. The scale was planned primarily for use with students having low vision who might previously have been considered unable to use their low vision for learning purposes; it may be useful also for those with less severe visual problems who have difficulty discriminating specific types of detailed material or whose difficulties are related to perceptual problems. Many teachers now use it as a screening measure that can be administered in 10–15 minutes, before a more comprehensive assessment of visual potential. Many states now require that a functional vision assessment be a part of the battery for all students who have light perception or more extensive visual responses; a variety of checklists and criterion-referenced measures may be used for this purpose, and the recommendation generally is that this be done by the teacher of students with visual handicaps or a clinical vision specialist.

The revision and expansion of the VES resulted in publication of a *Program to Develop Efficiency in Visual Functioning,* suitable for developmental ages 3 to adult (Barraga & Morris, 1980). This program, which is the most comprehensive functional vision assessment procedure available for children in this mental age range, includes a complete instructional guide for teachers, observation checklists, and a book. Criterion-referenced assessment tasks are used to evaluate a wide variety of functional vision skills, from the beginning stage of visual development to the visual reading stage. Field testing indicated a high (.94) reliability coefficient and established the sequential nature of the items in eight broad categories (Berla, Rankin, & Willis, 1980; Collins & Barraga, 1980). The instructional program provides 150 lesson plans to use as a guide in planning individual learning programs. The source book contains general knowledge needed by persons working with low vision learners, as well as sources for many commercial materials available for use in the instructional tasks. The program was designed for use by direct service personnel, such as teachers and therapists, as well as psychologists/psychometrists, orientation and mobility instructors, and other eye specialists. It is used extensively worldwide and has been translated into at least four languages.

For children who are totally blind and those with severe low vision, evaluation of their use of the tactual sense is of paramount importance. The *Roughness Discrimination Test* (RDT) was designed to measure the development of the ability to make coordinated tactual discriminations with the hands and fingers, which is important in learning to use braille (Nolan & Morris, 1965). The measure was validated with groups of first-grade children, and showed that children who did well on the RDT at the beginning of the first grade tended to be successful in learning to read braille, whereas those who did poorly were less likely to be successful (Nolan & Morris, 1965). The American Printing House for the Blind (APH) has made available tactual discrimination worksheets, which may be used to assess skill in discriminating geometric forms, lines, angles, and braille characters, all of which are indicators of readiness to perceive and understand braille symbols. The RDT and the worksheets not only assess the tactual discrimination ability of young children accurately, but are designed to be administered by teachers in the classroom. The advantage is that no special training is required for administration and no clinical interpretation is necessary. However, because the stimuli are made from different gradations of sandpaper, some children may not wish to touch specific items.

Because braille reading involves far more than simply discriminating tactile characters, Caton (1977) concluded that there was need for a means of identifying specific deficits in knowledge of concepts acquired by children who were blind. Obviously, mastery of basic concepts is necessary for success in first- and second-grade learning-to-learn and learning-to-read tasks. Caton developed and evaluated a tactile analog to the *Boehm Test of Basic Concepts* (Boehm, 1971). The tactile analogs are simple geometric shapes in raised form for tactual perception. The format and arrangement of the shapes are comparable to the visual pictures on the original test. Use of these two measures, the RDT and the *Boehm Tactile Test of Basic Concepts* (Caton, 1980), will provide information regarding the readiness of young children for using braille in reading, and teachers may find them useful prior to the introduction of braille reading material.

Children's knowledge of body image and spatial concepts is of critical concern to teachers and to orientation and mobility instructors. Cratty and Sams (1968) developed a screening test to determine knowledge of body parts, planes, and movements. This test, the *Body Image of Blind Children Screening Test,* is available from the American Foundation for the Blind. Hill and Hill (1980a, 1980b) have validated and revised the *Hill Performance of Selective Positional Concepts* for assessing the spatial conceptual abilities of children aged 6–10 years.

Other special skills assessment measures and tools are available, although many lack specific standardization or reliability criteria. The *Revised Children's Manifest Anxiety Scale* (Reynolds & Richmond, 1985) is considered useful in identifying global anxiety and was the basis of a study by Wilhelm (1989) with both low vision and blind children. Another measure designed for a doctoral dissertation, *Children's Fear Survey Schedule–Revised* (Ramirez, 1986), is a self-report survey purported to identify specific fears evidenced by children with visual impairments. Hackney (1986) found the *Piers–Harris Children's Self-Concept Scale* (Piers & Harris, 1969) useful with gifted children in determining the attitudes and concerns they had about themselves as individuals. Several measures are designed to assess the speed and efficiency of manipulation with tools and materials, and may be quite helpful as prevocational evaluations. A complete listing of all measures for assessment may be found in measures of psychological, vocational, and educational functioning in students who are blind and visually handicapped (Scholl & Schnur, 1976).

SPECIAL CONSIDERATIONS IN EVALUATION AND ASSESSMENT

Regardless of the type of professional doing the evaluation and the purpose for which the child is being assessed, several critical variables may affect whether the evaluation provides meaningful information. If a child is totally blind, then it is important to know whether the vision was lost through a deteriorating condition (Ching Lan) or whether the blindness was present from birth (Carlos). If the loss of vision occurred after the child had learned to function visually, the age of onset of blindness is an important factor. For students who are totally blind to feel at ease and to understand the nature of the task and the examiner's expectations of them, there needs to be a special method of presentation. Standard instructions used with sighted persons are often inappropriate and confusing, leaving the child to wonder what to do as well as how to do it. Instructions should be clear and concise, permitting only one interpretation of the task to be performed. If the task is to be timed, the child should be told this so that it is clear that work is to be done with the greatest possible speed and efficiency. If various objects are to be used, the child should have time to examine them tactually and determine their location as well as the space in which they are displayed before the timing begins.

The information gathered from children who have some vision and are performing a primarily tactual task may be less easily interpreted, because it is difficult to know to what degree low vision has enhanced their performance. An effective procedure might be to ask the student to close his or her eyes so as to obtain more valid results. However, this may be a disadvantage to children who have not relied solely on tactual learning in the past. In contrast, when the task is primarily visual and the person has limited visual capability, it is hard to determine whether the inability to perform a task is related to the visual impairment or whether there is lack of understanding of what was to be done. This poses another dilemma related to using evaluative materials designed for sighted individuals, especially if the performance of those who are visually limited is compared with that of their sighted peers, which would be highly inappropriate. Those with visual impairment may be perfectly capable of performing the same task, but are likely to require more time.

COMPREHENSIVE ASSESSMENT PLAN FOR USE IN EDUCATIONAL SETTINGS

An extensive plan of behavioral evaluation includes information from many disciplines, representative samples of behavior in numerous situations, and both observational and objective data from parents, social workers, teachers, educational diagnosticians/psychometrists/psychologists, and medical specialists. The objective of assessment and evaluation at any age is to make practical judgments and decisions regarding appropriate interventions to increase performance and determine the effectiveness of previously used strategies.

Weiner (1967) suggested that behavioral responses might be considered in the following contexts:

1. *Level of performance,* which indicates how much development has taken place in any dimension and the point from which to design future learning tasks. The length of time required to achieve a certain stage of development or learning is indicative of the rate at which gains may be expected.

2. *Range of behavior,* which suggests the array of learning opportunities provided for functioning in a broad spectrum of activities. Accuracy or behavioral adequacy in relation to speed of performance characterizes the efficiency of achievement to be anticipated.

3. *Autonomy,* which can be perceived as independence when self-initiated and self-directed tasks are approached and executed without instruction. Approach and completion of assigned tasks also give insight into the ability to work toward a specific goal.

Assessment Through Observation

Skills such as speed, independence, and accuracy may be evaluated through observing and recording general and specific behavioral patterns. This process can be a valuable procedure at the beginning of assessment, especially with young children or those who have numerous problems or impairments. For teachers, observing students on a one-to-one basis and in groups is probably the simplest means of gathering information about present levels of functioning. Teachers of students with visual handicaps may wish to use observation freely and consistently as a supplement to more structured procedures or information from objective measures. To become a sophisticated observer may require time to learn to select appropriate situations for observation, significant behaviors and responses, and practical means for recording what is seen. Observation permits the immediate assessment of the task or objective by use of a rating scale or by evaluating mastery or nonmastery of a response criterion (Silberman, 1981). Some writers use the term "ecological assessment" to describe the gathering of information under different conditions and in various environments.

For example, children may be observed in free play in various totally unstructured settings; or the environment and the materials available for use may be semistructured to limit to some extent the behaviors possible or to encourage certain desired responses; or the situation may be structured to require a specific type of task performance or interaction. Children who have disabilities often undergo numerous medical examinations and educational assessments. It is important for them to enjoy a sense of anonymity at times and not feel as though they are continually being assessed. Older students should have all assessments explained to them at their level of understanding.

Whatever the setting or situation, knowing what to observe is the key. Each observer may be interested in assessing particular behaviors and consequently focus exclusively on those. Observing the following behaviors can provide pertinent information about children with visual handicaps: (1) awareness of, and attention to the surrounding environment and those within it; (2) seeking and exploratory patterns of movement; (3) use of senses (especially vision and touch) in moving and acquiring information; (4) use of language to elicit contact or to respond to encounters; (5) nature and variety of cues used for self-directed and independent actions; and (6) the extent to which the child originates behavior or adapts to materials or to people. These few suggestions may stimulate teachers and others to develop their own ideas about what to observe.

Carefully recording the observations on checklists or scales can help estimate the functional status of children across all developmental dimensions, including sensory (especially visual development); motor; language; cognitive; social, emotional, and self-help; and academic skills (Chase, 1986a, 1986b; M. A. Moore & McLaughlin, in press). A chart or profile plotted or drawn across all behavioral domains may give the teacher a basis for determining some reasonable short-term objectives and for planning appropriate tasks or interactions to begin instruction pending more comprehensive and ongoing assessments.

For some children, observational evaluations may be the most desirable procedure for quite some time, whereas others may be ready for more extensive or other types of assessment techniques using carefully selected criterion-referenced and/or standardized measures. The following section provides a sequential summary of procedures and instruments mentioned earlier, which may provide a possible guide for gathering assessment information about children with visual handicaps from the time of identification (as soon after birth as possible) until they leave school and are a part of the larger society. The assessment and evaluation procedure is followed by a period of instruction, after which additional assessment and evaluation on an ongoing basis are conducted as required by present legislation. The listings presented are not intended to include all the possible instruments or approaches to assessment, but serve as a beginning, and may be helpful to teachers and less experienced examiners in knowing measures from which selections may be made.

Preschool Assessment

Eligibility requirements for service delivery to infants and toddlers specified in PL 99-457 necessitate the establishment of "developmental delay" in one or more of the following areas: physical, cognitive, speech–language, psychosocial, and self-help; children at risk due to environmental or biological factors are also eligible. Careful assessment of each dimension is required before any delay can be documented. The ideal is for a team of specialists in all these areas to work with the parents in making the determination and evaluation. The approach to assessment in the infant and preschool age might include information gathered from the following sources:

- *Medical information:* The nature and severity of the visual impairment and the prognosis as to whether the condition is stable, treatable, or deteriorating can be acquired from diagnostic files and/or consultation with the eye specialist, who can clarify the uses for prescribed lenses and/or optical devices.

- *Family history and experience:* A home visit by a case worker, social worker, and/or teacher can assess family attitudes and parenting skills of the family members. A complete analysis of these findings may give an idea of the general patterns and expectations to include in future evaluations.

- *Checklists or developmental scales:* The use of these may be begun during a home visit and completed on subsequent visits or other contacts. A wide variety of these are available to evaluate physical, personal–social– emotional, and language development.

- *Selected instruments:* The *Vineland Adaptive Behavior Scales–Expanded Form* and the *Maxfield–Buchholz Social Maturity Scale* may be administered during a home visit, but verification is suggested by future observations in other environments. The *Reynell–Zinken Developmental Scales, Langley's Functional Vision Inventory,* and the *Diagnostic Assessment Procedure* all were designed specifically for children with low vision. The *Callier–Azusa Scale* has been validated for use with children who are deaf–blind, as well as others with multiple disabilities. Portions of the following standardized (on sighted populations) instruments may be selected for specific children as appropriate: *Bayley Scales for Infant Development, Battelle Developmental Inventory, Uzgiris–Hunt Ordinal Scales, Kaufman Assessment Battery for Children,* and the *Wechsler Preschool and Primary Scale of Intelligence.*

Primary and Elementary Assessment

The following materials are recommended for assessing primary and elementary students with visual handicaps.

- *Teacher observation and checklists:* Teachers often find it valuable to record information derived from both informal and formal observation of movement behavior, use of hands in exploration, use of low vision, and responses to sound and auditory stimuli. Teacher-made or selected checklists may be useful also for documenting personal and social skills observed, and other functional behaviors considered desirable. The *Reynell–Zinkin Developmental Scales* and the *Callier–Azusa* may be used with children who have multiple disabilities. Other recommended instruments include the *Peabody Model Vision Project Scales* (Harley, DuBose, & Bourgeault, 1980), the *Peabody Mobility Kits for Multihandicapped* (Harley, Wood, & Merbler, 1980), and the *Developmental Activities Screening Inventory* (DuBose & Langley, 1977).

- *Available and appropriate instruments* (all or portions):
  — Mental Development
  Wechsler Scales—WPPSI or WISC–R, Verbal and Performance subtests, as desirable.
  The Blind Learning Aptitude Test—for students who are blind or near-blind.
  McCarthy Scales—selected subtests as appropriate.
  — Readiness/Achievement
  Boehm Test of Basic Concepts—for students with low vision.
  Boehm Tactile Test of Basic Concepts—for students who are blind.
  Peabody Picture Vocabulary Test—screening measure for word meanings.
  Stanford Achievement Test—in braille/large print.
  Iowa Test of Basic Skills—in braille/large print.
  Brigance Scales—selected subtests as appropriate.
  — Visual Functioning
  Visual Efficiency Scale—screening measure.
  Diagnostic Assessment Procedure.
  — Tactile Discrimination
  Roughness Discrimination Test.
  — Body Image/Orientation
  Body Image of Blind Children Screening Test.
  Hill Performance Test of Selected Positional Concepts.
  — Others
  Piers–Harris Children's Self-Concept Scale.
  Revised Children's Manifest Anxiety Scale.

High School and Young Adult Assessment

The following instruments are useful for assessing high school students and young adults who are visually handicapped:

- *Haptic Intelligence Scale for Adult Blind* (Shurrager, 1961)

- *Stanford–Ohwaki Kohs Block Design Intelligence Test for the Blind* (Suinn & Dauterman, 1966)

- *Wechsler Adult Intelligence Scale*

- *Scholastic Achievement Test* in braille and large print

- Selected special skills tests or criterion-referenced measures

Assessment and evaluation at the secondary level are valuable for counseling regarding the student's potential for advanced academic work or for specific vocational goals. Determining attitude and interest in specific vocations is important as a basis for selecting training, and could minimize the tendency to try to fit students into vocations rather than helping them identify the vocations for which they are best suited. Continued assessment should be made of family attitudes, personal management skills, and the competencies necessary for independent living. The more information young people are given, the greater their likelihood of success in the future.

Excellent guidelines for assessment have been written by Chase (1986a, 1986b), Bradley-Johnson (1986), and VanderKolk (1981). Valuable suggestions for educational and psychological assessment (Glenshaft, Dare, & O'Malley, 1980) stress important concerns that should be considered by diagnosticians/psychometrists/school psychologists.

SUMMARY

Even though federal legislation specifies that appropriate instruments and procedures of assessment be administered by qualified persons, tremendous discrepancies exist across and within states regarding interpretation of the guidelines. The types of behaviors to be assessed and the measures to be used vary from school to school even within states. These facts indicate that there is little consistency in assessment and evaluation of students with visual handicaps. This variation may not be entirely negative, but some minimal universal standards might be useful. Nevertheless, many positive trends have been observed, including expansion of the range of behaviors assessed, a greater role by teachers in the process, and more measures included in the assessment.

The suggestions for assessment and evaluation outlined in this chapter are to be considered as a guide from which professionals and parents may choose in designing the most feasible plan for each child. The choices may reflect the quality of information considered to be most helpful to teachers in planning the child's instructional program.

9

Curricular Adaptations and Media

As Ching Lan, who is rapidly losing her vision, continues her education in the public school, she will meet teachers who react in different ways to their responsibility to instruct a student with visual impairment. If they have never taught such a student before, they may have many questions about whether Ching Lan can learn effectively in their classrooms: Will she be able to get all her books in braille in time for her classes? How can she participate in classes such as physical education or art, which involve special activities and materials? Can she continue to read printed material even after she has started to use braille as her major reading medium?

In the education of students with visual impairments, two key questions must be addressed: What should be taught, and how should that content be presented? This chapter addresses both questions. The first section, Specialized Curriculum, focuses on what should be taught, and the second section, Methods and Materials, summarizes how the curriculum should be presented. In both areas, instructional decisions are highly individualized and require the IEP team to balance the importance of minimizing adaptations for greater normalization with the need to present learning in a form that can be best interpreted by a child with a visual limitation.

SPECIALIZED CURRICULUM

The general practice in educational programming for students with visual handicaps, especially in public schools, has been to parallel the academic curriculum of the sighted students, but to provide different materials, equipment, and teaching devices. The underlying assumption is that this practice enables students to learn the same academic subjects as sighted peers; however, this assumption is not based on an objective appraisal of the student's functional achievement.

In residential schools, this tendency has been less prevalent. Although residential schools offer the same or similar academic subjects as do public schools, they usually include many other subjects not considered necessary or appropriate for students with visual handicaps who attend some public schools (e.g., homemaking, vocational education, computer skills). After federal legislation provided funds to establish teacher education programs across the entire field of special education and to expand educational research through colleges and universities, as well as through the American Printing House for the Blind, increasing evidence indicated that greater attention should be given to selecting a specialized curriculum regardless of the type or location of program.

Spungin (1984) and Hazekamp and Huebner (1989) identified unique curricular areas that children with visual handicaps may need to benefit optimally from education. In the following sections, six broad classes of content are discussed: communication; orientation, movement, and physical skills; social skills; daily living skills; skills in the development and use of vision; and career–vocational skills. Specific issues in each area are described below.

Communication

Communication skills refer to the special types of competencies required for reading, writing, listening, and communicating through speech, gestures, or manual sign language. These skills relate strongly to emotional, social, motor, and cognitive development. The more efficient an individual is in communicating with other people, acquiring information, and functioning in all aspects of learning and living, the more his or her confidence and feelings of self-worth will grow.

For most students with visual handicaps, spoken language will be the primary form of communication with others; however, for some children with additional handicaps, oral communication may not be an option.

These children will be taught to express themselves through the use of natural gestures, augmentative communication systems such as a communication board, or a formal manual language such as American Sign Language (ASL). Regardless of the system, communication methods should be adapted to make them accessible to each child with a visual impairment; one child may require the use of symbols with high contrast on a communication board, whereas another may need instruction in receiving signs and gestures tactilely.

For the student who uses speech as a primary form of communication, development of skills in the effective use of spoken language will contribute to success in the academic environment as well as in the workplace during later years. Because students with visual handicaps are usually unable to see a speaker or an audience to perceive nonverbal cues, such skills as "eye contact," organized expression of thought, and changing topics appropriately may need to be developed through planned strategies. A course in spoken communication for junior or senior high school students is essential. It could include the following topics, as suggested by Simon (1974): interviewing, conversation, small-group communication, listening and receiving information and responding, appropriate language and expression, and nonverbal communication. For older students, planning, organizing, and presenting a public speech for communicating an idea is a useful project.

Listening is another critical area of specialized knowledge for the student with visual impairment. Exercises in listening skills should begin in the early school years and receive increased emphasis as children with visual handicaps progress through the school years. Even though junior high and high school students continue to use braille or print reading for most of their school learning, data on efficiency in acquiring information suggest that these students should begin to rely more on listening as a primary source of information. The process of listening actively for learning, which is called "auding," can be taught through the use of gradually more complex and independent tasks.

At the early levels, students develop readiness for formal listening experiences. Harley, Truan, and Sanford (1987) and Heinze (1986) described the skills that may develop a foundation of listening ability: awareness, identification, and discrimination of sound; ability to detect similarities and differences in words; development of a listening vocabulary; ability to follow directions; and ability to follow a sequence and associate meaning with sound.

Later, students develop critical listening skills, learn note-taking skills, and develop the ability to summarize information and identify the most important points. Heinze (1986) emphasized the importance of "active" listening to increase comprehension. This approach encourages the student to react to the material being heard through the use of note-taking, review, or problem solving.

Many students with visual handicaps will master technological devices, which offer them more control over material to which they are listening. The Kurzweil optical scanner translates printed material into sound, but skill and practice may be required to comprehend its mechanical speech efficiently and to understand the small percentage of irregular words that may be mispronounced by mechanical translators, which depend on phonetic rules in producing speech. Speech synthesizers, which produce an auditory version of computer programs, may also require some practice for efficient comprehension.

Students may want to try several forms of rapid speech and measure their comprehension when information is provided at a faster rate. This may be done by simply accelerating the speed of standard recording devices; however, with increased speed, the pitch also accelerates and creates a "chipmunk voice" effect. Devices to produce compressed speech are available; through this variation, pitch is not raised, although speed is increased. The "pitch down" effect is included in the recorders provided for auditory readers by the American Printing House for the Blind (APH) and the National Library Service. Some students can manage increased speed produced on a standard tape recorder and can maintain comprehension up to 275–300 words per minute (Harley, Truan, & Sanford, 1987; Swallow & Conner, 1982).

Nolan (1966) compared braille reading with listening and found that listening to recorded materials required only about one-third the time required for tactual reading of the same material and that no loss in comprehension was experienced. Several studies have indicated that there is no difference in comprehension of material presented at a normal rate of speed, material presented at a compressed rate, and material read in braille. Studies do show, nevertheless, that "reading" by listening to compressed speech was more efficient from the standpoint of both speed and comprehension than either reading through braille or reading by listening to a recording at a normal rate of speech.

The nature of the material seems to have some relationship to comprehension through listening, whether the material is presented at a normal rate or an accelerated rate (Gore, 1969; Tuttle, 1972). Comprehension of scientific and other abstract material decreased as the rate increased. More recent research (Foulke, Hollyfield, & Nolan, 1977; Swallow & Conner, 1982) has focused on identifying and teaching the skills needed to perceive and associate material presented aurally, and designing index codes for more efficient access to taped material (Chandler, 1986). Without special devices for slowing or accelerating the speed of taped materials, the listener has little control over the rate at which reading is done; it is difficult to listen ahead or repeat material already heard; and fewer contextual cues are available from listening than from either print or braille. Despite the lack of detailed knowledge regarding efficiency, specialists generally agree that skill in listening for the purpose of reading is an important part of the educational program for all students with visual handicaps.

Several standardized assessment instruments are available to assist in evaluating a student's listening abilities. The *Durrell Listening–Reading Series* has been adapted for use with the student who is visually handicapped and is available in both braille and large type (Morris, 1976). Correlations between this test and the *Stanford Achievement Test* were good (Wood, 1979). The *Stanford Achievement Test,* the *Listening Comprehension Tests,* and the *Sequential Tests of Educational Progress* are available in braille and large type, and can assist in measuring listening comprehension for elementary and early secondary students (Harley, Truan, & Sanford, 1987).

Study skills are also an important part of a curriculum in communication skills within an academic environment. A student's ability to set priorities by outlining material, taking notes, and summarizing important points is critical in both listening and reading. In addition, a student's ability to schedule study time efficiently and to manage assignment deadlines plays a part in academic success. As a child grows older, responsibilities such as locating and scheduling readers and maintaining equipment also influence the efficiency of learning.

Written language forms pose some special challenges to the student with visual impairment, because of either the need for adaptations in writing standard print or the need to learn a separate writing system through braille. Students with severe visual handicaps almost always require specialized instruction in written language during the elementary years. This is universally true for students to become braille readers, because instruction in the mechanics of the braille code, skills in proper reading and writing techniques, and the rules for appropriate usage of braille symbols are not taught in the regular classroom. New technology, described later in this chapter under Methods and Materials, has made braille materials more widely available and has made the process of braille translation possible for anyone who has a knowledge of keyboard skills; therefore, it is likely that braille will become an even more important medium for those students who do not have sufficient vision to manage print efficiently.

During the first few years when children are learning to read print and/or braille, there is little difference in reading speed between braille and print reading (Nolan & Kederis, 1969); however, after the mid-elementary years, even the best braille readers are unable to achieve the same reading speed as the sighted reader. Efficiency in braille reading requires thorough knowledge and recognition of the symbols; therefore, training in recognizing braille symbols as a means of increasing reading speed should be emphasized very strongly by teachers. Several professionals have explored the importance of efficient mechanical and motor training in developing the movements that are important for braille reading (Mangold, 1978; Wormsley, 1981). Mangold created a set of materials designed to train students in the efficient use of hand movements and knowledge of concepts necessary for successful braille reading.

There have been recent concerns about the process of deciding whether a child is to be a braille reader or a print reader. These concerns may be influenced in part by the emphasis on visual development skills over the past 20 years, as described by Rex (1989); she underscored the importance of a balanced perspective in encouraging literacy in the most efficient media. Jones (1961) found a wide variation in the reading medium (braille or print) in children with varying degrees of visual acuity. Some children with very low acuity were found to be print readers, whereas other children with much higher visual acuity were found to be braille readers. Children who have limited visual functioning and whose visual reading is slow and requires specifically prepared materials and optimal lighting conditions may learn to read in both print and braille; while print can serve them for brief, functional tasks such as reading labels on food packages or short notes or assignments, braille may remain their primary reading medium for larger quantities of information, such as novels or textbooks.

The decision about which media are appropriate for a child cannot be based on visual acuity alone; a variety of factors must be considered. Mangold and Mangold (1989) identified five major considerations in the selection of reading media, including working distance, portability, reading rate, visual fatigue, and assessment results. These authors recommended consideration of braille for students who are not reading print faster than 60 words per minute by late elementary school. Koenig and Holbrook (1989) described a detailed diagnostic approach to support the determination of reading media for the young student who is visually impaired. APH has published a brochure focusing on literacy for students with visual handicaps, which includes a set of guidelines for teachers in the decision-making process related to selection of learning media, especially for students with low vision for whom there may be a question.

Visual media are preferred for children who can develop sufficient speed and endurance while reading print. Studies (Ashcroft, Halliday, & Barraga, 1965; Barraga, 1964, 1980b) have indicated that, when given an appropriate program in visual perceptual development and use of vision, many children with low vision can be effective visual learners. This may be a long process for some children, depending on their other characteristics, such as motivation, intelligence, and the readiness to learn visually. Although children used to be blindfolded or in some other way prevented from looking at braille so as not to read with their eyes, it is now generally accepted that, if a child can read braille with the eyes, then something easier to read visually than braille should be provided. The provision of optical devices probably would permit such a child to do some visual reading and satisfy the innate desire to use whatever vision is available.

Writing skills are another aspect of communication that require particular emphasis. For children who are totally blind, braille writing usually begins after the child has been exposed to the braille reading system, understands that the symbols produced through writing can carry meaning, and can follow basic instructions and attend well enough to operate a braille writer. It is not necessary to delay braille writing until the child can read letters and words; in fact, there has been some tendency to teach reading and writing of braille simultaneously with selected children. The student who is blind will transfer skills to the slate and stylus, usually at about mid-elementary school, so as to provide a more portable writing method as content demands increase in school and the need for making notes in other settings becomes more necessary. Two advantages of the braille writer for the younger child are that less fine motor coordination is required to use the writer and the child's braille productions are immediately available in an upright position for examination and feedback. In contrast, paper must be turned over and the slate removed to read what is written by the stylus, because the dots are depressed. Using the slate and stylus also requires that the student understand the process of reversal with respect to the braille cell, since each letter is written as a mirror image of the readable cell. For this reason, learning the braille symbols by dot numbers may make writing much easier. Writing with the slate and stylus is done from right to left since the braille dots are punched down instead of up, unlike with the braille writer. Developing efficiency in braille writing is necessary for all students who are totally blind so that they will be able to monitor sentence structure for academic work and also to communicate among themselves.

Handwriting may pose special challenges for the student with low vision, and the techniques used may vary. Rather than teaching manuscript letters from the beginning, it is often more appropriate to begin with the cursive or a modified method of cursive such as the D'Nealian script. This precludes the child from having to lift the pen or pencil from the paper each time a letter is completed. Harley, Truan, and Sanford (1987) identified the cursive letters b, v, w, and o as particularly difficult since they terminate at midline rather than on the baseline. In addition, because spacing is hard to estimate when vision is poor, learning from the start to connect letters in cursive writing is easier and more logical. However, learning to form the letters and to join them may take longer than for normally sighted children and will require more assistance. Some teachers have found that beginning the writing process at the chalkboard makes it easier for the student with low vision to see at eye level and to use larger (gross motor) movements when forming the letters. Legibility rather than perfection is the goal. Heinze (1986) cautioned that although cursive writing may be easier for a visually handicapped child to produce, it may be less easily read; therefore, decisions about the most appropriate method need to be made based on an individual child's visual and motor ability.

For the student who is blind, handwriting is a functional skill that should be taught so that a legible signature can be produced. This can begin when the child has an interest in the use of the pencil and motivation to produce a readable signature. Some teachers advocate teaching handwriting along with braille writing to acquaint children with both braille and print symbols as a means of facilitating the association between them. From the standpoint of motor development, it would be appropriate to teach students who are blind (as suggested for those with low vision) to write on the chalkboard first, because gross movements are easier than the finer movements required by pencil and paper. Once they have learned the letter formations, they can transfer the skills to pencil and paper. Some materials are designed specifically to produce raised lines that are tactually distinguishable. Some children without any vision learn to write script well and can thereby communicate with their sighted classmates through writing. Students with very low vision or those with additional motor problems may write script only for personal reasons and do most of their schoolwork using the typewriter for the sake of legibility and efficiency.

For most students with visual impairment, typing (keyboarding) is also an essential part of the curriculum. It can be introduced as early as third grade, when the child has learned a basic writing vocabulary. Introducing typing as early as seems appropriate for the individual may be valuable for strengthening spelling skills and perhaps also for fostering mental memory, because the visually handicapped typist must remember not only what has been typed, but also what is to follow in order to become aware of location within the paragraph and on the page. As soon as children in public schools become efficient in typing, they can prepare their own work much more independently. This ability may influence the extent to which they can be integrated with sighted peers and achieve success in the classroom. It is the responsibility of the teacher of the visually handicapped to teach touch typing to the child who is ready for this skill.

With the increasing early use of computers in the elementary school, a variety of technological options are available for keyboard instruction and practice that provides immediate feedback to the students. Speech synthesizers and screen review programs allow the child to hear the computer speak the name of the letter just pressed or read the sentence just written. In addition, the lighter touch required on computer keyboards may encourage children to master keyboarding skills at an earlier age. The variety of highly motivating software and the opportunity for immediate feedback through computer instruction make typing a skill that may be more readily attainable, at a younger age, for the learner with a visual impairment. Ely (1989) emphasized the value of computer systems as writing and composition tools for the visually impaired individual, and the capability to write and edit a document as a unified process makes mastery of keyboarding skills a critical issue for the young student who is visually impaired.

In all areas of communication, the child with a visual handicap may require alternative curricular approaches; however, with appropriate materials and motivation, the potential to communicate effectively and to develop a refined knowledge of the spoken and written word is unlimited.

Orientation, Movement, and Physical Skills

A second aspect of the specialized curriculum is instruction in basic skills and concepts related to orientation within the environment, travel, and physical activity requiring endurance and agility. Chapter 3 presented a more thorough discussion of orientation and movement skills under the topic of development of movement and exploration.

As students acquire basic knowledge of the body and its relationship to environmental space, mobility instructors can teach them to move within that environment without assistance. Students must be taught how to move independently by using a cane or dog guide, and how to assess unfamiliar environments to anticipate appropriate movement patterns. Acquiring efficient travel skills requires long and intensive attention to physical activities and skills from a qualified travel instructor.

Because of the lack of visual feedback and confidence in moving through space, children with visual disabilities frequently are less physically active and develop poor tone, physical posture, and stamina. Literature in this area reflects the poor physical development of many students with visual handicaps (DePauw, 1981). Even students with visual handicaps who participated in a quality program of physical education demonstrated a poor general quality of physical development and problems of overweight, poor muscle tone and stamina, and lack of motivation to participate in physical exercise, according to a study by Jankowski and Evans (1981).

Appropriate programming in physical skills may be an area of special concern in the educational program of children with visual impairments. Because of the large sizes of many public school physical education classes and the frequent emphasis on team sports with a strong visual component, students with visual impairments may be involved only to a limited degree, without opportunities to become active participants. Teachers may assume that these students are incapable of participation or that they have no need to acquire certain skills. The students themselves may be reluctant to participate in activities that are physically challenging, and the teacher may not encourage participation.

Although PL 94-142 requires participation in physical education or the provision of an adapted program for students who are visually handicapped, many do not receive quality opportunities to improve physical skills and to participate in regular physical activity (Craft, 1986). Many physical activities and most competitive sports need to be modified or adapted for some students with visual handicaps, but their participation provides social interaction as well as a positive body image for the development of a stronger self-concept. The use of environmental connectors (e.g., ropes or railing), the location of consistent auditory cues for orientation, and the establishment of tactile boundaries can provide sufficient information to allow a student who is totally blind to function in a gymnasium. No adaptation other than modeling or verbal description is required for such activities as calisthenics, tumbling, swimming, or the standing broad jump. Minor adaptations are made in wrestling, requiring that contestants maintain body contact. Considerable adaptation must be made in competitive running or games requiring visual accuracy. As long as the specialist teacher instructs the students on basic body movements and skills and explains how to follow verbal directions, there is no reason why the majority of children and youth who are visually handicapped cannot participate fully in regular physical education activities and, in some cases, competitive events.

Physical education is important also for children who have multiple disabilities, including those who may not have independent locomotion. Activities can be modified to permit them to use their physical skills in satisfying leisure activities, such as throwing and rolling balls toward an auditory target, as in modified bowling; tug-of-war; wheelchair or scooter board races; and relays involving several children in different tasks. Despite physical differences, the child with multiple handicaps should not be relegated to being a spectator or a scorekeeper; physical participation at an appropriate level is important.

Families and friends can play a critical role in encouraging students to pursue physical leisure time activities such as dancing, hiking, swimming, and bicycling. Parents who participate in active recreation with their children provide effective models of physical activity and will communicate satisfaction with physically challenging pursuits. The importance of physical and recreational activities for the child who is visually disabled cannot be overemphasized because of the importance of this area in the health and life adjustment of adults. Unfortunately, too little attention is given to these activities, and many students with visual impairments do not pursue physical skills beyond the structured environment presented in their school setting.

Social Skills

The area of social–emotional adjustment has received increasing attention over the last 10 years, and there is mounting evidence that many students with visual impairments in mainstream settings may need special instruction to acquire the skills that will enable them to interact appropriately with peers and adults in the school setting. A study by Hoben and Lindstrom (1980) reported significantly fewer interactions by students with visual impairments in a regular school classroom, based on detailed observations of 22 students whose vision ranged from total blindness to acuities better than 20/100. In this study, 61% of classroom teachers saw these students as spending more time alone than other students in the class. Corn and Bishop (1984) reported lower than normal scores for students who were visually disabled on the *Test of Practical Knowledge,* which includes social knowledge among its subtests. In her 1986 study of factors that influence success in the mainstream, Bishop found that respondents rated peer acceptance and social skills as the second and third most important variables in determining success, outranked only by the role of an accepting classroom teacher.

For children with visual disabilities, both with and without multiple disabilities, acquiring functional skills related to socialization may take precedence over academic learning in the beginning, especially if the children are expected to spend time in the regular classroom. Social amenities of how to respond to others and how to behave in certain social situations may be unknown to children who are unable to monitor the environment or to see the social behavior they are expected to imitate. Such social skills must be practiced with understanding teachers.

The curricular goals in social skills for students who are visually handicapped have received increasing attention in the literature. Corn (1985a) proposed an independence matrix for learners, which promotes decision-making strategies for students in the areas of resources, problem solving, self-advocacy, and social skills. Corn stressed the importance of student initiative and independence in managing problems as they arise. Read (1989) presented an observational checklist for preschoolers with visual impairments, which specifies behaviors in the areas of participating in actions with others, maintaining relationships, assertiveness skills, classroom skills, and cafeteria skills. Huebner (1986) identified major areas of concern in social skills for students with visual handicaps as stereotypic behaviors and nonverbal communication, including body motion, physical characteristics, touching behavior, voice qualities, proxemics, artifacts or objects that provide nonverbal cues, and the environment.

In these and other areas, students may require specific instruction and feedback in generalizing what they have learned into a natural setting. With respect to nonverbal communication, for example, students may work with their teacher on the appropriate use of the hands to express excitement or conviction while speaking. The instruction may begin with the student touching the adult's hands and modeling the gestures until they can be produced with appropriate timing and fluency; then the student can begin to use those gestures with friends and family who can provide feedback about the appropriateness of the gestures; and finally, the student can begin to use them with unfamiliar people and in formal speaking situations until they look quite natural.

Other areas in which students with visual impairments may need additional feedback and practice include the establishment of eye contact (or apparent eye contact); entering and exiting from conversations, since spatial and nonverbal cues may not be read easily; communication through space decisions (e.g., in a theater, one does not select a seat right next to the only other person); and voice control according to the size of the room and the group receiving the information. Awareness of social routines in these areas will help a student to appear more like schoolmates and will make others feel comfortable during informal interactions.

For the student who experiences unusual difficulties related to socialization, the educational program should provide support services to help in dealing with short- and long-term needs. These may include counseling for the student and, in some cases, referrals for families to assist them in working with difficulties or crises within the family structure. Ching Lan's family, for example, may want some support during the time that their daughter is experiencing an unpredictable loss of vision. Family referral to genetic counseling may be of assistance when there is a question about the origin of the child's visual disability; the provision of additional information or options in this area may contribute to the well-being of the entire family.

Human sexuality is also an area of social skills that requires special attention in the curriculum of the child with a visual handicap; Huebner (1986), Spungin (1984), E. Scott (1982), and Neff (1982) all emphasized the importance of sexuality education in the unique curriculum. An awareness of oneself as a sexual being begins early for all children; attitudes and understanding related to normal sexual development are formed according to whether, and in what way, questions arising from a child's normal curiosity are answered or ignored (Dickman, 1975; Knappett & Wagner, 1976; Neff, 1982; Tait & Kessler, 1976). The nature of these attitudes emerges through interplay of three factors: (1) the child's own impression of a sexual self; (2) the visible, audible, and tangible expressions of all those around the child; and (3) the child's own desire for sex education. Typical experiences of the sighted child, such as seeing a young baby bathed, unclothed brothers or sisters, and men and women in pictures and in television and movies, cannot be experienced by blind children.

By the time children with visual handicaps reach high school and begin to think about relationships (and marriage), they may have incomplete or erroneous ideas or even be totally ignorant of the basic facts regarding body parts and functions. Distorted ideas or lack of information about the consequences associated with sexual relationships could have unfortunate results. Courses in sex education and preparation for marriage and family life are absolutely necessary for children and youth with visual impairments. Suggestions and guidelines for planning courses can be found in the entire May 1974 issue of *The New Outlook for the Blind,* as well as in Neff (1982).

Many concepts related to sexuality can be presented in alternative ways for students with visual handicaps. Differences in clothing and hairstyles of males and females, for example, may need to be explained to a young child with a visual impairment and can be confirmed through touch and conversation. Other concepts, particularly those related to anatomy and reproduction, are more difficult to present concretely because of society's taboos on touch as it relates to gathering information in these areas. Anatomical models are available from a number of companies, as well as from local Planned Parenthood organizations; these can be helpful in presenting concepts such as reproduction and birth control when a student is ready to learn about these processes.

Sexuality and social skills are a necessary part of the curriculum for the child who is visually handicapped. Because this student often misses information about the world that others may gain incidentally, it takes careful planning to provide the student with the skills needed to interact appropriately with others. Even for children as young as Carlos and Lucy, parents and teachers should begin to include information about social events beyond the children's immediate scope, and to provide opportunities in which the children can actively participate and monitor interactions with other children of their age as well as with adults.

Daily Living Skills

Many of the things a sighted child learns about managing daily routines may not be learned incidentally by a child with a visual impairment. For example, children who are blind cannot watch others tie their shoes before beginning to do it. They may not be aware of how to open a milk carton or prepare a sandwich unless others call attention to these activities through verbal description or actual participation. Instruction in such areas as dressing and clothing care, eating, grooming, food preparation, housecleaning, safety skills, and home maintenance may be necessary as a part of the educational program that will move students with visual disabilities toward independence.

Attention to daily living skills should begin during the preschool years. At this age, children should learn mealtime, toileting, and dressing routines. They should be able to use eating utensils at similar stages to sighted children, and they should be able to dress themselves fully by school age, with the possible exception of difficult fasteners and shoe tying. Also by school age, a child with a visual impairment and no additional disabilities should be able to manage toileting routines independently.

During the elementary years, children will take increasing responsibility for managing self-care and their own possessions. Activities that an elementary school child can learn include selecting clothing according to preferences and weather conditions; washing and caring for his or her own hair; participating in household routines, such as laundering clothing and shopping for food; and handling small amounts of personal money. Frequent communication between home and school about self-care responsibilities is important at this time to ensure consistency in instructional approaches and program priorities.

By high school, students should be taking primary responsibility for their own grooming, self-care, and organization of personal possessions. This includes ordering and maintaining special devices and equipment, such as braille writers. In addition, the older student should be able to apply social skills appropriate for different settings (e.g., be aware of the differences between behaviors expected at a fast-food restaurant and those at a formal restaurant).

Instruction of specific skills related to daily living often can be accomplished through breaking the task into its component substeps, called task analysis. The sighted instructor may be able to distinguish the components of the task that require adaptation by personally attempting the task while wearing occluders. It is surprising to discover that many familiar tasks (e.g., opening a jar or tying a shoe) provide sufficient tactile feedback to accomplish the tasks successfully without the use of vision. Other tasks (e.g., threading a needle or putting on makeup) may require use of alternative strategies or equipment to accomplish the tasks without the feedback normally provided by vision.

In some public school settings, students with visual impairments are discouraged from participating in subject areas such as home economics and industrial arts, in which these students should have the opportunity to learn practical skills to help them be independent. McConnell (1984) described some approaches for integrating children with visual impairments into industrial arts classes, and he suggested resources to facilitate this integration. He stressed the importance of teacher and classmate attitudes, availability of a special teacher, limitation of class size, and use of special devices as factors that could enhance the student's ability to gain from participation in such specialized classes.

Students with visual impairments in public schools usually have busy schedules that must encompass regular curricula as well as disability-specific skills. Frequently, instructional activities in daily living skills are set aside, and emphasis is placed on keeping up with peers in academic subjects. It is the responsibility of the teacher of students with visual handicaps along with the child and the family to advocate for instruction in daily living skills and to convince the greater school community of the importance of these skills, which will contribute to the long-term success and independence of the student.

Development and Use of Vision

Recognition that the use of vision is not automatic but must be learned requires that attention be given to "learning to see." If the visual system is not used by looking, storing visual images, and coordinating vision with movement, there is no activity in the occipital area of the brain (the portion that receives visual information), and no visual perceptions are formed. Although most children with low vision gather their major information through vision, their perceptions may not be organized or consistently accurate. Therefore, a planned program of visual perceptual development and visual learning needs to be part of the specialized curriculum for all those with visual potential, regardless of whether they will become visual readers. Functional vision for use when traveling, moving, performing daily living skills, and relating to others and the world is one of the most important personal characteristics to be developed (Barraga, 1980c).

Instruction in the use of low vision can be infused either in the general program or presented as a separate instructional area by the teacher of children with visual handicaps. For students who need specific instruction in visual or perceptual skills, such as discrimination, separate instruction may be the most efficient approach. For the child with multiple handicaps or the child who needs to apply vision in functional situations, such as travel or self-care activities, coordination between the classroom teacher and specialist is necessary for the most effective learning. The process for learning to use vision is described in Chapter 6.

Career and Prevocational Preparation

The process of preparation for an adult role begins early in life for all children. Information about what people do, how they do it, and what is required of an individual to perform a certain job is not commonly available to children with visual disabilities. In providing a student with the skills to pursue a satisfying career as an adult, the school needs to teach the relationship of academic subjects to job preparation.

Four steps that are necessary for the student with a visual impairment to attain career goals are awareness of career opportunities and requirements, exploration of possible work roles, preparation through the development of competencies, and placement in a preferred career role (Simpson, 1986). The process of career development is described in detail in Chapter 10. Career development should be infused at every level of the educational program, both within the regular classroom and with support from specialists, such as the vocational counselor and work experience coordinator.

Students with visual handicaps may require specialized approaches or curricula in the six areas described above. In many instances, success and efficiency of the learning process may depend on the use and availability of specialized equipment, materials, or techniques. The second part of this chapter describes techniques and equipment commonly needed during the instructional process by students with visual impairments.

METHODS AND MATERIALS

Itinerant teachers of children with visual handicaps often comment that they can be identified best by their personal vehicles, because the back seats and trunks are full of the bags, boxes, and kits of equipment that enable them to meet the needs of students of various ages and educational needs. Because the limitations imposed by a visual impairment often are manifested in the child's inability to use standard educational materials, the choice of appropriate equipment and the use of efficient instructional methodology can make a critical difference in success in learning for the child with visual disabilities.

For many years, students who were blind and visually handicapped were the only group in special education that had materials manufactured exclusively for their use authorized by the U.S. Congress. Presently, federal funds are being provided for other groups of students with special needs in a similar manner.

In 1879, the federal government designated the American Printing House for the Blind (APH) in Louisville, Kentucky, as the producer of books for blind students (Koestler, 1976). APH has continued to be the major worldwide producer of materials for students with visual handicaps. It is supported in part by federal funds, which are allotted to states under a quota system on a per-student basis. Other countries may purchase materials from APH as desired. Materials produced by APH include books in braille and large type, instructional computer materials, materials and equipment for students with low vision, and manipulables for preschoolers and students with multiple disabilities.

The recent surge in technology has encouraged private enterprise in the production of materials for students with visual impairments. Independent efforts funded through federal and private grants and by the private sector have become more common; some have focused on the production of one particular device, whereas others produce a variety of technological products. In technology and in the distribution of optical devices, the potential for the development of a competitive market has just begun to be tapped.

Providing educational materials for children with visual handicaps that are comparable to the wide variety of materials available for normally seeing students has posed problems throughout the years, and many of these have yet to be solved. The educational materials explosion has motivated increased research into the learning processes of students with visual handicaps and has created an impetus for greater experimentation and adaptation of media and materials.

Methods and Materials for Students Who Are Blind

Braille Codes. After years of controversy, the basic braille cell of six dots designed by Louis Braille has been accepted internationally as the one graphic symbol for use by blind readers. The 63 possible dot combinations form the basis for a literary braille code, a music code, a mathematical code, and a scientific code. The variety of codes developed from this basic six-dot braille cell and all the possible combinations thereof have been likened to a series of foreign languages. The multiple arrangement of symbols, the use of the same symbols with a variety of meanings depending on their relation to other symbols or their spatial position, and the many arbitrary rules for using these symbols, make all braille codes complex language systems for interpretation. A sophisticated system of braille shorthand in the form of contractions, letter combinations, and shortened forms of words saves space and usually time in reading. Although it increases efficiency in reading more familiar material, such extensive abbreviation may increase the time required for interpretation and recognition of new words in unfamiliar contexts (Henderson, 1973; Lowenfeld, 1973; Nolan & Kederis, 1969). Despite the fact that rapid reading skills seem to improve braille reading speed for some learners, there is no evidence of its effectiveness for all braille readers, or even the majority of them (Olson, Harlow, & Williams, 1977). In braille codes, it is impossible to maintain the sound–symbol relationship found in print symbols; this sound–symbol inconsistency poses an additional difficulty in symbol recognition.

The importance of early exposure to braille as a reading system has been emphasized in recent literature related to braille learning. During the preschool years, before a child is ready to decode or understand the construction and pronunciation of words, the opportunity to experience braille in the immediate environment, such as in a book being read by a parent, on labels of favorite objects, or on name tags placed on personal possessions, is a valuable precurser to braille reading. D. Miller (1985) described activities that encouraged her daughter to become motivated as a braille reader, namely, use of objects related to stories being read, tactile books, and experiential stories.

An important factor in the development of successful reading skills appears to be as early introduction as possible to the mechanics of braille reading. Mangold (1978) designed a reading program that suggested precision teaching of braille through a graduated sequence of activities; she emphasized the importance of accompanying the traditional program in word recognition and decoding with a foundation program in the mechanics of braille reading. Wormsley (1981) examined the effects of motor training on braille reading speed among elementary-aged students; although her training program in hand movements did not result in gains in reading efficiency among the children involved, she noted a decrease in inefficient hand movements among her younger students and suggested that strong association of motor and perceptual training at the early levels is important for later efficiency in reading.

Direct translations into braille of printed books used in the early school years present a serious problem because words easily recognized by sight may be difficult when transcribed into braille. The difficulty level of reading materials in the first few school years may suggest the use of "controlling symbols," or special reading materials for those children who will use braille, in order to introduce gradually the perplexing word symbols of the braille literary code (Rex, 1970). Long-term research projects should be designed and conducted to evaluate the efficiency of various braille literary code abbreviations in facilitating learning to read. *Patterns,* the braille reading series produced by APH, includes controlled vocabulary and introduction to braille symbols and contractions. Research related to effectiveness of reading instruction with this approach may provide more information about the importance of planned introduction of braille symbols.

Regardless of the process of learning or the methodologies used, the braille reading learner will be required throughout the school years to refine recognition skills and knowledge of the various aspects of the code and its multiple uses. Those young people who intend to continue in academic and literary pursuits beyond high school will find even greater challenges in the use of Grade 3 braille, an even more abbreviated but more efficient and space-saving form for adult use.

Tangible Materials. Until the recent development of extensive recorded materials, the most lasting products of the work of students who were blind have been tangible ones. Therefore, materials and devices that provide feedback through touch are an essential part of learning for students without vision.

Recent research has provided some enlightenment on the discriminability of tactile information by learners with visual handicaps. With a greater variety of options for creating tactile displays, such as the *Tactile Graphics Kit* distributed by APH (Barth, 1982), teachers can now prepare many graphs, charts, and diagrams for students without vision for their use in the regular classroom.

With the increase in technological innovations, there are new alternatives for providing tactile displays of materials, which are presented two-dimensionally for the sighted student. Graphs and diagrams are still reproduced manually by the teacher in some cases. This may be done with a tracing wheel and stiff paper; with an applied substance, such as a white glue or "Puff Paints," which leave a raised line when dry; or through the use of a manufactured kit, such as the *Sewell Raised Line Drawing Kit* from the American Foundation for the Blind. The use of a fluid pen that creates a raised line on a special paper has also been explored but not finalized.

Durable and complex versions of charts and diagrams can be produced using the *Tactile Graphics Kit*, which provides aluminum sheets and a variety of tools for creating tactile lines and spaces. Such materials are most often copied using the thermoform machine, which reproduces tangible reproductions using a heat press and a plastic paper to create multiple copies. A recent innovation known as the stereocopier can reproduce printed material in raised format on a special paper; although it provides a faithful reproduction of the printed copy, the cost of this device is still well beyond the reach of individuals and of many agencies.

The challenge of performing mathematical computations has been facilitated by a number of devices designed for use by students who are blind. Early approaches included the Taylor slate, which involved the placement of tiny six-sided pegs in rows to indicate numbers, and the cubarithm, which required the positioning of cubes with raised dots on them in a plastic grid to represent numbers. The adapted abacus was developed by Cranmer, of APH, in 1962; this abacus is used widely in the instruction of mathematics for students who are blind and provides a method of examining each step of the calculation process as a problem is solved. Lewis (1979) found that 66% of school programs were using the abacus; however, more recently, Rossi (1986) noted that "the brailler is still the most popular device for working out computations" (p. 370). Brothers (1972) noted that arithmetic computation continued to be a critical concern among educators. He suggested that there seemed to be several possible alternatives:

> (1) the use of the numberaid or other concrete manipulative devices at the third and fourth grade level; (2) providing an opportunity for all students to become proficient with the abacus by the completion of grade six; and (3) placing much less emphasis on the braille writer as a computational aid." (p. 7)

More recently, the talking calculator has assumed a role in the process of mathematical calculation. Although it provides a rapid method of solving problems and many students without vision are able to keep pace with their classmates in complex computational activities, the calculator does not teach the process of problem solving and it allows the student to attain an answer without being aware of the process. Most teachers of students with visual handicaps prefer to introduce calculators at the same time that sighted classmates are being allowed to use them in the classroom; however, they plan the mathematics curriculum to include instruction on the abacus and with brailled numerals to assure the student's understanding of the calculation process.

Although the problems in computation for students who are blind have not yet been resolved, it is clear that easy-to-handle computational devices, as well as sets of real objects and manipulatives, must be widely available during the child's early school years for arithmetic concepts to be understood. These tools also may be useful for children with low vision—for example, numberaid and abacus may supplement paper-and-pencil computational skills to increase efficiency. No single process or device has been identified as the most appropriate for all children. Thus, teachers should continue to experiment with various approaches to permit children with severe visual handicaps to acquire computational skills and to achieve in arithmetic at a level comparable to that of their sighted peers.

Concrete objects and materials known as *realia* play an important part in the learning process for the student who is blind. These may be purchased commercially or gathered from environmental sources; they are valuable in providing experience with basic concepts to blind students and should be a part of every classroom, especially during the early educational years. Carlos can never know the form and texture of a bird unless he has the opportunity to touch a live bird or to examine a taxidermist's model. He cannot observe a picture of a starfish or compare photographs of seeds in his science book, and he can understand these organisms well only if he can handle and examine them himself.

In the first few grades, models and three-dimensional representations of objects appear to have little use because of the discrepancy in size and texture between the model and the real object. The visually handicapped child whose ability to generalize is not well developed may only be confused by a small, solid representation of an animal that is actually large, furry, and warm. As students grow older and are able to make the association and transfer through abstract thinking, models may come to have some use, especially for representing large or inaccessible objects. Harley, Truan, and Sanford (1987) presented a hierarchy of abstraction that can be helpful in selecting the appropriate materials for the instruction of a student; the levels range from the child's own body as the most concrete through the use of the object itself, various models and representations, and verbal descriptions as the most abstract.

Basic geographic concepts (J. W. Miller, 1982) and adaptations of science activities (DeLucchi & Malone, 1982) have been welcome additions to curricula for students with visual handicaps. Provision of tapes for teaching concepts and a kit of hands-on materials may make it easier to teach social studies and science activities to these students within regular classroom settings, especially at junior and senior high school levels (Davis & Hawke, 1978). Curricula such as *Science Activities for the Visually Impaired* (DeLucchi & Malone, 1982) or *Laboratory Science and Art Curriculum for the Blind* (Hadary, 1977) have been developed to promote the use of the inquiry method of science instruction for students with visual handicaps. These activity-based approaches can enhance the understanding of science for all children, not only those who have special learning needs.

In art, as in science and social studies, direct experience with objects and materials is vital to the learning process. A study by Rubin (1975) emphasized that the aesthetic experience of the blind student is different from that of sighted students, because it depends on a tactile reference system. Rubin found that young children who are blind preferred the sculptures of other blind students, whereas students with low vision preferred sculptures created by others with similar vision. Swenson (1987) suggested the inclusion in curriculum of simple, familiar materials that encourage creativity. Particularly at the early stages, the purpose of art activities is to provide experiences in manipulation and control of materials, rather than to produce a product.

Availability of simple, durable materials that offer children without vision the opportunity to participate in and control experiences will encourage greater enthusiasm for tactile activities. Although these materials are made commercially, sometimes to instruct the child in a particular concept, as with the abacus, they may be simple, ordinary household materials, such as styrofoam packing worms or ice cream sticks, which can be counted, sorted, and arranged in original and pleasing ways. The use of manipulable materials is most critical at the early level, but the practice should continue at all levels for students who are blind, particularly when new concepts are being introduced or when participation and motivation are crucial to the understanding of an idea.

Auditory Materials. The increasing production of auditory materials for students with visual impairments and other disabilities has facilitated information availability, particularly at the secondary and postsecondary educational levels. Since the Pratt–Smooth Act in 1931, the National Library Service, a federally funded branch of the Library of Congress in Washington, D.C., with many regional libraries, has provided recreational listening materials for individuals with visual handicaps (Koestler, 1976). Recently, most books loaned by the library are on cassette tape, and each individual who qualifies receives on loan a cassette player for use with these tapes. Students may receive tape recorded versions of textbooks through application to Recording for the Blind, a privately funded agency in Princeton, New Jersey, with numerous regional studios that provide educational materials in recorded form to persons who are visually handicapped.

Auditory materials in other forms increasingly have expanded options to students with visual handicaps. Audio-card readers, speech synthesizers that translate computer programs into speech, and reading machines can provide increasing independence to the student in the classroom. With such equipment, teachers may prepare individual instructions for students or provide their work on a computer disk. The relative benefits of using prepared instructional material with students having visual handicaps have been explored only minimally; however, the continued interest of engineers and other specialists in developing technological alternatives for learning will ensure further refinement of materials and processes to enhance the learning and functioning of students with severe visual handicaps.

Technology. The world of communication through braille has broadened with the introduction of many technological options that increase the speed of braille production and the ease of translation. Braille can now be produced by a typist who does not know the braille code; print can be translated into braille using a personal computer and the appropriate software; and braille can be mechanically printed at speeds up to 100 characters per second. Technology has made the braille system more universally available and has offered increasing options for braille use in educational and professional settings.

Technology for individuals who are blind began to emerge with the development of the optacon in 1965 (Linville & Bliss, 1966). The refinement of the optical-to-tactile conversion instrument, now manufactured by Telesensory Systems, Inc., provided the first method by which a blind person could access the printed word without a sighted intermediary. In the optacon, a tiny camera passes over printed symbols, and the image is converted to a tactual representation of the letter shape through vibrating pins, which are perceived on the forefinger of the person.

As a reading device, the optacon is limited to less than 100 words per minute. Success with the device depends on a number of variables (Bliss & Moore, 1974; M. Moore, 1973; Terzieff, Stagg, & Ashcroft, 1982), which include intelligence, effectiveness of training, consistency of use, and motivation. For many individuals who are blind, the optacon represents a means of primary access to the printed word; it enables people to read their own mail, labels on food containers, or personal messages. Perhaps more importantly, it represents the first innovation in an explosion of technological options that are now available for the person who is blind.

For the student in school, this explosion of technology provides a greater number of options for learning. For taking notes, students without vision can consider a laptop computer with speech capabilities or a portable braille notetaker. The student can prepare papers for class using a preferred computer or a paperless brailler, and then edit them using a refreshable braille display or a screen review program that provides spoken output. The student can produce a brailled or printed copy of classwork, and can access print materials independently through the use of an optical scanner.

Despite the array of technological options for students who are visually disabled, some issues must be considered in applying these options with a particular student. The cost of the equipment that would allow students to function most efficiently is often prohibitive; teachers and other professionals may find that their role also requires them to make time to seek out appropriate funding sources to provide equipment for their students. The choice of technology must be made with each student's needs in mind, and the need for instructional and practice time on the devices must be available so that students become proficient in using them.

Scadden (1984) presented a perceptive analysis of the implications technology may have for the individual who is blind. For this individual to benefit from advancing technology, according to Scadden, it is critical that attention be given to preparing professionals to instruct students and clients in the use of technology, the increased development of software and personal computers that are accessible to readers who are blind, and the expansion of standard microcomputers that can be used by them. For the student who is visually impaired, the right choices in technology and training may make the difference between success and failure in school and in the job market.

Methods and Materials for Students with Low Vision

Children with low vision rely mainly on visual information during the learning process, even though the visual environment may vary from that of normally sighted children. If students with low vision learn to use vision efficiently, they will need to interpret incomplete or unclear images, draw conclusions about the identity and relationship of objects in the environment, increase individual visual advantage through the use of positioning as well as optical and nonoptical devices, and make decisions about the use of vision in conjunction with other senses. These students must develop a sense of self as individuals with a unique reference system that is not mainly tactile and auditory, as that of a person who is blind, and that is not a damaged version of the world as seen by a normally sighted person. Instead, it is a separate reference system that combines broad configurations and images with the knowledge and awareness of detail that can be learned through experience.

The environment can be made more accessible by the individual with low vision in three ways: (1) increasing the size of the material itself, (2) bringing the image or the material closer to the eye, or (3) using a device or projection to magnify the size of the material. When selecting an approach to facilitate the visual environment, the student and the team should consider a number of factors, such as cost, versatility, social acceptability, physical strength and endurance, visual needs, and convenience, which all may play a part in the choice of an adaptation to enhance the visual environment.

Adaptations for children with low vision may be either optical or nonoptical. Nonoptical adaptations generally are less expensive and involve the adjustment or alteration of the environment to make it more accessible. Corn (1983) identified environmental cues that can be altered to create differences in the visual environment. Increasing color differences in material to be viewed, altering viewing distances, or intensifying lighting to increase contrast are methods that Corn suggested can be used to provide a more visually accessible environment.

For younger children, these adaptations may involve controlling materials presented to emphasize the use of simple patterns and high contrast materials. Consistent presentation of certain familiar patterns and forms will enable children to begin to generalize these to more complex, poorly contrasted configurations that are a natural part of the environment (L. Harrell & Akeson, 1987).

Holding material closer to the eyes to reduce viewing distance enlarges the size of the image. Contrary to popular notion, holding materials even a few inches from the eyes is not harmful and can enhance the clarity of material for the reader. Decreasing the reading distance enlarges and clarifies the image without requiring the use of specialized materials or devices. The use of an easel to hold the book at an angle or varying the reading position to reduce neck strain can enable children to maintain a reduced distance comfortably while doing close work.

The assumption often is made that the student with low vision requires enlarged materials for most efficient functioning in school. For a number of reasons, this may not be true. Enlargement of materials automatically imposes spatial inconvenience; materials occupy more space and become heavier; more head movement and adaptive positioning is required of the large-print reader; large-print readers look so different from standard books that some children are embarrassed to use them; and, particularly for the student with a major field loss, less material can be presented at once. Producing large-type books is expensive, and the pictures in these textbooks are more difficult for children with limited vision to use than the color pictures in regular textbooks. Because of the expense, the number of titles available in large print is limited (Goldish, 1968).

The use of enlarged materials, such as books with large type, is now considered a last resort, less desirable than either the reduction of reading distance or the use of optical devices. For a number of years, it was assumed that the child with low vision would find it easier to see large-type materials; however, studies have reported inconclusive and often contradictory evidence regarding the size of print most easily read (Eakin, Pratt, & McFarland, 1961; Nolan, 1959). Further studies relating to school achievement and the effect of type size on reading and achievement (Bateman & Weatherall, 1967; Birch, Tisdall, Peabody, & Sterrett, 1966) have suggested that type size has little to do with reading speed or comprehension in students with low vision.

Two ophthalmologists, Faye (1970) and Fonda (1966), wrote that many children have been encouraged or even forced to read large-type materials when they could have more easily read materials in regular print size, either with or without magnification. Sykes (1971, 1972) found that high school students, when provided with magnifying devices and special lamps and/or lighting arrangements, were just as efficient with regular-sized print materials as they were with large-print materials. Reading standard print was found to be no more tiring than reading large print, implying that the concern should not be with the size of the type, but with the quality of the print and the illumination.

Use of optical magnifying devices is frequently the most efficient approach to enlarging or enhancing an image for the individual with low vision. The refinement in the quality of nonprescription magnifiers and the development of low vision clinics that prescribe aids for children have resulted in a trend toward the increasing use of magnifying devices. Neither visual acuity measurements nor the nature of the visual impairment seems to have any relationship to the student's preference and efficiency with low vision optical devices or large print. However, the teacher's training in knowledge and use of optical devices may be a critical factor (Corn, 1980).

For many reasons, magnification devices are preferable to the use of large-type books for the student with low vision. Not only do they provide access to a larger selection of material and eliminate the expense of enlarging every piece separately, but they also are less obtrusive and easier to carry and store. Corn and Ryser (1989) surveyed the teachers of 351 children with visual handicaps in Texas with respect to the use of optical devices and large type. They found that students who used optical devices increased their reading levels and speeds with age; that there were no differences in fatigue between users of large type and optical devices; and that magnifying devices appeared to be more cost-effective over time.

When children cannot be fitted with spectacle lenses that enable them to function with some visual efficiency, using hand-held or stand magnifiers is the most feasible solution. There is still worldwide controversy regarding large-print and visual devices. It is more logical to consider both for children to function more efficiently visually than to take an either/or position. The decision should be based on the individual child, the visual condition, and the motivation to function with either large type or magnification of regular-sized materials and still maintain speed and comprehension.

The style, spacing, and density of print are significant variables to consider. Teachers need to provide many varieties of print sizes and styles to enable children to choose what is best for them. Because the letters appear to run together, large, bold type with letters spaced close together is more difficult to read than smaller type with letters spaced farther apart.

Letters with low density are difficult to discriminate. The most visible print is simple in style, moderately bold, and well spaced. Lighting also is critical; some children need more light or light directed onto the material, whereas others can function more efficiently with less direct or intense light. Again, teachers should let children try many different lighting conditions to determine those that are optimal.

All optical devices and many magnifiers require considerable practice for children to use them effectively. Proper use of optical devices, including magnifiers, cannot be left to chance. Such tools should be prescribed after a thorough examination by a low vision specialist, who explores the practical requirements of the consumer. It is not the role of the teacher of students with visual handicaps to prescribe visual devices. Once these have been prescribed by the low vision specialist, the educator may provide the training the child needs to use the device.

It is important that this training to use visual devices begin with high interest, motivating materials, particularly with younger children, to assure acceptance of whatever device is prescribed. Introduction of distance devices can begin as young as 4 or 5 years of age to provide the child with a means of identifying objects at a distance and, later, with a method of copying material from the chalkboard at school. Generally, training begins with practice in handling, focusing, and storing the device. The child then experiments with scanning and locating (spotting) a stationary object, tracking a moving object, and finally using the monocular for complex tasks such as reading a bus sign or scanning the faces of performers at a concert.

Technological innovations have provided expanding opportunities for the individual with low vision to access printed material, as well as to read and edit his or her own material. Some technology that is most useful in learning settings is described below.

Closed circuit televisions (CCTVs) are among the most common technological devices in use. Through the use of a camera, the CCTV enlarges printed material on a monitor similar to a television screen. A source of light illuminates the material, which is presented on a viewing table. The viewer can alter the size and contrast of the material, and specialized devices allow the CCTV to be connected with a typewriter or a computer so that an individual can read and edit materials being written. Recently, some companies have developed a camera that can project an enlarged image from a distance onto the monitor screen.

DeWitt, Schreier, and Leventhal (1988) recommended that a closed circuit television be purchased only after an individual has a thorough low vision evaluation. They described five major design features that should be considered in the purchase of this equipment: image, reliability, cost, versatility, and portability.

The development of computer options for the user with low vision has expanded over the last 10 years. An individual who wishes to vary print size may choose a computer with built-in enlargement capabilities, a software program that enlarges the type size on a conventional computer, or a magnifying device that is placed over the screen to enlarge the image (Goodrich, 1984; Harley, Truan, & Sanford, 1987; Todd, 1986).

Most students with low vision use various combinations of optical and nonoptical devices at different times during their school years. In working with such a student, educators should stress the importance of a regular low vision evaluation, the options a student has in gathering information, and the student's responsibility for selecting the most appropriate environmental adaptation.

For children with visual impairments, the selection of appropriate instructional approaches and materials can facilitate the learning process and increase motivation and independence in learning. The opportunities that have become available through technology have multiplied the choices in learning media, but also have presented additional challenges. Ultimately, the most important skill that students with visual impairments can acquire is to take responsibility for the selection of approaches and methods that facilitate personal learning.

SUMMARY

For children with visual impairments, an individualized curriculum and specialized materials are often necessary to facilitate the learning process. Unique curricular areas may include content related to communication, movement and physical skills, social skills, daily living skills, skills in the use of vision, and career–vocational skills. For students who are blind, appropriate learning materials include classroom and supplementary materials in braille, as well as tangible objects that enhance the understanding of concepts. In addition, auditory materials and technological equipment can facilitate the learning process. For students with low vision, the availability of optical and nonoptical devices is critical; technology such as closed circuit television has been developed to make printed information more readily accessible. For any child with a visual handicap, the combination of identifying priorities in curriculum with acquiring practical materials is important to efficiency in learning.

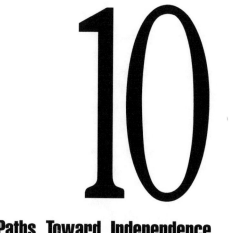

Paths Toward Independence

Education for any student ultimately should provide preparation for an adult life that includes a satisfying occupation and lifestyle, as well as give a feeling of success early in childhood and throughout the years. For students with visual impairments, this preparation may involve not only the development of skills in a chosen career field, but also skills in life management and in communicating effectively with others.

In the lives of most children, youths, and some adults with visual handicaps, conflicts may seem to exist between the goals of education and rehabilitation. Each of these sectors, at different times, may seem to give too little consideration to the individual's personal desires and needs. The prevailing assumption of most school programs is that their primary role is to ensure that each child achieves the maximum intellectually, often disregarding personal and vocational development. These programs invest much time and effort in academic pursuits, even when the student's potential for independent living and functioning may be limited.

Premature decisions to prepare for one occupational skill or vocation may pose an equally perplexing dilemma, however, for the youth who leaves school and finds that no opportunities are available to practice limited skills. Service delivery systems in rehabilitation for persons who are blind have been geared traditionally toward blinded adults who have already become part of the workforce or who previously have established vocational or professional goals. Their only major problem is loss of vision (Organization for Social and Technical Innovation, 1971). Only recently have rehabilitation systems begun to expand their services to meet the needs of individuals who are congenitally visually impaired and whose awareness and experience related to the work world may be limited and of people with multiple disabilities for whom competitive employment may not be an option.

In the past, community and state agencies tended to provide a set of undifferentiated services defined by the agency itself and not necessarily related to the clients' needs. Also, educational programs and specialized schools had their own traditional, although not necessarily realistic, objectives for individual students or for career possibilities (R. Scott, 1969). Services increasingly reflect that education, as well as rehabilitation, begins at birth and continues until death. Conflicts between them are artificial and detrimental.

This fact is recognized increasingly in building transitional programming to pave the way from primary to elementary to junior high to high school and on into the adult world. Program features, such as summer work programs at residential schools and rehabilitation centers, supported work experiences, written Individual Transition Plans (ITP), and mentoring programs, encourage students to develop skills to prepare them for adulthood during the time that their academic preparation is still taking place. In addition, professional preparation programs have initiated a renewed focus on the skills that will allow teachers and rehabilitation counselors to facilitate the transition of their students from school to adult life (Irwin & Macdonnell, 1988).

Educators must learn a great deal more about the occupational, vocational, and career world in which the rehabilitation counselor functions. Counselors in agencies must learn more about educational and school philosophies, curriculum offerings, social and recreational opportunities, vocational programs, and the scope of mobility programs. The present gap between education and rehabilitation might be bridged if both were to consider a broader range of variables affecting all children and youth with visual handicaps. This chapter will examine some of those variables within the context of occupational, personal, and social skills.

OCCUPATIONAL AND ECONOMIC CONSIDERATIONS

Career and vocational preparation is related closely to economic factors. If federal and state governments were to invest funds for acquainting people who are visually disabled with careers and vocations in which there is a high probability of success, not only would society be required to spend less for habilitation after the school years, but also greater productivity from goods, services, and taxes would be provided by persons who are congenitally visually impaired. Independence, or even partial independence, at an earlier age would reduce the need for many of the economic expenditures associated with caring for these people in later years.

In addition to the economic benefits, the human considerations are important. Tuttle (1984) described the importance of appropriate employment in maintaining the self-esteem of persons with visual impairments: "The degree to which a blind individual has attained or regained a status equal to his peers with comparable abilities is the degree to which he is likely to achieve self-acceptance and self-esteem" (p. 261). Knowing that one has economically valuable skills and that using those skills provides personal satisfaction can be motivation for increasing independence.

Developing realistic attitudes about the facts of a visual disability is as much a part of vocational preparation for independence as is acquiring skills and knowledge. Medical costs may be substantial in some cases because of eye conditions; living expenses may be proportionately higher for personal services and travel expenses in some careers; and reduced income is regrettable but a real possibility. Young adults need to understand these facts, but also to gain confidence in their ability to make the decisions that will best enhance their personal success. Counseling courses, as well as frequent contacts with adults who are visually handicapped, as friends or mentors, can be very informative, because young people who are visually disabled are often naive about the responsibilities, the demands, and the stresses experienced in many occupations.

Simpson (1986) emphasized the importance of early career development for students with visual impairments. According to Simpson, this process should begin during the early school years, and the Individualized Education Program (IEP) should include objectives related to career awareness and planning from the earliest stages. Early in elementary school, students should be exposed to a wide variety of career possibilities. Because students who are blind may not learn incidentally about the working world around them, it is important to involve workers within and outside the school, as well as to plan field trips to encourage awareness of various occupational fields. The occupations observed should reflect a range of skill and income levels, and students should be encouraged to develop respect for every occupation that allows a worker to be employed actively at an appropriate skill level.

Some studies have indicated a difference in occupational expectations among students who are visually impaired. A 1988 study by Bush-LaFrance indicated that adolescents who are legally blind may have lower occupational expectations as a whole; however, with the respondents to this study, the expectations were lower among students who were legally blind but who had more vision. This phenomenon may be related to the fact that students who were totally blind were not considered for occupations with visual demands, whereas students with functional vision were. A 1985 study by Corn and Bishop noted a high interest in artistic expression but a dislike of selling, performing, and nature-related occupations among 8th to 12th graders. More extensive investigation is needed into the ways in which a visual impairment impacts a student's perception of possible and desirable occupations, as well as how realistic those expectations are.

There is a paucity of studies of adults with visual handicaps, but one surveyed graduates from both local and residential school programs (Luxton, 1980–1981). The information indicated that a high percentage are either overeducated and underemployed or show a greater inconsistency in job stability far beyond that of the general population. It may be that some youths with visual handicaps have no philosophical understanding of work as an integral part of a full life. Work can be viewed in two ways: as a goal and as a process. Perhaps education should also be viewed as a goal and a process. Any process is a continuum of skill, training, experience, evaluation, and reevaluation directed toward both general and specific goals. To the present time, most school programs have been concerned with the narrow goal of teaching academic subject matter. The time may have come to consider an array of options within education, including specialized programs within cities or states that will allow students to pursue a chosen field of study according to their life goals.

The first step in effective career development is the implementation of specific and detailed assessment processes in the area. Use of specific instruments, such as the *Occupational Aptitude Survey and Interest Schedule* (Parker, 1983), provide the student with the opportunity to evaluate the suitability of a particular work situation for individual skills and interests. In addition, assessments that lead to skill development and mastery, such as the *Vocational Readiness Curriculum* (McCarron & Hurst, 1985), are being applied more frequently to identify specific areas of strength and weakness.

A proactive approach, in which the student takes initiative in seeking out resources and information about prospective careers, should be encouraged from the beginning. The student should consider the options for careers based on personal interests and skills, not on stereotyped notions of what people with visual handicaps can do. Too many adolescents leave high school with a nebulous dream of being a musician or a disk jockey, without a realistic concept of the competition in those occupational fields. Their repertoire of vocational–career knowledge is limited, and they can picture themselves only in the roles of well-known adults who are visually handicapped. Professionals and parents are responsible for making students aware of the wide array of job roles that are available, as well as emphasizing the dignity of work of any kind, regardless of whether it is a glamorous or high status profession.

Current studies of what is available and what is desirable in preparing students who are visually disabled for careers indicates that there still is a wide gap between needs and opportunities. In a study of career needs and resources for people who are visually impaired, Bagley (1985) surveyed students, parents, teachers, rehabilitation personnel, and adults with visual impairments; she noted a high perceived need for resources in career development, but an inaccessibility of many of these resources. Likewise, Graves and Lyon (1985) noted in a study of the perceptions of ninth graders with visual impairments that most of these students did not feel that schools were meeting their needs in the career discovery process. Clearly, there is agreement that career development is important; however, effective planning in this area is just beginning to emerge.

In response to this concern, specialized programs that focus on career development skills are becoming more widely available, particularly at the secondary level. Alternatives such as independent living programs based at residential schools (Stewart, van Hasselt, Simon, & Thompson, 1985; Venn & Wadler, 1988) or weekend programs that involve families in the career planning process (Houser, Moses, & Kay, 1987) recognize the importance of combining career and life skills preparation with the development of formal education for secondary students. Postsecondary programs, such as the Job Readiness Clinic at The University of Texas at Austin, use a problem-solving approach to develop skills in job seeking and long-term career development (Wolffe, 1985); students are encouraged to view their career as an ongoing, long-term process rather than only as a source of immediate income. Alternative programs such as these may supplement or intensify the career development experience, providing the specialized skills that are not a regular part of the high school curriculum.

As alternative approaches for preparing students for careers evolve, it is critical that professionals evaluate the success of these programs with respect to employment and life satisfaction. Heiden (1989) presented follow-up information on one residential program, which indicated a 44% employment rate for graduates of the Wisconsin School for the Blind, a higher percentage than the national average of 31%. According to this study, graduates found classes in adaptive living, orientation and mobility, and word processing to be most useful in their preparation for adulthood; most reported satisfaction with their quality of life. This type of follow-up is critical to the planning of appropriate programs that will lead students to effective career choices.

When students are planning to attend college after high school, a precollege program may be quite useful. The college campus is quite different from a residential school or a local high school, not only in terms of relationships, but in academic and social demands. The personal responsibilities may be overwhelming for those who are not prepared to handle such chores as laundry, money management, and communication of needs to professors and others. Most of these topics are included in such orientation seminars.

For some students entering the adult world, a self-supporting, independent work role will not be an option. However, this does not mean that the world of work is closed to the student with severe disabilities. There are various opportunities for occupational roles (summer and part-time employment) that can provide income and self-satisfaction to the individual with motor, cognitive, or behavioral differences.

The supported employment model is becoming more widely applied for those individuals with severe disabilities. In this model, a job is identified in a setting with nondisabled employees, and a job coach supports the disabled individual until the skills needed to accomplish the tasks have been mastered. Others prefer a sheltered workshop setting, which employs only those with disabilities. In such a setting, adaptations for visual and other differences are available quite readily. Some adults with severe disabilities attend day activity centers, in which they are involved in recreational, occupational, and life skills activities appropriate to their functional level.

For an appropriate placement to be available by adulthood for those with severe disabilities, work must begin during early adolescence. Vocational counselors from involved agencies should be invited to the annual IEP meeting, and care should be taken to make the student's program functional and focused on realistic adult goals. Family involvement will broaden to include long-term concerns, such as guardianship and estate planning; it is important that families seek legal counsel in making the decision about these issues. Only with this type of careful planning can an individual be assured of the placements and opportunities that will provide a satisfying adult lifestyle.

LIFE SKILLS

Parents and professionals often stress the importance of career planning in preparing a student for a viable career. In the planning process, the importance of general life skills training can become secondary to the goal of attaining a job. However, skills in personal and life management are equally important; they may determine whether a student is able to live independently or with minimal assistance, or they may ensure that a student is a contributing member of the family unit.

The student with visual impairment should develop the skills that will allow maximum independence and quality of life as an adult. These include personal care and management routines, such as choosing and caring for clothing, styling one's own hair, personal hygiene, preparing and storing food, and cleaning and caring for the home. Several resources are available that provide practical ideas for the acquisition of daily living skills (Swallow & Huebner, 1987; Wehrum, 1977; Willoughby & Duffy, 1989).

Skills related to personal care and home management also must involve those that require problem solving and complex choices: When is it more practical to grocery shop with sighted assistance as opposed to ordering groceries to be delivered? How should a resident respond when a smoke alarm buzzes in an apartment? How should spilled liquid be wiped from different surfaces? An individual must be able to anticipate and manage unexpected events and must perceive the choices implicit in every situation, as well as know how to follow routines.

In addition, financial management is an important factor in preparation for maximum independence. The skills of maintaining a checking account, making long-term financial plans, paying bills, and building financial security are important for any young adult. For the student who is blind, specific concerns must be addressed: What procedures will be used for signing checks and maintaining account records? When sighted assistance is needed, who can provide trusted and reliable help? From elementary school, the student who is visually handicapped, like all students, should have the opportunity to manage money and experience the decisions that go along with spending and saving. The ability to make financial decisions and to be aware of their consequences is critical for financial responsibility.

For the individual with severe additional disabilities, life skills are equally important, although priorities may be different. The emphasis is on teaching those skills representing tasks that otherwise would have to be performed by others; where independent performance or adapted independence is not an option, partial participation and/or cooperation become the goals. The presence of a visual impairment makes it even more critical to establish routine, provide cues for future events, and make symbols for choice available so that the individual can control some aspects of daily living. Even relatively small increments of learning can enable an individual to be perceived more positively by caregivers and to maintain some control over routine activities.

SOCIAL AND ADVOCACY SKILLS

The final element to a satisfactory adult life is the acquisition of skills that allow the student both to act and interact with ease and confidence. Not only must a young adult with a visual impairment develop general social skills that may not be learned incidentally, but the individual also must learn to manage the specialized social decisions that result from a visual impairment; these disability-specific skills may include understanding the sighted world's reaction to an individual with a visual impairment and using devices or materials that enhance visual efficiency or travel skills (Corn, 1989b). The individual with a visual impairment must be comfortable in responding to strangers who are oversolicitous or who offer too much help, as well as in dealing with aspects of a visual impairment that are unfamiliar to others.

Another necessary skill is the ability to advocate effectively to fulfill one's needs in the larger community. A young adult with a visual impairment must be assertive in interacting with others and in stating needs. R. Harrell and Strauss (1980) described techniques for a person who is visually impaired to apply in entering conversations, making requests for services or assistance, and handling anger in an interaction.

Along with the assertiveness to advocate for oneself, an individual must have the skills to acquire information necessary for self-advocacy. This includes knowledge of the organizations and agencies that provide services or information, as well as the ability to use the telephone and library to locate information about important resources. To be a self-advocate, one needs an understanding of governmental agency support that is available for those with visual impairments; many states have a service unit for individuals who are blind and visually handicapped that provides frequently needed vocational counseling and guidance, home teaching, family support, and other public services.

Of particular importance are the social skills that will enable a young adult to seek a job successfully. Problems posed by the interview process can be overcome by careful planning and practice; specific preparation in such skills as asking appropriate questions and using positive "I" statements can contribute to an individual's effectiveness in a job interview (Howze, 1987). The individual with a visual impairment must decide how and at what point to disclose the fact of a visual impairment in order to emphasize strengths and overcome the initial apprehension of prospective employers.

Many people with visual impairments choose to join an organization of other individuals with visual impairments to share experiences and knowledge about services, gain emotional support, and collaborate on issues of mutual concern. The two largest of these consumer organizations, the American Council of the Blind and the National Federation of the Blind, each publish a newsletter or journal for their members and hold regular meetings and conferences on topics of common interest. They are active in advocacy for the rights of persons who are blind as well as in the initiation of new services, such as radio reading.

For an individual with functional delays or additional disabilities, social skill instruction is critical. The ability to turn toward a speaker, to use voice or sign to indicate desires, or to enter into reciprocal interactions with others creates a social support system and enables that individual to be even more functional.

SUMMARY

The young person with a visual impairment faces new challenges upon leaving the more protected environment of the school setting and entering the adult world. A strong network of support between educational and rehabilitative systems will facilitate movement into adulthood for the young person with a visual impairment. These systems need to establish a collaborative relationship that provides early exposure to career awareness and an educational plan that has as its goal successful employment in a chosen field. With a solid foundation in career awareness and experience, support from transitional service systems, and appropriate preparation in life skills and social skills, there is no reason why each young person should not have a satisfying life that includes a variety of choices and opportunities. Professionals have an obligation to ensure that school experiences are planned to provide a clear pathway to the future.

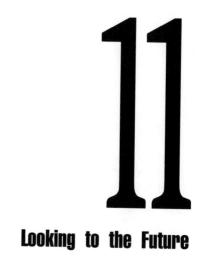

Looking to the Future

What is actually known about learning and behavior in children and youth with visual impairments remains a controversial issue among psychologists, medical and optical specialists, and educators. The hope of reaching agreement is an illusion that often inhibits understanding of the present and clouds visions of the future. However, this should neither deter attempts to identify issues that are of paramount importance at the present time nor minimize efforts to anticipate topics that, inevitably, will need attention early in the next century.

Previous chapters presented facts about present knowledge and practices; however, not all the information available is being utilized fully, and numerous unresolved issues remain. Some concerns that have not yet achieved consensus among professionals and/or parents may be summarized under the following general topics: low vision, braille literacy, early intervention, multiple disabilities, orientation and mobility, and placement and service delivery. As indicated in the following subsections, critical questions being asked in each of these areas may call attention to the need for resolution of controversy, despite the empirical and research evidence.

Low Vision

- When there is indecision about whether children with low vision should use print or braille materials, is it appropriate to think in terms of either/

or? Could it be that the selection of a medium takes precedence over exploring the most efficient means for the child to learn as much as possible by acquiring available information through a variety of media depending on the environmental conditions?

- Why do many professionals recommend large print, when a multitude of research evidence indicates that most learners with low vision can read as comfortably and efficiently by using regular print with or without magnification?

- Are teachers and/or parents being fair to children with severe low vision by insisting only on print (even when closed circuit television is required) and depriving them of learning braille as either a primary or a supplementary medium?

- Conversely, why do some professionals and/or parents require many students with moderate low vision to learn braille when they are just as efficient (if not more so) in print reading? Print materials are far more accessible than braille.

Braille Literacy

- What factors have contributed to the concern about braille literacy? Has the widespread mainstreaming concept deprived some children with visual handicaps of the specialized services necessary to acquiring basic learning skills?

- Should regular class teachers who have braille-reading children in their classrooms be required to learn the braille code? Or should educational regulations mandate that all children who need braille have a specially trained teacher available to them on a regular basis?

Early Intervention

- Is legislation (federal or state) needed to *mandate* services to all children with visual impairments from birth as an extension or supplement to PL 99-457, which only provides the *option* from birth to 3 years? Some states are serving children from 3 to 5 years, and are giving no consideration to providing services from birth. Evidence accumulating from neonatal nurseries using evoked response techniques, along with studies of children with visual impairment in the first 2 years of life, validate the effectiveness of early intervention in preventing many lags in the various dimensions of development.

- What types of early intervention need to be available, and which professionals should be responsible for the intervention—education, medicine, health, or possibly a combination of all of these disciplines? What can be expected of parents (or other caregivers), especially when the number of working mothers and single parents continues to increase? Can intervention services be a part of day care centers that serve children with impairments? Can the public be convinced of the cost-effectiveness of such programs and provide public monies?

Multiple Disabilities

- Who should be involved in the identification and diagnosis of children with multiple disabilities? Should one condition (mental retardation, visual impairment, cerebral palsy, deafness, etc.) take precedence over others as primary, and other conditions be ignored in terms of reporting and provision of services?

- Are there legal and moral issues that are influencing decisions about children with multiple impairments? Are children being labeled prematurely in order to secure services? Should all children be maintained for long years on life support systems simply because the technology is available? Whether to sustain life of some damaged infants is becoming a decision of the courts, often against the wishes of the parents. Has the medical community made any strides in coming to terms with the ethical issues surrounding infants severely damaged at birth?

- Should there be some guidelines for the appropriate use of residential schools and public schools where children with multiple disabilities are involved? Who makes the decisions? Are the decisions based on best care and education of the children, or on what is least expensive or administratively expedient?

Orientation and Mobility

- With what children at various ages can electronic travel devices be useful?

- Are there identifiable personal characteristics that can be associated with success in the use of particular devices?

- Are electronic devices, in fact, useful enough to warrant the time, expense, and effort required to learn to use them efficiently?

- At what age should children learn to use a cane for travel? Are there individual characteristics that override the age issue?

- Should persons with visual impairments be certified as mobility instructors, and can they teach outdoor travel safely?

Many more related issues have been discussed by Hill and Jacobson (1985), but not all can be addressed in this overview.

Placement and Service Delivery

- What process determines the appropriate placement and the nature of the services to be delivered to children with visual impairments? Are specially trained persons involved in the decisions and the development of IEPs?

- Are some children being deprived of needed skills because the school administration does not make the effort to find the trained specialists or refuses to expend the funds to secure them?

- Is placement in a regular classroom (least restrictive environment) taking precedence over the most appropriate setting for some children with visual impairments? How can these two concepts be considered equally in the best interests of children?

Many more questions could be raised, each of which might seem more important in some local areas and less important in others. The preceding questions are being debated in the literature and in professional meetings, but as yet have not received universal consensus, although empirical evidence is available to assist in resolution in the very near future.

Unfortunately, only a few institutions of higher education have professors engaged regularly in research that can be applied to improvement in classroom instruction. Even fewer researchers are investigating basic human attributes that influence learning and functional behavior. Valuable contributions have been made by these sources, but much more needs to be done.

The American Printing House for the Blind maintains a research division that studies the usefulness of certain academic and tangible materials and methods of instruction as a precursor to the issuance of educational materials. Other research activities are conducted by private nonprofit and for profit agencies, relating primarily to devices and equipment that can be marketed to individuals, schools, and agencies with the funds to purchase them.

FORCES OF THE FUTURE

The 21st century is upon us! Are we ready to accept the challenges and understand the realities that indicate a very different world? Huebner (1989) has addressed some of the forces that will be shaping the educational needs and intervention indicated in response to the social changes occurring. The survival rate of high risk births is likely to increase significantly the numbers of children with visual impairments. The decrease of persons choosing teaching as a career is likely to cause an even greater shortage of trained teachers than there is now. One suggestion is that teachers will need to have multiple certifications to better serve children with visual impairments, most of whom are being placed in regular school settings. In discussing the future of low incidence training programs, Head (1989) introduced the idea of a national network of university training programs, a thought to be considered seriously.

In June 1989, a symposium entitled Through the Looking Glass was held at The University of Texas at Austin. Participants examined the next 25 years in terms of four major issues: education, families, learning environments, and technology. Speakers suggested some of the variables professionals in the future need to consider when "charting the course" for the next century. In his presentation, Bina (1989) reminded us that "We often set a lofty goal in our field and start traveling before we plan our trip." Without careful planning, we may become frustrated and waste time and money. He emphasized that we need to work smarter by achieving political know-how and management skill, in order to collaborate with professionals in other fields and understand their literature so as to apply the principles to education. Bina also stressed the need to be more assertive and to be positive agitators so as to challenge rather than succumb to the tough problems. He called for teachers to educate the medical community; begin transitional services much earlier; consider regional centers for training and service delivery; and work toward a national program of evaluation, accreditation, and accountability.

In looking at families in the future, Stotland (1989) projected that the sociological makeup of families would be dramatically different: younger, poorer, and of numerous "minority" cultures. The medical trend suggests that there will be increasing numbers of children with multiple impairments, in addition to those born to drug-using mothers. These predictions, if they come true, may require changes in the entire field of visual handicaps, from early intervention and service delivery to teacher preparation and adult care facilities.

Additional issues were addressed by Spungin (1989) in her discussion of environments. The struggle for generational equality, greater emphasis on employment skills, and a longer school year of at least 11 months, are likely to alter the entire school environment in terms of learning settings, curricula, and academic emphasis. More bilingual teachers will be needed, and all teachers will be required to have sophisticated knowledge of devices and software systems, and to have the skills to be case managers in cooperation with the parents.

According to Loshin (1989), the future in sophisticated technology for use by human beings is likely to have tremendous impact, particularly on persons with low vision. He indicated that a new generation of electro-optics is already beginning, and may result in much improved optical devices, such as head-borne miniature television cameras to expand a visual image on the retina or to completely remap the visual image to counter the person's type of impairment.

As a part of the symposium, and in a following survey, a futures research project was conducted by The University of Texas at Austin using a force-field analysis technique. The plan for such an approach utilized a three-part questionnaire. The first part identified 25 events or issues to be studied, and determined the likelihood of their occurrence and the degree of impact. The second part took the seven issues or events of highest likelihood and impact and determined the desirability or undesirability of these events in relation to the impeding or facilitating forces, and finally matched the force weight with desirability or undesirability of each. The third part used five event statements with weak forces not likely to bring about desired outcomes, identified strategies to modify strength or weakness of the forces, and specified how these could be implemented so as to control the outcome of events (Bishop, 1990).

A pool of 547 potential respondents was chosen from active medical/educational/rehabilitation professionals/parents in the field of visual handicaps throughout the United States and internationally. Only five major statements of predicted future events remained after the first two rounds had been completed:

1. An increased understanding of brain and neurological functioning as it related to sight and seeing has resulted in improved methods of teaching those with visual impairment.

2. Due to increased litigation and bureaucratic constraint, teachers have less contact with families during the educational program planning process.

3. Child care and early intervention programs for children with visual impairments are required to have specially certified teachers.

4. Disability labels no longer exist relative to education; therefore, individualized assessment of specific disabilities is no longer required.

5. State schools and other institutions exclusively for persons with visual impairments serve only the most severely involved children with multiple disabilities.

In the final analyses, the first statement (neurological) elicited highly positive forces, and numerous strategies were suggested, such as increased cooperation between medicine and education, and the need for research findings to be incorporated into teacher preparation and in-service training courses and activities. The second statement (family contact) showed strong positive forces, with emphasis on better communication with parents and more effective resolution of conflicts among professionals as a means of counteracting the possibility of less contact with families. Early intervention services to young children with visual impairments by certified teachers of visually handicapped was the third statement. Although considered to be an event of high likelihood and positive force, much work is needed to inform the general public and regular educational personnel (including early childhood specialists) of the devastating effects of severe visual impairment on the early developmental years; additionally, a strong need to teach parents how to advocate effectively and to use their power with a collective voice was expressed.

The fourth statement (elimination of disability labels) was projected to be a highly positive force, but numerous strategies must be implemented to achieve the desired result. The major factors influencing such elimination related to the trend for a generic philosophy and services, assessment approaches and tools, and a continuing shortage of teachers with the specialized skills needed to serve children with severe visual impairments. The final statement, regarding the role of the residential school in the future, proved to be the most controversial projected event with great negative force. Strategies to stop the event from occurring included the need for modification of the residential school, clarification of the concerns with mainstreaming, assignment of children to the least restrictive environment, and determination of the most appropriate placement.

Two surprising issues were not included in the final future considerations: low vision and technology. Bishop (1990) speculated that respondents might have thought it impossible to project the future in technology and thus avoided the issue entirely. Possibly, those who participated thought (erroneously) that the issues relating to low vision were no longer of major importance, having been addressed successfully in recent years. Generally, the final five topics seemed to reflect fears of diminishing control and lack of identity as a specialized field in need of continuing research and creative strategy planning.

DREAMS OF THE FUTURE

In the final presentation at the symposium, Barraga (1989) painted a much broader picture of possible dreams to be realized in the 21st century. She emphasized the need to expand communication linkages with colleagues locally, nationally, and internationally as machines and telecommunications continue to become more sophisticated; exchange research and literature with professionals in related disciplines so that the best of all knowledge can be applied to persons with visual impairment; learn, share, and participate in exchange programs with teachers around the world so as to experience a variety of cultural and political settings; and find ways to determine how to ensure that children with multiple impairments develop and use all their capacities to promote the highest possible quality of life.

THE CHALLENGE

Based on presentations at the symposium and findings of the futures project, it is evident that new discoveries about the development and learning of children with visual handicaps will be influencing programs and services far into the next century. Unfortunately, educational practices do not always keep abreast with and utilize all available knowledge. Some teachers who do not attend in-service sessions or workshops on critical topics or read professional literature may not have ready access to new ideas or, without help and encouragement, may have difficulty translating them into practice. More probably, the lag in putting new knowledge into practice arises from a reluctance to question traditional attitudes and methods (complacency) or from a lack of courage to take the risks implied in making dynamic and innovative changes. Even though there continues to be a shortage of specially trained teachers for children and youth with visual impairments, those entering the profession in the next century are likely to be bright and capable, acquainted with new information about the learning and functioning potential of human beings, and qualified to provide the leadership needed to move beyond the traditional strategies to those more appropriate for the future. Lowenfeld (1990), in giving a charge to beginning teachers, said,

> Learn as much as you can from the experience of others; and if you incorporate that with your own ideas and inclinations you cannot only apply the knowledge that is generally available, but you can also bring to your own profession the freshness of your own individual approach. (p. 149)

The children and youth in our educational programs deserve educational services appropriate to their present level of functioning and designed to help them move, step by step, up the ladder of independence to a life of freedom and dignity. Parents and teachers, LET'S DO IT!

References

Abel, G. L. (1959). Problems and trends in the education of blind children and youth. In G. L. Abel (Ed.), *Concerning the education of blind children* (pp. 79–81). New York: American Foundation for the Blind.

Anater, P. F. (1980). Effect of auditory interference on memory of haptic perceptions. *Journal of Visual Impairment and Blindness, 74,* 305–309.

Anderson, D. W. (1984). Mental imagery in congenitally blind children. *Journal of Visual Impairment and Blindness, 78,* 206–210.

Anderson, D. W., & Fisher, K. P. (1986). Nominal realism in congenitally blind children. *Journal of Visual Impairment and Blindness, 80,* 896–900.

Arnheim, R. (1969). *Visual thinking.* London: Faber & Faber.

Ashcroft, S., Halliday, C., & Barraga, N. (1965). *Study II: Effects of experimental teaching on the visual behavior of children educated as though they had no vision.* Nashville, TN: George Peabody College for Teachers.

Ashcroft, S. C., & Zambone-Ashley, A. M. (1980). Mainstreaming children with visual impairments. *Journal of Research & Development in Education, 13,* 22–36.

Ayres, A. J. (1981). *Sensory integration and the child.* Los Angeles: Western Psychological Service.

Bagley, M. (1985). Service providers assessment of the career development needs of blind and visually impaired students and rehabilitation clients and resources available to meet those needs. *Journal of Visual Impairment and Blindness, 79,* 434–443.

Baird, A. S. (1977). Electronic aids: Can they help blind children? *Journal of Visual Impairment and Blindness, 71,* 97–101.

Barraga, N. (1964). *Increased visual behavior in low vision children.* New York: American Foundation for the Blind.

Barraga, N. C. (Ed.). (1970). *Visual Efficiency Scale.* Louisville, KY: American Printing House for the Blind.

Barraga, N. C. (1973). Utilization of sensory–perceptual abilities. In B. Lowenfeld (Ed.), *The visually handicapped child in school* (pp. 118–154). New York: John Day.

Barraga, N. C. (Ed.). (1980a). *Program to develop efficiency in visual functioning: Design for instruction.* Louisville, KY: American Printing House for the Blind.

Barraga, N. C. (Ed.). (1980b). *Program to develop efficiency in visual functioning: Diagnostic Assessment Procedure (DAP).* Louisville, KY: American Printing House for the Blind.

Barraga, N. C. (Ed.). (1980c). *Source book on low vision.* Louisville, KY: American Printing House for the Blind.

Barraga, N. C. (1983). *Visual handicaps and learning* (2nd ed.). Austin, TX: PRO-ED.

Barraga, N. C. (1986). Sensory perceptual development. In G. T. Scholl (Ed.), *Foundations of education for blind and visually handicapped children and youth: Theory and practice* (pp. 83–98). New York: American Foundation for the Blind.

Barraga, N. C. (1989, June). Dreams of the future. In A. L. Corn (Chair), *Through the looking glass.* Symposium conducted at The University of Texas at Austin.

Barraga, N. C., Collins, M., & Hollis, J. (1977). Development of efficiency in visual functioning: A literature analysis. *Journal of Visual Impairment and Blindness, 71,* 387–391.

Barraga, N. C., & Collins, M. E. (1979). Development of efficiency in visual functioning: Rationale for a comprehensive program. *Journal of Visual Impairment and Blindness, 73,* 121–126.

Barraga, N. C., Dorward, B., & Ford, P. (1973). *Aids for teaching basic concepts of sensory development.* Louisville, KY: American Printing House for the Blind.

Barraga, N. C., & Morris, J. (1980). *Program to develop efficiency in visual functioning.* Louisville, KY: American Printing House for the Blind.

Barth, J. (1982). The development and evaluation of a tactile graphics kit. *Journal of Visual Impairment and Blindness, 76,* 269–273.

Bateman, B. (1965). Psychological evaluation of blind children. *The New Outlook for the Blind, 59,* 193–197.

Bateman, B., & Weatherall, J. L. (1967). Some educational characteristics of partially seeing children. *International Journal for the Education of the Blind, 17,* 33–40.

Bayley, N. (1969). *Bayley Scales of Infant Development.* San Antonio, TX: Psychological Corp.

Behar, M. P., & Zucker, D. R. (1976). Sensory awareness exercises for the visually handicapped. *The New Outlook for the Blind, 70,* 146–148.

Bell, J. (1986). An approach to the stimulation of vision in the profoundly handicapped, visually handicapped child. *British Journal of Visual Impairment, 4,* 46–48.

Bentzen, B. L., & Peck, A. F. (1979). Factors affecting traceability of lines for tactile graphics. *Journal of Visual Impairment and Blindness, 73,* 264–269.

Berla, E. P., Rankin, E. F., & Willis, D. H. (1980). Psychometric evaluation of the low vision Diagnostic Assessment Procedure. *Journal of Visual Impairment and Blindness, 75,* 297–301.

Bina, M. (1982). Morale of teachers of the visually handicapped: Implications for administrators. *Journal of Visual Impairment and Blindness, 76,* 121–128.

Bina, M. J. (1989, June). Futures in education of visually impaired children. In A. L. Corn (Chair), *Through the Looking Glass.* Symposium conducted at The University of Texas at Austin.

Birch, J., Tisdall, W., Peabody, R., & Sterrett, R. (1966). *School achievement and effect of type size on reading in visually handicapped children* (Cooperative research project No. 1766, U.S. Office of Education). Pittsburgh: University of Pittsburgh Press.

Birns, S. L. (1986). Age at onset of blindness and development of space concepts: From topological to projective space. *Journal of Visual Impairment and Blindness, 80,* 577–582.

Bishop, V. E. (1986). Identifying the components of success in mainstreaming. *Journal of Visual Impairment and Blindness, 80,* 939–945.

Bishop, V. E. (1990). *Futures in low vision research project.* Unpublished report, Department of Special Education, The University of Texas at Austin.

Blackhurst, A. E., & Berdine, W. H. (1985). *Introduction to special education.* Boston: Houghton-Mifflin.

Bliss, J. C., & Moore, M. (1974). The Optacon reading system. *Education of the Visually Handicapped, 6,* 98–102.

Boehm, A. E. (1971). *Boehm Test of Basic Concepts: Test manual.* San Antonio, TX: Psychological Corp.

Boldt, W. (1969). The development of scientific thinking in blind children and adolescents. *Education of the Visually Handicapped, 1,* 5–11.

Bower, T. G. (1977). Blind babies see with their ears. *New Scientist, 73,* 255–257.

Bradley-Johnson, S. (1986). *Psychoeducational assessment of visually impaired and blind students: Infancy through high school.* Austin, TX: PRO-ED.

Braley, A. E. (1962). The problem of definition of blindness. *Proceedings of the 36th Convention of the American Association of Workers for the Blind.*

Brigance, A. H. (1978). *Inventory of Early Development.* North Billerica, MA: Curriculum Associates.

Brigance, A. H. (1981). *Brigance Diagnostic Inventory of Essential Skills.* North Billerica, MA: Curriculum Associates.

Brigance, A. H. (1983). *Brigance Diagnostic Comprehensive Inventory of Basic Skills.* North Billerica, MA: Curriculum Associates.

Brothers, R. J. (1972). Arithmetic computation by the blind: A look at current achievements. *Education of the Visually Handicapped, 4,* 1–8.

Brown, D., Simmons, V., & Methvin, J. (1978). *The Oregon project for visually impaired and blind preschool children* (rev. ed.). Medford, OR: Jackson Education Service District.

Bruner, J. S. (1966). *Toward a theory of instruction.* New York: Norton.

Buktenica, N. A. (1968). *Visual learning.* San Raphael, CA: Dimension.

Bullard, B., & Barraga, N. C. (1971). Subtests of evaluative instruments applicable for use with preschool visually handicapped children. *Education of the Visually Handicapped, 3,* 116–122.

Bush-LaFrance, B. (1988). Unseen expectations of blind youth: Educational and occupational ideas. *Journal of Visual Impairment and Blindness, 82,* 132–136.

Campbell, P. (1987). The integrated program team: An approach for coordinating professionals of various disciplines in programs for students with severe and multiple handicaps. *Journal of the Association for Persons with Severe Handicaps, 12,* 107–116.

Cartwright, G. P., Cartwright, C. A., & Ward, M. E. (1989). *Educating exceptional learners* (3rd ed.). Belmont, CA: Wadsworth.

Caton, H. (1977). The development and evaluation of a tactile analog to the Boehm Test of Basic Concepts. *Journal of Visual Impairment and Blindness, 71,* 382–386.

Caton, H. R. (1980). *The Tactile Test of Basic Concepts.* Louisville, KY: American Printing House for the Blind.

Caton, H., Bradley, E. J., & Pester, E. (Eds.). (1982). *Patterns: The primary braille reading program*. Louisville, KY: American Printing House for the Blind.

Chandler, J. (1986). An introduction to voice indexing. *Education of the Visually Handicapped, 17*, 154–156.

Chase, J. B. (1972). Evaluation of blind and severely visually impaired persons. In M. D. Graham (Ed.), *Science and blindness: Retrospective and prospective* (pp. 53–58). New York: American Foundation for the Blind.

Chase, J. B. (1975). Developmental assessment of handicapped infants and young children: With special attention to the visually impaired. *The New Outlook for the Blind, 69*, 341–349, 364.

Chase, J. B. (1986a). Application of assessment techniques to the totally blind. In P. J. Lazarus & S. S. Strichart (Eds.), *Psychoeducational evaluation of children and adolescents with low-incidence handicaps* (pp. 75–102). New York: Grune & Stratton.

Chase, J. B. (1986b). Psychoeducational assessment of visually impaired learners. In P. J. Lazarus & S. S. Strichart (Eds.), *Psychoeducational evaluation of children and adolescents with low-incidence handicaps* (pp. 41–74). New York: Grune & Stratton.

Cobb, E. S. (1977). Learning through listening: A new approach. *Journal of Visual Impairment and Blindness, 71*, 302–308.

Cohen, S. E., & Beckwith, L. (1979). Preterm infant interaction with the caregiver in the first year of life and competence at age two. *Child Development, 50*, 767–776.

Coleman, C. L., & Weinstock, R. E. (1984). Physically handicapped blind people: Adaptive mobility techniques. *Journal of Visual Impairment and Blindness, 78*, 113–117.

Colenbrander, A. (1977). Dimensions of visual performance. *Archives of American Academy of Ophthalmology, 83*, 335.

Collins, M. E., & Barraga, N. C. (1980). Development of efficiency in visual functioning: An evaluation process. *Journal of Visual Impairment and Blindness, 74*, 93–96.

Cook-Clampert, D. (1981). The development of self concept in blind children. *Journal of Visual Impairment and Blindness, 71*, 233–238.

Corn, A. (1980). *Development and assessment of an in-service training program for teachers of the visually handicapped: Optical aids in the classroom*. Unpublished doctoral dissertation, Teachers College, Columbia University, New York.

Corn, A. (1983). Visual function: A theoretical model for individuals with low vision. *Journal of Visual Impairment and Blindness, 77*, 373–377.

Corn, A. (1985a). An independence matrix for visually handicapped learners. *Education of the Visually Handicapped, 17*, 3–10.

Corn, A. L. (1985b). Strategies for the enhancement of visual function in individuals with fixed visual deficits: An interdisciplinary model. *Rehabilitation Literature, 46*, 8–11.

Corn, A. (1989a). Employing critical thinking strategies within a curriculum of critical things to think about for blind and visually impaired students. *Journal of Vision Rehabilitation, 3*, 17–36.

Corn, A. L. (1989b). Instruction in the use of vision for children and adults with low vision: A proposed program model. *RE:view, 21*, 26–38.

Corn, A. L., & Bishop, V. E. (1984). Acquisition of practical knowledge by blind and visually impaired students in grades 9–12. *Journal of Visual Impairment and Blindness, 78,* 552–556.

Corn, A. L., & Bishop, V. E. (1985). Occupational interests of visually handicapped secondary students. *Journal of Visual Impairment and Blindness, 79,* 475–478.

Corn, A., & Ryser, G. (1989). Access to print by students with low vision. *Journal of Visual Impairment and Blindness, 83,* 340–349.

Craft, D. H. (1986). In K. Huebner (Ed.), Curricular Adaptations. In G. Scholl (Ed.), *Foundations of education for blind and visually handicapped children and youth: Theory and practice* (pp. 395–403). New York: American Foundation for the Blind.

Cratty, B. J. (1971). *Movement and spatial awareness in blind children and youth.* Springfield, IL: Charles C. Thomas.

Cratty, B. J., & Sams, T. (1968). *Body image of blind children.* New York: American Foundation for the Blind.

Cress, P. J., Spellman, C. R., DeBriere, T. J., Sizemore, A. C., Northam, J. K., & Johnson, J. L. (1981). Vision screening for persons with severe handicaps. *TASH Journal, 6,* 41–50.

Curry, S. A., & Hatlen, P. H. (1988). Meeting the unique educational needs of visually impaired pupils through appropriate placement. *Journal of Visual Impairment and Blindness, 82,* 417–424.

Davidson, F. W. K., & Simmons, J. N. (1984). Mediating the environment for young blind children: A conceptualization. *Journal of Visual Impairment and Blindness, 78,* 251–255.

Davis, J. E., & Hawke, S. (Project directors). (1978). *Materials adaptation for visually impaired students in social studies (MAVIS).* Boulder, CO: Social Science Education Consortium.

Dekker, R., Drenth, P. J. D., Zaal, J. N., & Koole, F. D. (1990). An intelligence test series for blind and low vision children. *Journal of Visual Impairment and Blindness, 84,* 71–76.

Del Frari, P. (1978). Meeting the O & M needs of the multiply handicapped blind individual. *Journal of Visual Impairment and Blindness, 72,* 324–325.

DeLucchi, L., & Malone, L. (1982). SAVI (Science Activities for the Visually Impaired). In S. Mangold (Ed.), *A teacher's guide to the educational needs of blind and visually handicapped children* (pp. 72–93). New York: American Foundation for the Blind.

DePauw, K. (1981). Physical education for the visually impaired: Review of the literature. *Journal of Visual Impairment and Blindness, 75,* 162–164.

DeWitt, J., Schreier, E., & Leventhal, J. (1988). A look at closed circuit television systems (CCTV) for persons with low vision. *Journal of Visual Impairment and Blindness, 82,* 151–160.

Dickman, I. (1975). *Sex education and family life for visually handicapped children and youth: A resource guide.* New York: American Foundation for the Blind.

Dodds, A. G. (1983). Mental rotation and visual imagery. *Journal of Visual Impairment and Blindness, 77,* 16–18.

Dodds, A. G., & Davis, D. P. (1989). Assessment and training of low vision clients for mobility. *Journal of Visual Impairment and Blindness, 83,* 439–446.

Dodds, A. G., Howarth, C. E., & Carter, D. C. (1982). The mental maps of the blind: The role of previous visual experience. *Journal of Visual Impairment and Blindness, 77,* 5–12.

Downing, J., & Bailey, B. (1990). Developing vision use within functional daily activities for students with visual and multiple disabilities. *RE:view, 21,* 209–220.

DuBose, R. F., & Langley, M. B. (1977). *Developmental Activities Screening Inventory.* Boston: Teaching Resources.

Duehl, A. N. (1979). The effect of creative dance movement on large muscle control and balance in congenitally blind children. *Journal of Visual Impairment and Blindness, 73,* 127–133.

Dunn, L. M. (1965). *Peabody Picture Vocabulary Test.* Circle Pines, MN: American Guidance Service.

Eakin, W., Pratt, R., & McFarland, F. (1961). *Type-size research for the partially seeing child.* Pittsburgh: Stanwix House.

Easton, R. D., & Bentzen, B. L. (1980). Perception of tactile route configurations by blind and sighted observers. *Journal of Visual Impairment and Blindness, 74,* 254–265.

Eichel, V. J. (1979). A taxonomy for mannerisms of blind children. *Journal of Visual Impairment and Blindness, 73,* 167–178.

Ely, R. (1989). Writing, computers, and visual impairment. *Journal of Visual Impairment and Blindness, 83,* 248–252.

Erhardt, R. P. (1987). Visual function in the student with multiple handicaps: An integrative transdisciplinary model for assessment and intervention. *Education of the Visually Handicapped, 19,* 87–98.

Erin, J. N. (1988). The teacher–consultant. *Education of the Visually Handicapped, 20,* 57–63.

Erin, J., Daugherty, W., Dignan, K., & Pearson, N. (1990). Teachers of visually handicapped students with multiple disabilities: Perceptions of adequacy. *Journal of Visual Impairment and Blindness, 84,* 16–20.

Faye, E. E. (1970). *The low vision patient.* New York: Grune & Stratton.

Faye, E. E. (Ed.). (1984). *Clinical low vision* (2nd ed.). Boston: Little, Brown.

Felix, L., & Spungin, S. J. (1978). Preschool services for the visually handicapped: A national survey. *Journal of Visual Impairment and Blindness, 72,* 59–66.

Ferrell, K. A. (1980a). Can infants use the sonicguide? Two years experience of Project VIEW. *Journal of Visual Impairment and Blindness, 74,* 209–220.

Ferrell, K. A. (1980b). Orientation and mobility for preschool children: What we have and what we need. *Journal of Visual Impairment and Blindness, 72,* 59–66.

Ferrell, K. A. (1984). A second look at sensory aids in early childhood. *Education of the Visually Handicapped, 16,* 83–101.

Ferrell, K. (1985). *Reach out and teach: Meeting the needs of parents of visually and multiply handicapped young children.* New York: American Foundation for the Blind.

Ferrell, K. (1987). State of the art of infant and preschool services in 1986. *Yearbook of the Association for Education and Rehabilitation of the Blind and Visually Impaired, 4,* 22–32.

Fieandt, K. (1966). *The world of perception.* Homewood, IL: Dorsey Press.

Field, T. M., Goldberg, S., Stern, D., & Sostek, A. M. (Eds.). (1980). *High-risk infants and children: Adults and peer interactions.* New York: Academic Press.

Fletcher, J. G. (1981a). Spatial representation in blind children: Effect of task variations. *Journal of Visual Impairment and Blindness, 75,* 1–3.

Fletcher, J. F. (1981b). Spatial representation in blind children: Effects of individual differences. *Journal of Visual Impairment and Blindness, 75,* 46–49.

Fonda, G. (1961). Definition and classification of blindness with respect to ability to use residual vision. *The New Outlook for the Blind, 55.*

Fonda, G. (1966). An evaluation of large type. *The New Outlook for the Blind, 60,* 296–298.

Foulke, E. (1968). Non-visual communication. *International Journal for the Education of the Blind, 18,* 77–78.

Foulke, E. (1981). Impact of science and technology on the early years. *Journal of Visual Impairment and Blindness, 75,* 101–108.

Foulke, E., Hollyfield, R., & Nolan, C. (1977). Index codes for tape recorded tests. *Journal of Visual Impairment and Blindness, 71,* 219–224.

Fraiberg, S. (1977). *Insights from the blind: Comparative studies of blind and sighted infants.* New York: Basic Books.

Fraiberg, S., Smith, M., & Adelson, E. (1969). An educational program for blind infants. *Journal of Special Education, 3,* 121–139.

Furth, H. G. (1969). *Piaget and knowledge.* Englewood Cliffs, NJ: Prentice-Hall.

Gallagher, W. (1988). Categorical services in the age of integration: Paradox or contradiction? *Journal of Visual Impairment and Blindness, 82,* 226–229.

Gardner, L. (1982). Understanding and helping parents of blind children. *Journal of Visual Impairment and Blindness, 76,* 81–85.

Gates, C. (1985). Survey of multiply handicapped, visually impaired children in the Rocky Mountain/Great Plains region. *Journal of Visual Impairment and Blindness, 79,* 385–391.

Gearheart, B. R., & Weishahn, M. W. (1984). *The exceptional student in the regular classroom.* St. Louis: Times Mirror/Mosby.

Gerhardt, J. B. (1982). The development of object play and classificatory skills in a blind child. *Journal of Visual Impairment and Blindness, 76,* 219–223.

Gipsman, S. C. (1981). Effect of visual condition on use of proprioceptive cues in performing a balancing task. *Journal of Visual Impairment and Blindness, 75,* 50–54.

Gleason, D. (1984). Auditory assessment of visually impaired preschoolers: A team effort. *Education of the Visually Handicapped, 16,* 102–113.

Glenshaft, J. L., Dare, N. L., & O'Malley, P. L. (1980). Assessing the visually impaired child: A school psychology view. *Journal of Visual Impairment and Blindness, 74,* 344–349.

Goetz, L., & Gee, S. (1987). Functional vision programming: A model for teaching visual behaviors in natural contexts. In G. Goetz, D. Guess, & K. Stremel–Campbell (Eds.), *Innovative program design for individuals with dual sensory impairments* (pp. 77–98). Baltimore: Brookes.

Goetz, L., Guess, D., & Stremel-Campbell, K. (1987). *Innovative program design for individuals with dual sensory impairments.* Baltimore: Brookes.

Goldish, L. (1968). *Teaching aids for the visually handicapped.* Watertown, MA: Perkins School for the Blind.

Goodrich, G. (1984). Applications of microcomputers by visually impaired persons. *Journal of Visual Impairment and Blindness, 78,* 408–414.

Gore, G. (1969). A comparison of two methods of speeded speech. *Education of the Visually Handicapped, 1,* 69–76.

Gottesman, M. (1976). Stage development in blind children. A Piagetian view. *The New Outlook for the Blind, 70,* 94–100.

Graves, W., & Lyon, S. (1985). Career development: Linking education and careers of blind and visually impaired ninth graders. *Journal of Visual Impairment and Blindness, 79,* 444–449.

Griffin, J. C., & Gerber, P. J. (1982). Tactual development and its implications for the education of blind children. *Education of the Visually Handicapped, 13,* 116–123.

Hackney, P. W. (1986). Education of the visually handicapped gifted: A program description. *Education of the Visually Handicapped, 18,* 85–95.

Hadary, D. (1977). Science and art for visually handicapped children. *Journal of Visual Impairment and Blindness, 71,* 203–209.

Hall, A. (1981). Mental images and the cognitive development of the congenitally blind. *Journal of Visual Impairment and Blindness, 76,* 281–285.

Hall, A. (1983). Methods of equivalence grouping by congenitally blind children: Implications for education. *Journal of Visual Impairment and Blindness, 77,* 172–174.

Hall, A., & Bailey, I. L. (1989). A model of training vision functioning. *Journal of Visual Impairment and Blindness, 83,* 390–403.

Hall, A. P., Kekelis, L. K., & Bailey, I. L. (1986). *Development of an assessment program and intervention guidelines for visually impaired children* (Final report). Sacramento: California State Department of Education.

Hallahan, D. P., & Kauffman, J. M. (1988). *Exceptional children: Introduction to special education* (4th ed.). Englewood Cliffs, NJ: Prentice-Hall.

Hamilton, K. W. (1950). *Counseling the handicapped in the rehabilitation process.* New York: Ronald Publishing.

Hammill, D., & Crandell, J. N. (1969). Implications of tactile–kinesthetic ability in visually handicapped children. *Education of the Visually Handicapped, 1,* 65–69.

Hanninen, K. A. (1976). The influence of preference of texture on the accuracy of tactile discrimination. *Education of the Visually Handicapped, 8,* 44–52.

Hardy, J. (1983). *Cerebral palsy.* Englewoods Cliffs, NJ: Prentice-Hall.

Haring, N. G., & McCormick, L. (1986). *Exceptional children and youth* (4th ed.). Columbus, OH: Charles Merrill.

Harley, R. K., DuBose, R. F., & Bourgeault, S. E. (1980). *Peabody Model Vision Project.* Chicago: Stoelting.

Harley, R. K., & English, W. H. (1989). Support services for visually impaired children in local day schools: Residential schools as a resource. *Journal of Visual Impairment and Blindness, 83,* 403–406.

Harley, R. K., Henderson, F. M., & Truan, M. B. (1979). *The teaching of braille reading.* Springfield, IL: Charles C. Thomas.

Harley, R., Truan, M., & Sanford, L. (1987). *Communication skills for visually impaired learners.* Springfield, IL: Charles C. Thomas.

Harley, R. K., Wood, T. A., & Merbler, J. B. (1980). *Peabody mobility kits.* Chicago: Stoelting.

Harley, R. K., Wood, T. A., & Merbler, J. B. (1981). *Peabody Mobility Scales.* Chicago: Stoelting.

Harrell, L., & Akeson, N. (1987). *Preschool vision stimulation: It's more than a flashlight.* New York: American Foundation for the Blind.

Harrell, R. L., & Curry, S. A. (1987). Services to blind and visually impaired children and adults: Who is responsible? *Journal of Visual Impairment and Blindness, 81,* 368–376.

Harrell, R., & Strauss, F. (1980). Approaches to increasing assertive behavior and communication skills in blind and visually impaired persons. *Journal of Visual Impairment and Blindness, 74,* 794–798.

Harris, D. B. (1963). *A revision and extension of the Goodenough Draw-a-Man Test.* New York: Harcourt, Brace & World.

Harris, L., Humphrey, G. K., Muir, D. M., & Dodwell, P. C. (1985). Use of the Canterbury child's aid in infancy and early childhood: A case study. *Journal of Visual Impairment and Blindness, 79,* 4–11.

Hatlen, P. (1990). Meeting the unique needs of pupils with visual impairments. *RE:view, 22,* 79–82.

Hazekamp, J., & Huebner, K. M. (1989). *Program planning and evaluation for visually impaired students: National guidelines for educational excellence.* New York: American Foundation for the Blind.

Head, D. N. (1989). The future of low incidence training programs: A national problem. *RE:view, 21,* 145–152.

Hebb, D. O. (1949). *The organization of behavior.* New York: John Wiley.

Heersema, D. J., & Hof-Van Duin, J. V. (1990). Age norms for visual acuity in toddlers using the acuity card procedure. *Clinical Vision Sciences, 5,* 167–173.

Heiden, J. (1989). A ten-year follow-up study of former students of the Wisconsin School for the Visually Handicapped. *RE:view, 21,* 81–87.

Heinze, T. (1986). Communication skills. In G. Scholl (Ed.), *Foundations of education for blind and visually handicapped children and youth: Theory and practice* (pp. 301–314). New York: American Foundation for the Blind.

Held, R., & Hein, A. (1963). Movement-produced stimulation in the development of visually guided behavior. *Journal of Comparative and Physiological Psychology, 56,* 872.

Heller, M. A. (1985). Tactual perception of embossed Morse Code and braille: The alliance of vision and touch. *Perception, 14,* 563–570.

Heller, M. A. (1989). Picture and pattern perception in the sighted and the blind: The advantage of the late blind. *Perception, 18,* 379–389.

Henderson, F. (1973). Communication skills. In B. Lowenfeld (Ed.), *The visually handicapped child in school* (pp. 185–219). New York: John Day.

Hieronymus, A. N., Hoover, H. D., & Lindquist, E. F. (1986). *Iowa Test of Basic Skills.* Chicago: Riverside.

Higgins, L. C. (1973). *Classification in congenitally blind children.* New York: American Foundation for the Blind.

Hill, E. W., Dodson-Burk, B., & Smith, B. A. (1989). Orientation and mobility for infants who are visually impaired. *RE:view, 21,* 47–60.

Hill, E., & Hill, H. M. (1980a). *Hill Performance Test of Selected Positional Concepts.* Chicago: Stoelting.

Hill, E., & Hill, H. M. (1980b). Revision and validation of a test for assessing the spatial conceptual abilities of visually impaired children. *Journal of Visual Impairment and Blindness, 74,* 373–380.

Hill, E. W., & Jacobson, W. H. (1985). Controversial issues in orientation and mobility: Then and now. *Education of the Visually Handicapped, 17,* 59–70.

Hill, E. W., Rosen, S., Correa, V. E., & Langley, M. B. (1984). Preschool orientation and mobility: An expanded definition. *Education of the Visually Handicapped, 16,* 58–72.

Hoben, M., & Lindstrom, V. (1980). Evidence of isolation in the mainstream. *Journal of Visual Impairment and Blindness, 74,* 289–292.

Hoover, R. E. (1962). Visual efficiency as a criterion of service needs. *Proceedings of the 36th Convention of the American Association of Workers for the Blind,* pp. 162–164.

Houser, L., Moses, E., & Kay, J. (1987). A family orientation to transition. *Education of the Visually Handicapped, 19,* 109–119.

Howze, Y. (1987). The use of social skills training to improve interview skills of visually impaired young adults: A pilot study. *Journal of Visual Impairment and Blindness, 81,* 251–255.

Huebner, K. (1986). Social skills. In G. Scholl (Ed.), *Foundations of education for blind and visually handicapped children and youth: Theory and practice* (pp. 341–362). New York: American Foundation for the Blind.

Huebner, K. M. (1989). Shaping educational intervention for blind and visually impaired learners in response to social change. *RE:view, 21,* 137–144.

Huebner, K. M., & Strumwasser, K. P. (1987). State certification of teachers of blind and visually impaired students: Report of a national study. *Journal of Visual Impairment and Blindness, 81,* 244–250.

Hull, W. A., & McCarthy, C. G. (1973). Supplementary programs for preschool visually handicapped children. *Education of the Visually Handicapped, 5,* 97–104.

Hupp, S., & Rosen, S. (1985). The team approach to designing instruction for visually impaired multiply handicapped children: A decision-making paradigm. *Education of the Visually Handicapped, 17,* 85–96.

Irwin, J., & Macdonnell, P. (1988). Access to transition services: Integral part of curriculum. *Journal of Visual Impairment and Blindness, 82,* 69–70.

Jan, J., Groenveld, M., Sykanda, A., & Hoyt, C. (1987). Behavioral characteristics of children with permanent cortical visual impairment. *Developmental Medicine and Child Neurology, 29,* 571–576.

Jankowski, L., & Evans, J. (1981). The exercise capacity of blind children. *Journal of Visual Impairment and Blindness, 75,* 248–251.

Jastrzembska, Z. S. (1982). *Model for a workshop on assessment of blind and visually impaired students.* New York: American Foundation for the Blind.

Jones, J. (1961). *Blind children—Degree of vision, mode of reading.* Washington, DC: U.S. Government Printing Office.

Jones, J. W. (1962). Problems in defining and classifying blindness. *The New Outlook for the Blind, 56,* 115–121.

Jones, J. W., & Collins, A. T. (1966). *Educational programs for visually handicapped children.* Washington, DC: U.S. Government Printing Office.

Jose, R. T. (1983). *Understanding low vision.* New York: American Foundation for the Blind.

Kates, L., & Schein, J. D. (1980). *A complete guide to communication with deaf-blind persons.* Silver Spring, MD: National Association for the Deaf.

Kaufman, A. S., & Kaufman, L. (1983). *Assessment Battery for Children.* Circle Pines, MN: American Guidance Service.

Kekelis, L. S., & Andersen, E. S. (1984). Family communication styles and language development. *Journal of Visual Impairment and Blindness, 78,* 54–65.

Keogh, B. K. (1973). Perceptual and cognitive styles: Implication for special education. *First Review of Special Education,* pp. 83–109.

Kershman, S. M. (1976). A hierarchy of tasks in the development of tactual discrimination. *Education of the Visually Handicapped, 8,* 73–82.

Kirchner, C., & Peterson, R. (1980). Multiple impairments among non-institutionalized blind and visually impaired persons. *Journal of Visual Impairment and Blindness, 74,* 42–44.

Kirchner, C., Peterson, R., & Suhr, C. (1979). Trends in school enrollment among legally blind school children, 1963–1978. *Journal of Visual Impairment and Blindness, 73,* 373–379.

Kirk, S. A., & Gallagher, J. J. (1989). *Educating exceptional children* (6th ed.). Boston: Houghton-Mifflin.

Klatzky, R. L., & Lederman, S. J. (1988). The intelligent hand. In G. H. Bower (Ed.), *The psychology of learning and motivation* (pp. 121–151). New York: Academic Press.

Klatzky, R. L., Lederman, S. J., & Metzger, V. A. (1985). Identifying objects by touch: An expert system. *Perception, 37,* 299–302.

Klatzky, R. L., Lederman, S., & Reed, C. (1987). There's more to touch than meets the eye: The salience of object attributes for haptics with and without vision. *Journal of Experimental Psychology, 116,* 336–369.

Knappett, K., & Wagner, N. N. (1976). Sex education and the blind. *Education of the Visually Handicapped, 8,* 1–5.

Knowlton, M. (1987). Directional sensitivity of the fingertip. *Education of the Visually Handicapped, 18,* 157–164.

Koenig, A. J., & Holbrook, M. C. (1989). Determining the reading medium for students with visual impairments: A diagnostic teaching approach. *Journal of Visual Impairment and Blindness, 83,* 296–302.

Koestler, F. (1976). *The unseen minority: A social history of blindness in the United States.* New York: David McKay.

Kratz, L. E., Tutt, L. M., & Black, D. A. (1987). *Movement and fundamental motor skills for sensory deprived children.* Springfield, IL: Charles C. Thomas.

Langley, M. B. (1979). Psychoeducational assessment of the multiply handicapped blind child: Issues and methods. *Education of the Visually Handicapped, 10,* 97–114.

Langley, M. B. (1980). *Functional Vision Screening Inventory for the Severely and Multiply Handicapped.* Chicago: Stoelting.

Lewis, M. (1979). Teaching arithmetic computation skills. *Education of the Visually Handicapped, 2,* 66–72.

Linville, J., & Bliss, J. (1966). *A direct translation reading aid for the blind* (Report SEL-65-055, TR No. 4819-1). Stanford, CA: Stanford Electronics Laboratories.

Loshin, D. S. (1989, June). Future potential image enhancement for low vision patients. In A. L. Corn (Chair), *Through the looking glass.* Symposium conducted at The University of Texas at Austin.

Lowenfeld, B. (1969). Multihandicapped blind and deaf–blind children in California. *Research Bulletin, 19,* 1–72. New York: American Foundation for the Blind.

Lowenfeld, B. (1973). History of the education of visually handicapped children. In B. Lowenfeld (Ed.), *The visually handicapped child in school* (pp. 1–25). New York: John Day.

Lowenfeld, B. (1981). The preschool child and his needs. In *Berthold Lowenfeld on blindness and blind people* (pp. 35–45). New York: American Foundation for the Blind.

Lowenfeld, B. (1990). Berthold Lowenfeld: An interview with a leader in the development of educational programs for the blind and visually impaired students. *RE:view, 22,* 137–149.

Ludel, J. (1978). *Introduction to sensory processes.* San Francisco: W. H. Freeman.

Luxton, K. (1980–1981). A jigsaw puzzle: Constructing a sound bridge to adulthood for visually handicapped adolescents. *Blindness,* 97–105.

Lydon, W. T., & McGraw, M. L. (1973). *Concept development for visually handicapped children.* New York: American Foundation for the Blind.

Mangold, S. (1977). *The Mangold developmental program of tactile perception and braille letter recognition.* Castro Valley, CA: Exceptional Teaching Aids.

Mangold, S. S. (1978). Tactile perception and braille letter recognition. *Visual Impairment and Blindness, 72,* 259–266.

Mangold, S., & Mangold, P. (1989). Selecting the most appropriate primary learning medium for students with functional vision. *Journal of Visual Impairment and Blindness, 83,* 294–295.

Mangold, S. S., & Roessing, L. J. (1982). Instructional needs of students with low vision. In S. S. Mangold (Ed.), *A teacher's guide to the special educational needs of blind and visually handicapped children* (pp. 29–34). New York: American Foundation for the Blind.

Maxfield, K. E., & Buchholz, S. (1957). *A social maturity scale for blind preschool children.* New York: American Foundation for the Blind.

McCarron, L., & Hurst, J. (1985). Vocational readiness curriculum: Preparing visually multi-handicapped students for the world of work. *Journal of Visual Impairment and Blindness, 79,* 450–457.

McCarthy, K. (1970). *McCarthy Scales of Children's Abilities.* San Antonio, TX: Psychological Corp.

McConnell, J. (1984). Integration of visually handicapped students in industrial arts classes: An overview. *Journal of Visual Impairment and Blindness, 78,* 319–323.

McGinnis, A. R. (1981). Functional linguistic strategies of blind children. *Journal of Visual Impairment and Blindness, 75,* 210–214.

McLaughlin, W. J. (1974). Reading attainment of blind and partially sighted children: A comparative study. *Teacher of the Blind, 2,* 98–106.

Millar, S. (1985). The perception of complex patterns by touch. *Perception, 14,* 293–303.

Miller, D. (1985). Reading comes naturally: A mother and her blind child's experiences. *Journal of Visual Impairment and Blindness, 79,* 1–4.

Miller, J. W. (1982). Development of an audio-tutorial system for teaching basic geographic concepts. *Education of the Visually Handicapped, 13,* 109–115.

Miller, S. E. (1982). Relationship between mobility level and development of positional concepts in visually impaired children. *Journal of Visual Impairment and Blindness, 76,* 149–153.

Moore, M. (1973). *Professional preparation of teachers of reading with the Optacon.* Pittsburgh: University of Pittsburgh Press.

Moore, M. A., & McLaughlin, L. M. (in press). Assessment of the visually handicapped preschool child. In E. V. Nuttall (Ed.), *Assessing and screening preschoolers: Psychological, social, and educational dimensions.* New York: Allyn and Bacon.

Moore, S. (1984). The need for programs and services for visually handicapped infants. *Education of the Visually Handicapped, 16,* 48–57.

Mori, A., & Olive, J. (1978). The blind and visually mentally retarded: Suggestions for intervention in infancy. *Journal of Visual Impairment and Blindness, 72,* 273–279.

Morris, J. E. (1974). The 1973 Stanford Achievement Test Series as adapted for use by the visually handicapped. *Education of the Visually Handicapped, 6,* 33–40.

Morris, J. (1976). Adaptation of the Durrell Listening Reading Series for use with the visually handicapped. *Education of the Visually Handicapped, 8,* 21–27.

Morse, J. L. (1975). Answering the questions of the psychologist assessing the visually handicapped child. *The New Outlook for the Blind, 69,* 350–353.

Murphy, L. B. (1972). Infants' play and cognitive development. In M. W. Pier (Ed.), *Play and development* (pp. 119–126). New York: Norton.

Myerson, L. (1963). Somatopsychology of physical disability. In W. M. Cruickshank (Ed.), *Psychology of exceptional children and youth* (pp. 1–52). Englewood Cliffs, NJ: Prentice-Hall.

Neff, J. (1982). Sexuality education methodology. In S. Mangold (Ed.), *A teachers' guide to the special educational needs of blind and visually handicapped children* (pp. 63–71). New York: American Foundation for the Blind.

Netupski, J. A., & Hamre-Netupski, S. M. (1987). An ecological approach to curriculum development. In L. Goetz, D. Guess, & K. Stremel-Campbell (Eds.), *Innovative program design for individuals with dual sensory impairments* (pp. 225–250). Baltimore: Brookes.

Newborg, J., Stock, J. R., Wnek, L., Guidabaldi, C., & Svinicki, J. (1984). *Battelle Developmental Inventory.* Allen, TX: DLM/Teaching Resources.

Newland, T. E. (1961). *The Blind Learning Aptitude Test.* Presented at the Conference on Research on Braille, New York.

Newland, T. E. (1979). The Blind Learning Aptitude Test. *Journal of Visual Impairment and Blindness, 73,* 134–139.

Nolan, C. (1959). Readability of large types—A study of type sizes and type styles. *International Journal for the Education of the Blind, 9,* 41–44.

Nolan, C. (1966). *Reading and listening in learning by the blind: Progress report.* Louisville, KY: American Printing House for the Blind.

Nolan, C. Y., & Kederis, C. J. (1969). *Perceptual factors in braille word recognition.* New York: American Foundation for the Blind.

Nolan, C. Y., & Morris, J. E. (1965). Development and validation of the Roughness Discrimination Test. *International Journal for the Education of the Blind, 15,* 1–6.

Nolan, C. Y., & Morris, J. E. (1973). *Aural study systems for the visually handicapped.* Louisville, KY: American Printing House for the Blind.

Office of Special Education. (1981). *Programs for education of the handicapped* (Federal Register, 5379). Washington, DC: U.S. Government Printing Office.

Olson, M. R. (1981). *Guidelines and games for teaching efficient braille reading.* New York: American Foundation for the Blind.

Olson, M. (1982). Play behavior of young preschoolers and its meaning for parents and teachers. *DVH Newsletter, 26,* 32–36.

Olson, M. R., Harlow, S. D., & Williams, J. D. (1977). An evaluation of McBride's approach to rapid reading for braille and large print readers. *Education of the Visually Handicapped, 9,* 16–23.

Organization for Social and Technical Innovation. (1971). *Blindness and services to the blind in the United States.* Cambridge, MA: OSTI Press.

Overbury, O., Goodrich, G. L., Quillman, R. D., & Faubert, J. (1989). Perceptual assessment in low vision: Evidence for a hierarchy of skills. *Journal of Visual Impairment and Blindness, 83,* 109–113.

Palazesi, M. A. (1986). The need for motor development programs for visually impaired preschoolers. *Journal of Visual Impairment and Blindness, 80,* 573–576.

Parker, R. (1983). *Occupational Aptitude Survey and Interest Schedule.* Austin, TX: PRO-ED.

Parsons, A. A. (1982). *An exploratory study of the patterns of emerging play behavior in young children with low vision.* Unpublished doctoral dissertation, The University of Texas, Austin.

Parsons, S. (1986). Function of play in low vision children: Emerging patterns of behavior. *Journal of Visual Impairment and Blindness, 80,* 777–784.

Pereira, L. M. (1990). Spatial concepts and balance performance: Motor learning in blind and visually impaired children. *Journal of Visual Impairment and Blindness, 84,* 109–110.

Piaget, J. (1966). *The psychology of intelligence.* Totawa, NJ: Littlefield, Adams.

Piaget, J. (1973). *The child and reality.* New York: Grossman.

Piers, E. V., & Harris, D. B. (1969). *The Piers–Harris Children's Self-Concept Scale (The way I feel about myself).* Nashville, TN: Counselor Recordings and Tests.

Pogrund, R. L., & Rosen, S. J. (1989). The preschool blind child can be a long cane user. *Journal of Visual Impairment and Blindness, 83,* 431–439.

Ramirez, S. (1986). *Children's Fear Survey Schedule-Revised.* Unpublished doctoral dissertation, University of Wisconsin–Madison.

Rasmussen, R. (1985, February). *Echolalia and the blind child.* Paper presented at Workshop, Texas School for the Blind, Austin, TX.

Read, L. (1989). Social skills of blind kindergarten children. *RE:view, 20,* 142–155.

Reiser, J. J., Guth, A., & Hill, W. E. (1982). Mental processes mediating independent travel: Implications for orientation and mobility. *Journal of Visual Impairment and Blindness, 76,* 213–218.

Rex, E. J. (1970). A study of basal readers and experimental supplementary instructional materials for teaching primary reading in braille. *Education of the Visually Handicapped, 2,* 97–107.

Rex, E. J. (1989). Issues related to literacy of legally blind learners. *Journal of Visual Impairment and Blindness, 83,* 306–313.

Reynell, J. (1980). *Reynell–Zinkin Developmental Scales for Young Visually Handicapped Children.* Chicago: Stoelting.

Reynolds, C., & Richmond, B. (1985). *Revised Children's Manifest Anxiety Scale (RCMAS) manual.* Los Angeles: Western Psychological Services.

Roberts, F. K. (1986). Education for the visually handicapped: A social and educational history. In G. T. Scholl (Ed.), *Foundations of education for blind and visually handicapped children and youth: Theory and practice* (pp. 1–18). New York: American Foundation for the Blind.

Robinson, L. (1982). *Growing up: A developmental curriculum.* Ogden, UT: Parent Consultants.

Rogers, S. J., & Puchalski, C. B. (1988). Development of object permanence in visually impaired infants. *Journal of Visual Impairment and Blindness, 82,* 137–142.

Rogow, S. M. (1978). Considerations in assessment of blind children who function as severely or profoundly retarded. *Child Care, Health and Development, 415,* 327–335.

Rogow, S. (1988). *Helping the visually impaired child with developmental problems.* New York: Teachers College Press.

Rossi, P. (1986). Mathematics. In K. Huebner, Curricular adaptations. In G. Scholl (Ed.), *Foundations of education for blind and visually handicapped children and youth: Theory and practice* (pp. 367–374). New York: American Foundation for the Blind.

Rowland, C. (1984). Preverbal communication of blind infants and their mothers. *Journal of Visual Impairment and Blindness, 78,* 297–302.

Rubin, J. A. (1975). The exploration of a "tactile aesthetic." *The New Outlook for the Blind, 70,* 369–375.

Sanctin, S., & Simmons, J. N. (1977). Problems in the construction of reality in congenitally blind children. *Journal of Visual Impairment and Blindness, 71,* 425–429.

Scadden, L. (1984). Blindness in the information age: Equality or irony? *Journal of Visual Impairment and Blindness, 78,* 394–400.

Scholl, G. T. (1981). *Self-study and evaluation guide for day programs for visually handicapped pupils: A guide for program improvement.* Reston, VA: Council for Exceptional Children.

Scholl, G. T. (Ed.). (1986). *Foundations of education of blind and visually handicapped children and youth: Theory and practice.* New York: American Foundation for the Blind.

Scholl G., & Schnur, R. (1976). *Measure of psychological, vocational, and educational functioning in the blind and visually handicapped.* New York: American Foundation for the Blind.

Scott, E. (1982). *Your visually impaired student: A guide for teachers.* Baltimore: University Park Press.

Scott, R. (1969). *The making of blind men.* New York: Russell Sage.

Seidenberg, B. H. (1975). Pediatric low vision. In E. G. Faye & C. M. Hood (Eds.), *Low vision* (pp. 117–129). Springfield, IL: Charles C. Thomas.

Shaffer, M. R. (Ed.). (1977). *Studies in mother–infant interaction.* New York: Academic Press.

Shurrager, H. (1961). *Haptic Intelligence Scale for Adult Blind.* Chicago: Illinois Institute of Technology.

Sicilian, S. P. (1988). Development of counting strategies in congenitally blind children. *Journal of Visual Impairment and Blindness, 82,* 331–335.

Sigelman, C. K., Vengroff, L. P., & Spanhel, C. L. (1984). Disability and the concept of life functions. In R. P. Marinelli & A. E. Dell Orto (Eds.), *The psychology and social impact of physical disability* (2nd ed., pp. 3–13). New York: Springer.

Silberman, R. K. (1981). Assessment and evaluation of visually handicapped students. *Journal of Visual Impairment and Blindness, 75,* 109–114.

Silberman, R. (1986). Severe multiple handicaps. In G. Scholl (Ed.), *Foundations of education for blind and visually handicapped children and youth* (pp. 145–164). New York: American Foundation for the Blind.

Silverstein, R. (1985). The legal necessity for residential schools serving deaf, blind, and multiply impaired children. *Journal of Visual Impairment and Blindness, 79,* 145–149.

Simon, J. D. (1974). A course in spoken communications for high school students who are visually handicapped. *Education of the Visually Handicapped, 6,* 41–44.

Simpkins, K. A. (1979a). Tactual discrimination of household objects. *Journal of Visual Impairment and Blindness, 73,* 86–92.

Simpkins, K. A. (1979b). Tactual discrimination of shapes. *Journal of Visual Impairment and Blindness, 73,* 93–101.

Simpson, F. (1986). Transition to adulthood. In G. Scholl (Ed.), *Foundations of education for blind and visually handicapped children and youth: Theory and practice* (pp. 405–422). New York: American Foundation for the Blind.

Smith, A., & Cote, K. (1982). *Look at me: A resource manual for the development of residual vision in multiply impaired children.* Philadelphia: Pennsylvania College of Optometry.

Sonksen, P. M. (1983). Vision and early development. In K. Wybar & D. Taylor (Eds.), *Pediatric ophthalmology: Current aspects* (pp. 85–94). New York: Marcell Dekker.

Sparrow, S. S., Balla, D. A., & Cicchetti, D. V. (1984). *Vineland Adaptive Behavior Scale.* New York: American Guidance Service.

Spungin, S. J. (1980). *Guidelines for public school programs serving visually handicapped children.* New York: American Foundation for the Blind.

Spungin, S. J. (1982). The future role of residential schools for visually handicapped children. *Journal of Visual Impairment and Blindness, 76,* 229–233.

Spungin, S. (1984). The role and function of the teacher of the visually handicapped. In *Quality services for blind and visually handicapped learners: Statements of position* (pp. 31–34). Reston, VA: Division for Visually Handicapped, Council for Exceptional Children.

Spungin, S. J. (1989, June). Assessment of future learning environments for students with low vision. In A. L. Corn (Chair), *Through the looking glass.* Symposium conducted at The University of Texas at Austin.

Stager, J. D. (1978). Assessing public school programs for visually handicapped students. *Journal of Visual Impairment and Blindness, 72,* 170–172.

Stephens, B. (1972). Cognitive processes in the visually impaired. *Education of the Visually Handicapped, 4,* 106–111.

Stephens, B., & Grube, C. (1982). Development of Piagetian reasoning in congenitally blind children. *Journal of Visual Impairment and Blindness, 76,* 133–143.

Stephens, B., Simpkins, K., & Wexler, M. (1976). A comparison of the performance of blind and sighted subjects, age 6–10 years on the rotation of squares test. *Education of the Visually Handicapped, 8,* 66–70.

Stewart, I., van Hasselt, V., Simon, J., & Thompson, W. (1985). The Community Adjustment Program (CAP) for visually impaired adolescents. *Journal of Visual Impairment and Blindness, 78,* 49–54.

Stillman, R. (Ed.). (1979). *The Callier–Azusa Scale.* Dallas: The Callier Center for Communication Disorders of The University of Texas at Dallas.

Stotland, J. (1989, June). Futures for families of visually impaired children. In A. L. Corn (Chair), *Through the looking glass.* Symposium conducted at The University of Texas at Austin.

Strelow, E. R., Kay, M., & Kay, L. (1978). Binaural sensory aid: Case studies of its use by two children. *Journal of Visual Impairment and Blindness, 72,* 1–9.

Suinn, R. M., & Dauterman, W. L. (1966). *Stanford–Ohwaki Kohs Block Design Intelligence Test for the Blind.* Los Angeles: Western Psychological Services.

Sussman, M. B. (1969). Dependent disabled and dependent poor: Similarity of conceptual issues and research needs. *Social Service Review, 42,* 383–395.

Swallow, R. M., & Conner, A. (1982). Aural reading. In S. S. Mangold (Ed.), *A teacher's guide to the special educational needs of blind and visually handicapped children* (pp. 63–71). New York: American Foundation for the Blind.

Swallow, R., & Huebner, K. (1987). *How to thrive, not just survive: A guide to developing independent life skills in blind and visually impaired children and youth.* New York: American Foundation for the Blind.

Swenson, A. (1987). Art experiences for young children with severe visual impairments. *Education of the Visually Handicapped, 19,* 120–124.

Sykes, K. C. (1971). A comparison of the effects of standard print and large print in facilitating the reading skills of visually impaired students. *Education of the Visually Handicapped, 3,* 97–105.

Sykes, K. C. (1972). Print reading for visually handicapped children. *Education of the Visually Handicapped, 4,* 71–75.

Tait, P., & Kessler, C. (1976). The way we get babies: A tactual sex education program. *The New Outlook for the Blind, 70,* 116–120.

Terzieff, I., Stagg, V., & Ashcroft, S. C. (1982). Increasing reading speed with the optacon: A pilot study. *Journal of Visual Impairment and Blindness, 77,* 17–22.

Texas School for the Blind. (1870). *Annual Report of the Texas School for the Blind, 1869–1870.* Austin, TX: Author.

Todd, J. (1986). Resources, media, and technology. In G. Scholl (Ed.), *Foundations of education for blind and visually handicapped children and youth: Theory and practice* (pp. 285–296). New York: American Foundation for the Blind.

Tronick, E., Als, H., & Brazelton, T. B. (1980). Monacid phases: A structural descriptive analysis of infant–mother face to face interaction. *Merrill-Palmer Quarterly, 26,* 3–24.

Tuttle, D. W. (1972). A comparison of three reading media for the blind. *Education of the Visually Handicapped, 4,* 40–44.

Tuttle, D. (1984). *Self-esteem and adjusting with blindness.* Springfield, IL: Charles C. Thomas.

Urwin, C. (1983). Dialogue and cognitive functioning in the early language development of three blind children. In A. E. Mills (Ed.), *Language acquisition in the blind child* (pp. 142–161). San Diego: College-Hill.

Uslan, M., Hill, E., & Peck, A. (1989). *The profession of orientation and mobility in the 1980's: The AFB competency study.* New York: American Foundation for the Blind.

Uslan, M., Malone, S., & De L'Aune, W. (1983). Teaching travel to multiply handicapped blind adults: An auditory approach. *Journal of Visual Impairment and Blindness, 77,* 18–20.

Utley, B., Duncan, D., Strain, P., & Scanlon, K. (1983). Effects of contingent and noncontingent vision stimulation on visual fixation in multiply handicapped children. *Journal of the Association for Persons with Severe Handicaps, 8,* 29–42.

Uzgiris, I. C., & Hunt, J. M. (1975). *Assessment in infancy: Ordinal Scales of Psychological Development.* Urbana: University of Illinois Press.

Valvo, A. (1971). *Sight restoration after long-term blindness: The problems and behavior patterns of visual rehabilitation.* New York: American Foundation for the Blind.

VanderKolk, C. J. (1981). *Assessment and planning with the visually impaired.* Baltimore: University Park Press.

Van Dijk, J. (1965). The first steps of the deaf/blind child towards language. *Proceedings of the Conference on the Deaf/Blind.* Boston: Perkins School for the Blind.

Van Weelden, J. (1967). *On being blind.* Amsterdam: Netherlands Society for the Blind.

Venn, J., & Wadler, F. (1988). Deaf–blind independent living project: A status report. *Education of the Visually Handicapped, 20,* 23–28.

Wan-Lin, M. M., & Tait, P. E. (1987). The attainment of conservation by visually impaired children in Taiwan. *Journal of Visual Impairment and Blindness, 81,* 423–428.

Warren, D. H. (1974). Early vs. late vision: The role of early vision in spatial reference systems. *The New Outlook for the Blind, 68,* 157–162.

Warren, D. H. (1984). *Blindness and early childhood development* (2nd ed.). New York: American Foundation for the Blind.

Weber, L. (1971). *The English infant school and informal education.* Englewoods Cliffs, NJ: Prentice-Hall.

Wechsler, D. H. (1963). *Wechsler Preschool and Primary Scale of Intelligence.* San Antonio, TX: Psychological Corp.

Wechsler, D. H. (1974). *Wechsler Intelligence Scale for Children–Revised.* San Antonio, TX: Psychological Corp.

Wechsler, D. (1981). *Wechsler Adult Intelligence Scale.* San Antonio, TX: Psychological Corp.

Wehrum, M. (1977). *Techniques of daily living: A curriculum guide.* Pittsburgh: Greater Pittsburgh Guild for the Blind.

Weiner, B. B. (1967). A new outlook on assessment. *The New Outlook for the Blind, 61,* 73–78.

Whitmore, J. R., & Maker, C. J. (1985). *Intellectual giftedness in disabled persons.* Rockville, MD: Aspen Systems.

Wiederholt, L., & Larsen, S. (1983). *Test of Practical Knowledge.* Austin, TX: PRO-ED.

Wilhelm, J. G. (1989). Fear and anxiety in low vision and totally blind children. *Education of the Visually Handicapped, 20,* 163–172.

Willoughby, D., & Duffy, S. (1989). *Handbook for itinerant and resource teachers of blind and visually impaired students.* Baltimore: National Federation of the Blind.

Witkin, H. A., Oltman, C. K., Chase, J. B., & Friedman, F. (1971). Cognitive patterning in the blind. In J. Hellmuth (Ed.), *Cognitive studies: Deficits in cognition* (pp. 16–46). New York: Brunner/Mazel.

Wolffe, K. (1985). Don't give those kids fish: Teach 'em how to fish! *Journal of Visual Impairment and Blindness, 79,* 470–472.

Wood, T. (1979). The usability of the adapted Durrell Listening–Reading Series with students in the intermediate grades. *Education of the Visually Handicapped, 4,* 33–38.

Wormsley, D. (1981). Hand movement training in braille reading. *Journal of Visual Impairment and Blindness, 75,* 327–331.

Wright, B. A. (1960). *Physical disability: A psychological approach.* New York: Harper, Row.

Zimmerman, G. A. (1985). *An exploratory study of preferred textures of objects for visually handicapped infants and young children.* Unpublished doctoral dissertation, The University of Texas, Austin.

Index

About the Authors

Natalie C. Barraga, Ed.D., is professor emerita of the Program for Visually Handicapped, Department of Special Education, The University of Texas at Austin. She is author of *Increased Visual Behavior in Low Vision Children,* previous editions of *Visual Handicaps and Learning,* several monographs and book chapters, numerous journal articles, and assessment instruments and instructional programs. She is active in state, national, and international professional organizations and activities, having conducted courses and seminars in a multitude of countries around the world.

Jane N. Erin, Ph.D., is assistant professor, Department of Special Education, The University of Texas at Austin, where she is undergraduate advisor and faculty liaison for student teaching in special education and an instructor in personnel preparation of visually handicapped. She is an experienced classroom teacher and supervisor in programs related to children with visual and multiple handicaps. She is the author of several articles and is active in state and national professional organizations in visually handicapped and multihandicapped, where she has held numerous leadership positions.